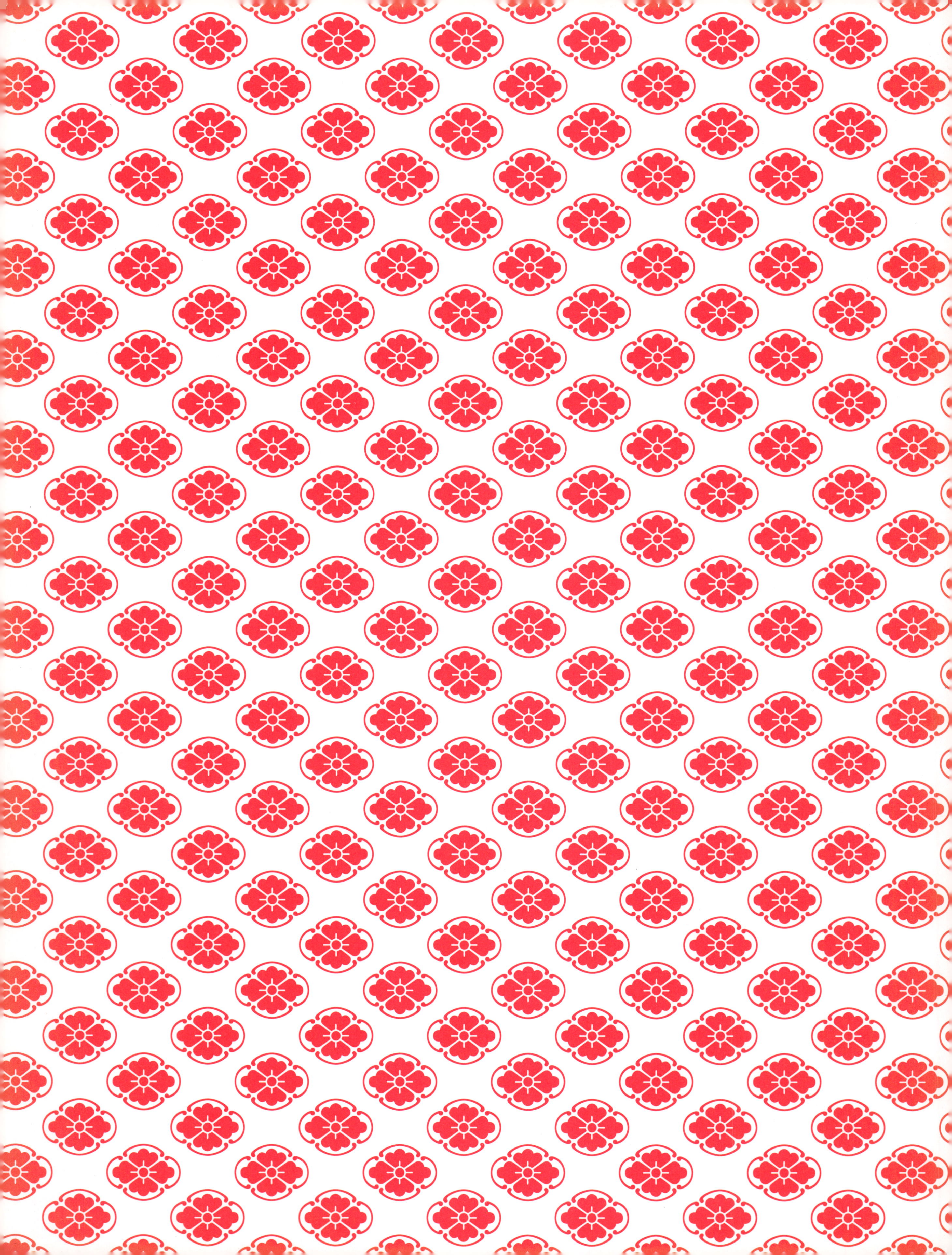

Geisha

A Photographic History

1872 – 1912

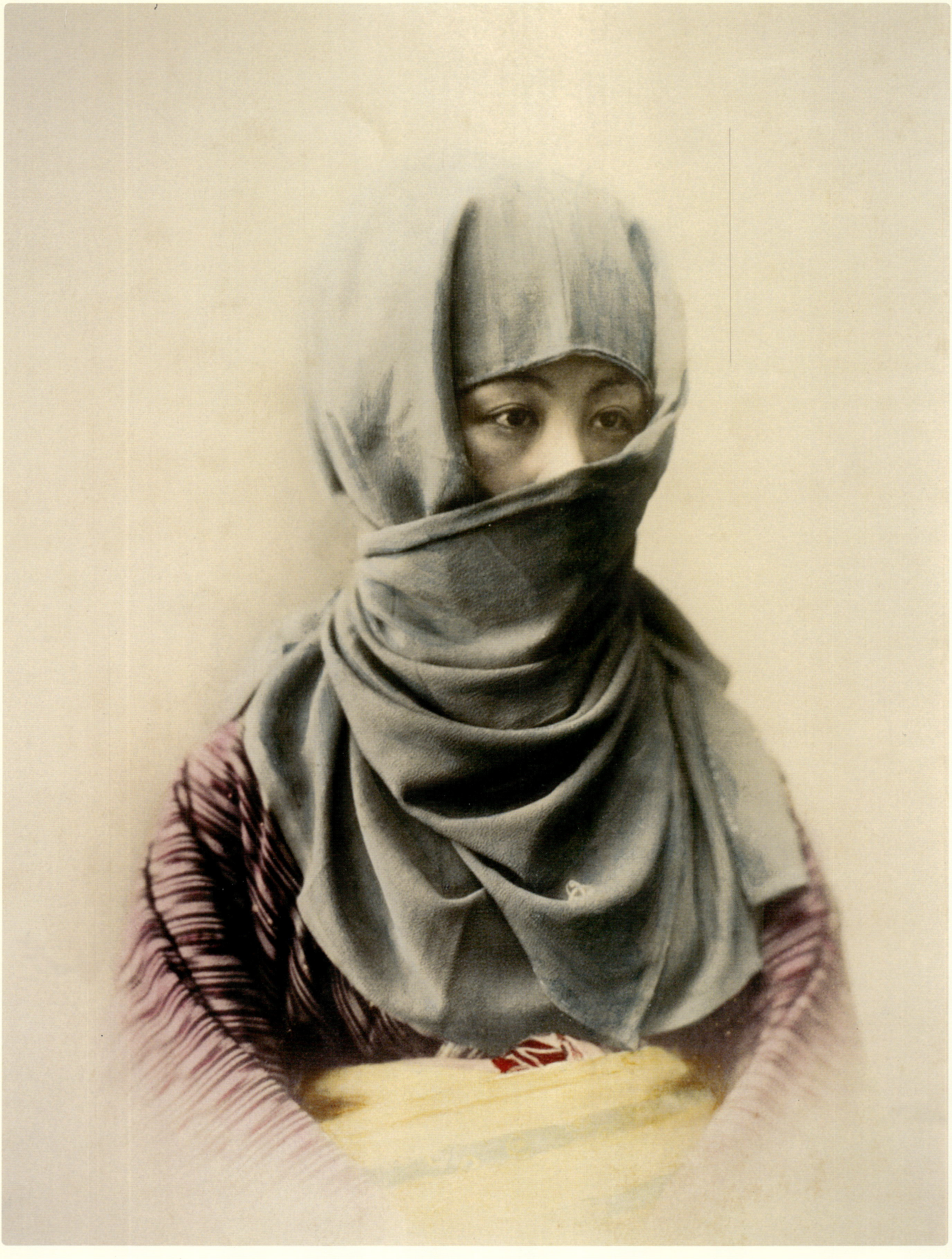

Geisha

A Photographic History 1872–1912

By Stanley B. Burns, MD
and Elizabeth A. Burns

A Burns Archive Book

pH powerHouse Books Brooklyn, NY

Front Cover: Geisha Looking at Flower (unattributed, c. 1890)

This young geisha contemplates a flower, which not only symbolizes spring and beauty, but the ephemeral nature of life. Geisha reside in *hanamachi*, literally "flower towns," and live in *karyukai*, the "flower and willow world." It is a place of escape and hedonism for those who visit. A world of pleasure and fantasy, where the realities of the outside may not enter. It is the whole universe of the geisha.

Back Cover: [Geisha] Singing Girl (U25)
(Kusakabe Kimbei, c. 1880)

The view of a geisha's back was significant, as it showed her obi, her hairstyle, and her neck. Kimonos were worn low, as exposure of the nape of the neck was considered erotic. They painted their faces white, as well as their upper back to the nape. The paint was shaped like a forked tongue or *W*, to show that there was flesh, and a real woman, beneath the white-painted fantasy. They received wages called *hanadai*, flower money, and also a tip called *shugi*, which was frequently placed in the back of her kimono. When serving drinks or conversing at a dinner party a geisha often sat in the middle of a U-shaped seating arrangement. Her back was what guests on the opposite side saw. It was crucial that their view of her was tantalizing.

Frontispiece: Winter Outfit (attributed Felice Beato, c. 1875)

This rare close-up photograph of a geisha resembles the familiar imagery of veiled Middle Eastern Arab women. Similarly, it evokes the mystery and eroticism of the exotic and unattainable woman. However this heavy woolen headwear was worn because of cold winters. This early photograph is most likely the work of Felice Beato, Japan's first successful commercial photographer, who vignetted his portraits. He was a noted war photographer who photographed the Crimean War (1855) and conflicts in India and China. He brought his aesthetic to Japan and established the hand-painted Japanese photograph tourist album trade. Felice is often confused with his brother, Antonio, also a noted photographer, who spent years in the Middle East photographing Arab life, and produced numerous images of veiled women.

Table of Contents

Preface

In an attempt to visually recreate the world of the nineteenth-century geisha, my daughter Elizabeth and I collect Japanese photography. As photographic historians drawn to visualizing past subjects, we work to recreate and explore the roots of modern events and culture using period photographs. Numerous books show geisha in the twentieth century, however none concentrate on the golden age of the geisha in the Meiji era.

I have always been a collector and historian. I am most intrigued by forgotten significant historical events and unusual cultural traditions. Prior to the 1970s, I collected written materials: books and ephemera. In the mid-1970s I began collecting photography, and by 1979 had established The Burns Archive—its main purpose to publish photographic historical works and prepare exhibitions about specific subjects. I have concentrated on opening up uncharted regions of photographic history. My interest in photographs springs from their function as historic documents. In Japanese, the word for photograph is *shashin,* which translates as "a copy of the truth." Original photographs are a unique source of information. They offer accurate recordings of events and provide enhanced comprehension. Some summarize events becoming visual icons.

Most photographic historians are interested in a particular photographer, a special collection, or a specific style or format of photograph. During the past three decades, my interest has been solely in subject matter. I am not interested in who took the photograph as much as I am interested in what was photographed. My collection of over 800,000 photographs is completely subject-oriented. If it contains a Matthew Brady or Lewis Hine photograph, it is because of the topic. Most of the photographs were taken as documentation, however due to the passage of time they are now perceived as art.

I have written over 20 texts. Two, on specific cultural subjects, were chosen "Best Photo-Historical Book of the Year." In 1990, *Sleeping Beauty: Memorial Photography in America* documented the cultural phenomena of photographing the dead. In 1995, *Forgotten Marriage: The Painted*

Tintype & Decorative Frame, A Lost Chapter in American Portraiture documented the practice of enlarging, copying, painting, and framing photographs. My study of painting tintypes was expanded in my exhibit *Color Before Color*, which explored the history of color photography as used around the world. My collection of hand-colored Japanese photography, accumulated over a period of 30 years, concentrates on specific topics. What intrigues me about these beautiful, colored photographs is the subject matter: the portrayal of geisha, samurai, shopkeepers, prostitutes, sumo wrestlers, and other professions that exemplified the feudal era of Japan.

My interest in the geisha tradition stems from deep within me. I studied history as a scientist to uncover truth and find a key to understanding the present. I was also intrigued with the past as a comfort zone. The concept of the good old days as better times is a worldwide phenomenon; in reality however, the good old days were not always good. The nostalgic illusion of prior times provides a sense of reassurance and contentment. Today we romanticize about a slower-paced time, and often seek escape from our hectic modern world. I joined the National Arts Club about 20 years ago to recapture the calmer, contemplative essence of a bygone era. The building, an 1876 mansion, situated on New York's Gramercy Park, was once the home of New York governor, and almost United States president Samuel J. Tilden. It imparts the splendor and elegance of the Victorian era. The club's mission is to further a wide range of art and artists in America. I wanted to spend my hours away from my busy medical practice in the art world. It is my oasis. It evokes a feeling of timelessness, similar to the geisha. She is an artist personifying traditional Japan.

I have enjoyed exploring another time and place while preparing this book, and plan, through exhibitions on geisha and Japanese photography, to continue this endeavor. I am delighted to share my discoveries and sincerely hope you enjoy looking at these photographs, as much as I have enjoyed collecting and studying them.

—Stanley B. Burns, MD

Introduction

This book presents a detailed look at the nineteenth-century geisha as portrayed by the commercial photographers of the treaty port cities of Japan, most notably Yokohama. The photographs are hand-colored albumen prints and artistically can be considered a continuation of the colored woodblock print: the ukiyo-e. Ukiyo-e documented the noted pleasure quarters and their numerous personalities, including geisha and prostitutes. But photographs offered a new reality, expanding the perception of Japanese culture. The Meiji era (1868–1912), considered by some the golden age of the geisha, was the period in which modern Japan was created. Social and cultural reforms were established that broke centuries-old traditions, the samurai were disarmed, the rule of the shoguns was over, and the fabric and philosophy of the nation changed. The feudal state gave way to a modern, industrialized society. These captivating images were taken during this period of transition—bringing historic and cultural context to one of Japan's most well known icons, the geisha.

In Asian cultures until about the mid-twentieth century, it was near-impossible for a woman of "common birth" to achieve wealth, status, and celebrity. Japan had the only cultural climate in which that was possible. With the creation of the geisha in the eighteenth century, women could gain fame, renown, and even independence. Impoverished families sold their children, not only for the money, but perhaps to give their child an opportunity for a better life.

Ukiyo-e prints granted celebrity. At the end of the nineteenth century, photographers such as Ogawa produced images of notable geisha—taking their celebrity to another level. In the early twentieth century, with the development of the photographic postcard, collecting images of geisha became a Japanese passion. At the end of this volume, examples are presented. The photographic postcard expands this study of geisha life. Many of the photographs taken in the nineteenth century were reproduced as photographic postcards. All commercial photographers exploited the postcard format, as it gave them a new market for their images. The photographic postcard granted worldwide dispersions of geisha imagery.

The collection of photographs presented show the range of geisha imagery available in the Meiji era produced by commercial photographers. There are images of geisha eating, sleeping, dancing, dressing, singing, and performing many other routines and activities of their daily life. This is the largest collection of these types of images ever compiled. Many of the photographs show activities in which there are several surviving views. The images chosen are highlights of the large (8 by 10 inch) photograph albums that were sold in the heyday of the tourist trade, from 1880 to 1900. Other published works concentrate on the very early images, 1862 to 1872, as photographs by the pioneers naturally fascinated photographic historians. By the mid-1880s, the competition between the Yokohama studios of Kusakabe Kimbei and Adolfo Farsari, two of the most renowned photographers of their day, resulted in the production of most exquisitely painted staged images. In the first decades of the twentieth century, Englishman Herbert Ponting and other Western photographers were sent to Japan to photograph the Russo-Japanese War. They created stereoviews and lantern slides of the people and the country. A page from Ponting's original sale book is reproduced. This work also concentrates on the use of photography in promotion of the geisha as representative of Japanese life and as a national icon.

It has been speculated by some photoprahic historians that women other than geisha posed for some of the photographs. If true, this still may not detract from the visual narrative of geisha life. The images chosen are all most likely (ostensibly) geisha. In the Peabody Essex Museum's 2004 text, *Geisha: Beyond the Painted Smile*, Allen Hockney and others point out that photographers purposely blurred the distinctions between geisha and other Japanese women. Therefore identifying geisha in nineteenth-century photographs is particularly tricky. Photographers created these staged tableaus to provide an accurate vision of the life of the geisha for Western audiences. What they created was a picture of Japan that has endured, enticed, and thrilled generations.

Since the late nineteenth century, the concept of the geisha has been misinterpreted by the Western world. To accurately present the life of the geisha, it is important to differentiate geisha from prostitute. There are many visual clues distinguishing them. This book includes a wide range of photographs of prostitutes, from courtesans to caged brothel workers, as well as an analysis of these images, granting new understanding of the profession. Photographs without text can be misinterpreted and/or misleading. The novels and periodicals of the end of the nineteenth century misguided the public as to the true role of the geisha. Photographers, who provided images of Japanese women, did not accurately label them, allowing the observer to come to his own conclusions and assumptions.

An advantage of presenting a specific subject is that isolation and concentration results in new understandings. A pleasure of researching using photographic sources as historic documents are the surprising discoveries that can be made when large numbers of images are analyzed. There have been several books on nineteenth-century Japanese photographic history, and most identify the obvious lower and higher levels of prostitute. However valuable connections between images of prostitutes have not been made, and this work illustrates for the first time an important categorization that will allow researchers, collectors, and curators to identify prostitutes and their establishments. We discovered the meaning behind the term "N° 9." N° 9 girls have been misidentified, most often as geisha. However, a N° 9 girl is a prostitute and she lives in a brothel: frequently with the street address N° 9.

After reviewing numerous albums, the connection became clear. Many photographs show groups of beautifully outfitted women, some majestically posed. The images are labeled "N° 9 Girls" or more frequently "New N° 9 Girls" (pages 42 and 49). It was obvious that building N° 9 in Yokahama was a brothel, as there were women in every window and balcony. Further study revealed that other N° 9 buildings were brothels. Perhaps the most significant photograph is of "Nectarine N° 9" It is clearly a brothel, as indicated not only by the presence of prostitutes but also the three men dressed in western garb entering the building (page 45, top).

The initial clue as to the identification of N° 9 girls as prostitutes was found in the album of a sailor. It was the only image he had from Japan. The photograph was labeled "New No. 9 Girls" and was taken indoors (page 43). The women in the image have their obi tied in front, the visual symbol of the trade. A fascinating photograph is labeled "New N° 9 Girls Kanagawa (An Eurasian)" (page 47). She is dressed in a fine kimono with her obi tied in back like a geisha. In a different album, the same woman in the same outfit is depicted with a group of women in the same hallway and in front of the same backdrop as the photograph from the sailor. It is labeled, "Eurasian, New N° 9 Girl." It is clear that the woman is a prostitute, and probably the pride of the brothel—in a nation that was isolated for over two and a half centuries, where commingling with foreigners was forbidden by law.

After examining more photographs, it became clear that "N° 9 girl" was a euphemistic term for prostitute. Many images had women in groups labeled "N° 9." And many were of buildings with women all around, undoubtedly brothels, showing the entrance with the address N° 9. In many societies, numbers have special connotations: in Japan the N° 9 is considered unlucky.

To provide background for a better understanding of Japanese history, culture, and art, several essays are presented. The first, on the history of Japan, discusses the opening and closing of the country to the rest of the world. The next is on the ukiyo-e woodblock print, then an analysis of commercial photography with a chronology and a history of the photographic postcard in Japan. The final essay is a study of the geisha, also with a chronology.

Japan is the only major nation that does not have a clear history of who introduced photography into the country, who took the first photographs, or how early photography developed. When photography was presented to the world in 1839, Japan was still a closed nation in self-imposed isolation. These hand-painted photographs, for many, represent Japanese photography in the nineteenth century. However these photographs were not primarily made by or for the Japanese. Western photographers pioneered the hand-colored photograph in Japan in the 1860s. They were produced for the foreign market, especially the images of "customs and costumes." The photographs were placed in albums as souvenirs of a trip or sojourn in Japan. When Japanese photographers took over the businesses of the Western photographers they continued to take and offer hand-colored images. The photographs were hand-painted with watercolors. They ranged in quality and many were so exquisitely and completely painted that they challenge the sensibilities of those accustomed to modern color photography.

When photography was discovered, exposure times were long, and there were no posing conventions. People had to learn how to sit for the camera. Having a photograph taken was often a once-in-a-lifetime event. Even as late as the 1890s, after faster film had been developed, posing for a photograph was a serious matter. As with most portrait photographs of the era, the subjects had sober facial expressions. Relaxed conventions in portraiture were not achieved until the twentieth century, and were the direct result of the development of amateur photography.

Many of the photographs are named by the photographer, as well as numbered. Some have only numbers or only names. When available, these titles are used. Many have the title "Singing Girl" or "Dancing Girl," which was the colloquial term for geisha. Almost all of the photographs presented are about 8 by 10 inches, with the exception of the images on pages 34, 43, 45 (top), 68, 94, and 104, which are 3 1/2 by 5 1/2 inches. At one time, all of these images were matted on board in albums. Also, all of the postcards are the standard 3 1/2 by 5 1/2 inches. Japanese names are listed with the family name first, as is traditional in Japan.

There have been numerous texts and essays detailing the history of the geisha and courtesans. The most revered is *Geisha* by anthropologist Liza C. Dalby—who in the mid-1970s became the first non-Japanese woman to become a geisha. Leslie Downer, Sheridan Prasso, Lisa Louis, and others have produced texts, each with an expanded view on one or more aspects of geisha life and history. Others, such as Arthur Golden, have written historical novels detailing geisha society. To supplement these works, this book covers the pertinent photographic history to create a visual history of the nineteenth-century geisha. Hopefully, the art and life of the nineteenth-century geisha will be better understood, and the hand-colored photographs that document their existence will be appreciated by a larger audience.

—Stanley B. Burns, MD & Elizabeth A. Burns

The Opening and Closing of Japan to Asian & Western Influence

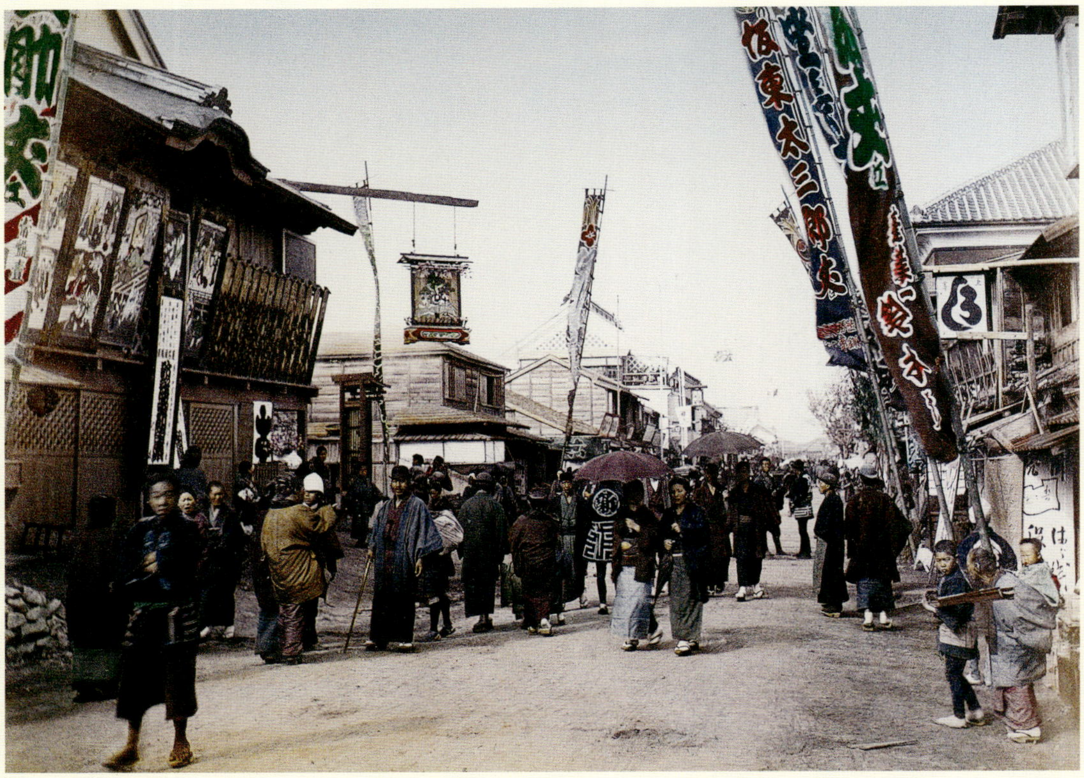

Theater Street Yokohama (566)
(attributed Kusakabe Kimbei, c. 1881)

Yokohama, the largest and most important treaty port open to foreigners, had over 1,200 foreigners living in the city in the 1880s. The city was basically divided into three sections. The large hill overlooking the city was where the Western businessmen and diplomats lived with their families. The area was essentially a ghetto with Western-style buildings, which included homes, hospitals, and private clubs. The area containing Western businesses and hotels, the Bund, was on the waterfront. The right side of the city was Japanese and had three main streets: Benten dori, the street for antiques, gift shops, and other Japanese goods; Honcho dori, the "main" street where the best shops were located, and Isezaki-cho, or "Theatre Street," pictured here. This was the entertainment and restaurant center of the city. By the 1880s, the Japanese penchant for Western garb began, and can be seen here on the men wearing derbies. Many photographers' studios were in the Bund the section of the city and others had their studios on Benten dori and other nearby streets.

Japan, an island nation, was geographically well situated to become isolated once a powerful military was established. Up until the ninth century, much of Japanese life was influenced by Chinese, as well as Korean, culture. The Heian Period, established in 794, began the decline of outside influence and the start of the fledgling nation's independent lifestyle. At the beginning of this era, the capital was moved to Kyoto, then known as Heiankyo (city of peace and tranquility). This dynasty lasted until 1192, and it was a period of unprecedented peace and security—as well as indulgence. During this time the arts flourished and the "entertainment" predecessor of the geisha was created.

The Heian era ended when families—essentially warlords with their own militias—began a civil war. The outcome was the creation of a new form of government: the shogunate. It was a significant step in the development of Japan. There were several shogunate dynasties, starting with the Kamakura (1192–1333), then the Muromachi (1338–1573), next the Azuchi-Momoyama (1573–1603), and finally the Edo (1603–1868). The shogunate had seized power from the imperial court and became the practical rulers of Japan until the Meiji Restoration in 1868. The shogun's administration became known as *bakufu*, literally translated as "tent government." Legally, the shogunate was under the control of the emperor, but in actuality it was a military dictatorship with the emperors as powerless figureheads.

During the Kamakura shogunate, the Mongols attempted to conquer Japan. In 1274, Kublai Kahn attacked the island nation with over 40,000 troops, but failed due to bad weather. Khan, recognizing that nature, not military incompetence, was the cause of his defeat, launched another assault seven years later, in 1281. He assembled a new armada consisting of two fleets with over 140,000 men. A typhoon destroyed the forces and it was interpreted as God's answer to the prayers of the Japanese and their Buddhist and Shinto priests. They called it *kamikaze*, "divine wind." The typhoon became an integral part of the legend and heritage of the country. (To evoke hope and success, the Japanese named their World War II suicide pilots kamikaze.)

Japan had been closed to outsiders for at least three centuries when, in the fourteenth century, limited trade was reestablished with the Chinese. Contact with Westerners began in 1542, when the Muromachi shogunate, also known as the Ashikaga shogunate, allowed the first European ship, a Portuguese vessel that had been blown off course, to land and develop trade. The Portuguese introduced Christianity, as well as firearms, to Japan. The Japanese were cautious in exposing their culture to foreign influence and only opened the port of Nagasaki and surrounding islands to the Portuguese and Chinese. A trade station was established, exposing the Japanese to limited European culture and vice versa. Western, "modern" scientific developments were introduced, including the microscope and telescope.

In 1549, Portuguese Jesuit priests led by Francis Xavier (later canonized) began to proselytize, and eventually converted thousands of Japanese to Christianity. In 1573, a new ruling era was established, the Momoyama shogunate—in which three military rulers began unifying the country. On July 24, 1587 a decree was issued ordering the Christian priests to leave.[1] Religious proselytizing was forbidden. In 1600, Dutch traders, and in 1613, English traders, succeeded in establishing rights to trade in Nagasaki and Hirado.

In 1600, the legendary Battle of Sekigahara brought the Tokugawa family to power, and in 1603, the Tokugawa shogunate, or Edo period, was established. It lasted until 1868. The castle town of Edo (Tokyo) was the home of the Tokugawa, and over the 250 years of their rule the town grew into the largest city in the world. Edo was known as the eastern capital, and Kyoto, the home of the powerless emperor, the western capital. The new shogunate began reversing the accomplishments of Westernization and forced the reconversion of its citizens back to Japanese religions. They called this policy of isolation *sakoku*. Restrictions were enforced throughout the country, regulating all aspects of the culture, including class structure. Every individual's place in society was defined and one could not move between classes. From 1616 to 1636, thousands of Christian Japanese and foreign priests were executed.[2] Businesses established by the English were unsuccessful, and they withdrew in 1623. In 1633, the shogunate forbade travel abroad. In addition, all foreign books were banned. In 1639, the Portuguese were expelled. For the next two centuries, Japan again isolated itself from the rest of the world, allowing only Dutch and Chinese traders to operate on Deshima Island near Nagasaki. The island was artificially constructed for isolating foreigners from the Japanese. The Dutch continued to gradually introduce Western scientific concepts and inventions to the Japanese, *rangaku*.

It was America who opened Japan to the world. The United States hoped for friendly ports for American whaling vessels in the far Pacific, as well as for trade with the mysterious island nation. On July 8, 1853, America's Commodore Mathew Perry sailed four black steam ships armed with canons into Tokyo harbor. He had a letter from President Millard Fillmore and refused to present it to anyone but the emperor or his highest emissaries, promising force if he was denied. Perry left with a promise to return, which he did in March of 1854, securing a treaty. An American consulate was created in Japan, which opened in 1855. As a result of the American intervention, the Japanese made preliminary agreements with the Dutch and Russians in the same year. By 1858, a treaty satisfactory to the Western nations was negotiated. It opened up trade and ports in Nagasaki, Hakodate, Kanagawa, Osaka, and Yokohama. French, Russian, British, Dutch, and American traders and diplomats finally had a foothold in the country.

Xenophobia, however, was rampant, and attacks against foreigners were common. The foreign enclaves in the treaty ports were the safest place for foreigners. The murder of a British businessman in 1862 in a town near Yokohama was the last straw, and forced England take action to protect its citizens. Unable to receive assurances of the safety of British citizens, an armed fleet was sent to Japan. The murder had been committed by members of the Satsuma clan. The British bombarded and destroyed their home town of Kagoshima, as the Japanese did not have canons to fight the fleet. They kept the ships in Japanese waters to control the seas and intimidate warring factions.

The British joined forces with three other countries and fought with the Chôshû clan, who controlled access to a strait leading to a major port. The Chôshû had hoped to drive out the foreigners, but they were easily beaten and realized that it would be almost impossible. So they changed their tactics. They shifted their loyalty from the shogunate to the emperor. The country was divided. The Chôshû forces joined with the Satsuma clan to challenge the shogunate's policies. In 1864, after a series of skirmishes, the clans entered the capital city of Kyoto and a battle ensued. A fire was started that destroyed over 28,000 buildings in the city. Civil war broke out in the country, which resulted in the resignation of the shogun in November of 1867. Fighting for control of the country became intense. When the last battles were over in late 1868, power reverted to the Meiji emperor and his allies, including the Chôshû and Satsuma rebels. The official capital was moved from Kyoto to Edo (Tokyo). Since 1868, there have been four reigning emperors. Japanese history is divided into the time period of the life of each emperor, Meiji (1868–1912), Taisho (1912–1926), Showa (1926–1989), and Heisei (1989–present).

The new government, in order to create unity and awareness of imperial rule, modernized the county with drastic laws that forever changed the nation. In 1869, the rigid feudal class structure was abandoned: the four lower classes were now equal and one could potentially move between them. Creating a modernized army under the control of the new government was a critical goal for them, and conscription of the lower classes was established in 1872. Under the strict Edo period caste system, the samurai were an unproductive warrior class who were not allowed to work, and were supported by taxation of other classes. The new government simply disenfranchised the samurai class, pensioned them off under unfavorable terms and forbade them to wear their swords, attempting to confiscate them in 1876. They rebelled. In 1877, the Seinan war, the uprising of the Satsuma clan, finally ended the ambitions of the samurai class.

To elevate the emperor's position as a spiritual leader, Shinto was made the state religion. Other economic and social changes created an entrepreneurial class. Reliance on the agricultural "wet rice" economy was gradually abandoned. Farming was very labor-intensive, and the plight of the peasant farmer did not improve until after World War II (1945). The Japanese first turned to manufacturing textiles, and then to more industrial endeavors. Foreign experts, *o-yatoi gaijin*, were employed to run the new enterprises and teach the Japanese manufacturing, engineering, and scientific processes. Japanese scholars were sent to American and European universities to be educated, returning to the country with modern expertise. Western-style civil codes were promulgated during the 1880s. In 1889, after a decade of contention, a written constitution was introduced. It was revised numerous times until Western influences were reduced, so that it was satisfactory enough for Western ideologies but also strong enough to assure Japan some international respectability. With the help of European politicians, the constitution gave the emperor extensive and absolute powers to ensure social order, command the army, and control the Diet (legislature). By the time of the war with China in 1894, Japan had become a determined and competent industrialized nation with modern steel, shipbuilding, and armament capabilities. The war with Russia in 1904 proved that to the rest of the world. Even though the country was opened to the world in trade and participated in some international endeavors, it would be a while before the hearts and minds of the Japanese ruling class would truly be open to Western ideas.

In the treaty ports, foreigners developed their own society, as they were not allowed to freely intermingle with the Japanese. The treaty port of Yokohama had large foreign enclaves, each with their own private clubs, businesses, entertainment areas, and housing. Initially they were small ghettos within the ports. Travel into the interior was forbidden, and if necessary, special passports were issued. Even then, carefully laid out routes and approved Western-style hotels were required. In the 1870s, foreigners were only allowed to travel about 20 miles inland from the port cities. Over the decades, as the country progressed economically, increased travel was permitted in the interior. In 1899, the passport system ended and travel restrictions were removed.

It was in the port cities that travelers were introduced to Japanese culture, and could take home as souvenirs the lacquered albums of hand-colored photographs. The Japanese carefully controlled the image of the country that was exported to the West. One can posit that the photographs offered to Westerners were carefully scripted images that Japan wanted to present. Foreigners were most impressed with Japanese art and design, which were presented at fairs and exhibitions worldwide, including London, Paris, Berlin, and Vienna. American fascination with Japan began with Perry's voyage. New Englanders were particularly interested because of the association with American whaling interests, which were instrumental in opening the country. They were among the early pioneer businessmen and travelers there. Herman Melville's *Moby Dick or The Whale* (1851) tells of a hunt of a powerful white whale. The story is set off Japan, and references to the closed, mysterious nation appear in the book.[3]

The first major American introduction to Japanese art and culture was at the Centennial Exhibition of 1876 held in Philadelphia. "Japonisme," Japanese-influenced design and decor, became fashionable in America in the late 1870s, and, furniture, picture frames, wallpaper, flatware, and other goods were decorated with Japanese motifs. There was also an exhibition at the 1884–5 New Orleans World's Industrial and Cotton Centennial Exposition. At the World's Columbian Exposition held in Chicago in 1893, a 60,000–square foot Japanese village was constructed, and sold Japanese products. In 1897, the J.B. Millet Company published a ten-volume set of books on Japan with tipped-in hand-colored photographs. The books were sold to collectors and a special edition was made for American department stores. In total, 37,500 volumes were produced.

In the 1904, the Louisiana Purchase Exposition was held in St. Louis, Missouri. It was to be the largest world's fair ever held. The Japanese presence was spectacular. One entered through a 150-foot reproduction of the 300-year-old Portal of Nikko (the gate to the sacred burial ground). It opened into a reproduction of a street in Tokyo's Asakusa district with gardens and 300 "natives." There were over 40 stores, a theatre seating 600, and several teahouses, with 40 geisha. Japanese participation also included a pavilion, in which was installed a replica of the summer home of Prince Pu Lun, a magnificent Japanese garden, and a reproduction of the emperor's imperial garden, including lagoons, seven buildings, and several pagodas.

Japanese art and culture, promoted by fairs and museum exhibits, resulted in a worldwide audience for all things Japanese. Photographs, prints, porcelains, textiles, and other such goods were the objects Japan wanted to offer the world as representative of their culture. In the United States, the Boston Museum of Fine Arts hired Japanese art expert Okakura Kakuzô as curator and cultural commentator of their Japanese collection, a position he held from 1904 to 1913. The museum, "then and now [contains] the greatest most comprehensive repository of Japanese art outside Japan."[4]

By the end of the Meiji era in 1912, Japan had become a quiet world power, having removed the shackles of feudalism. This period coincided with America's Gilded Age, in which the United States similarly became an industrialized nation and world power. Japan joined the United States and her allies in World War I against Germany, Turkey, and the other Central Powers. Within 30 years, however, the two nations would be at war. At the end of World War II, an American-dictated peace and democratic constitution would truly open Japan to the world. In the 1850s and again in 1940s, the paths of the two nations crossed. With each encounter, the feudal past and strict codes of Japanese society were rewritten.

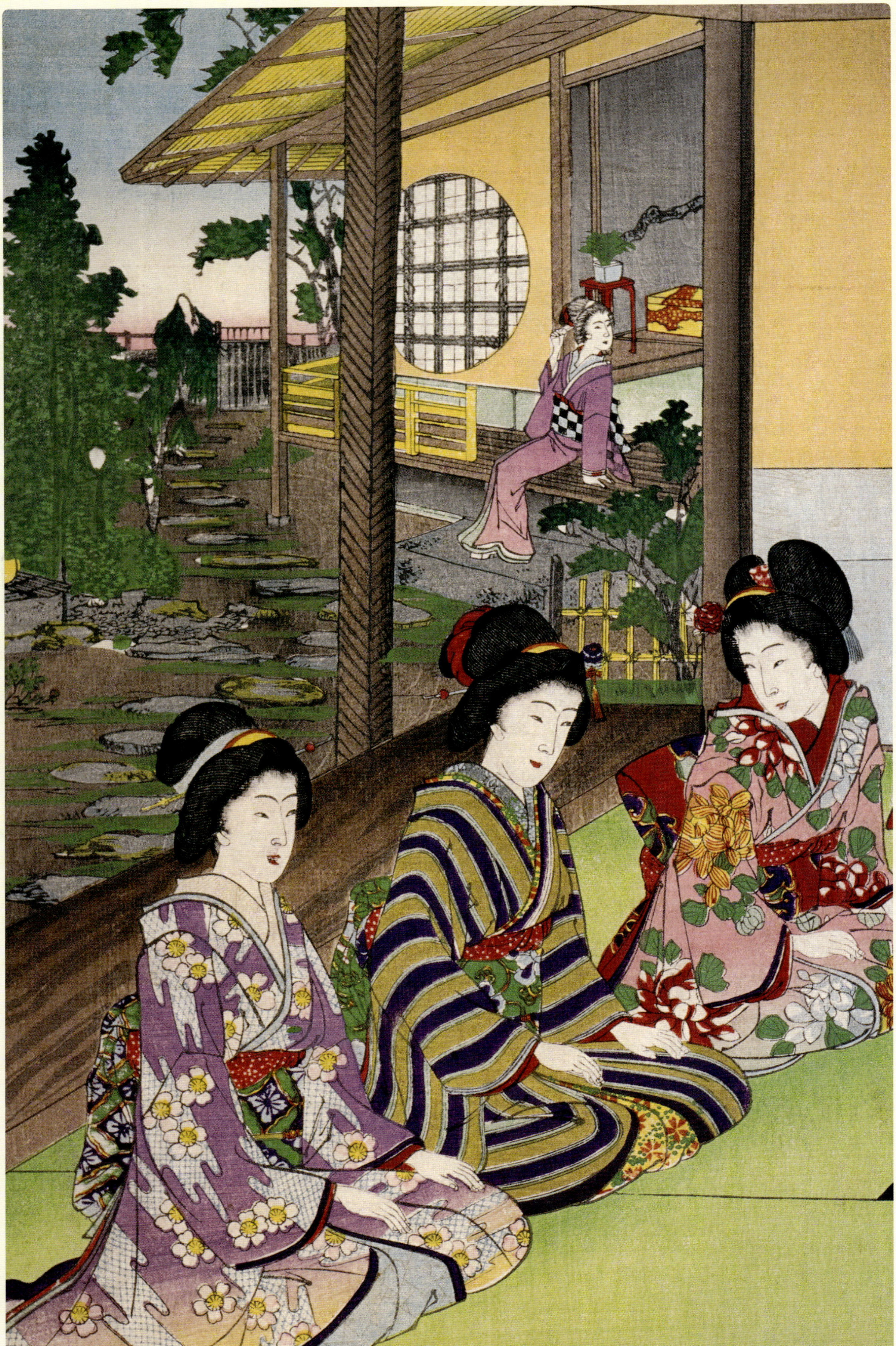

Ukiyo-e
Pictures of the Floating World

In the evolution and development of art, in any country, one would expect that revered subjects, themes, and compositions would flow from one era to the next. Advancements in science and technology do not hamper this stately flow. A new technology simply offers artists another way of viewing and expressing their familiar world. When photography was introduced into Japan, it became a popular and commercial success. Western photographers working in Japan were instrumental in establishing commercial photography for tourists and foreigners living in Japan. They adapted and followed the themes of prior artistic conventions, and most importantly created a unique format by having the images hand-colored in emulation of a centuries-old popular artwork that was identified with Japan—the ukiyo-e.

The ukiyo-e is a colored woodblock print. The print was developed in the early 1600s in Edo (Tokyo). Ukiyo-e were laden with allusions to and images of mythology, and emphasized life in the "floating world," the hedonistic and entertainment center of the city, the licensed Yoshiwara district. The pleasures of the teahouse, brothel, theatre, and restaurant, along with the cast of characters who inhabited, worked in, and enjoyed these establishments were the main themes of these early prints. Originally monochromatic and drawn with bold lines, in the 1700s, ukiyo-e began to be vividly colored. Woodblock printing enabled Japanese artists to mass produce images. These richly colored prints were strikingly graphic and visually appealing. By the nineteenth century, *bijin-ga* (images of beauties) become one of the central themes of ukiyo-e. The prints celebrated both real and idealized women, especially geisha and courtesans. Japanese feminine beauty in fashionable attire became a defining and recognizable image. With the opening of Japan in the mid-nineteenth century, these visual representations rapidly spread through the Western world and became symbolic of Japanese cultural iconography.

By the 1860s, ukiyo-e had become perhaps the major art form of Japan. The subject matter included an entire range of visual illustration, from fantasized mythological figures to landscapes and noted personages. Japanese participation in fairs and exhibitions worldwide influenced design, decoration, and the art world. Ukiyo-e prints provided new aesthetic conceptions for Western artists. The lines, colors, and bold strokes of the ukiyo-e provided inspiration for generations. Perhaps the best-known interpretation of the convention was that of French artist Henri de Toulouse-Lautrec (1864–1901). His poster for the Moulin Rouge of the cancan dancer La Goulue was in a dramatic new style. The highly stylized poses, bold colors, patterning, flattened perspective, and asymmetrical composition became a touchstone for future generations' artistic expression. The spirit of Japanese ukiyo-e had entered Western art.

Ukiyo-e (Chikanobu, c. 1870. Courtesy London Clark Gallery, Washington, DC)

This woodblock print depicts three geisha in a teahouse. It is by Chikanubu, who was born in Niigata Prefecture as Hashimoto Tadayoshi. He was trained in the Kano school of painting, and later studied with the Utagawa masters. His artistic activity began in the Bunkyu era (1861–4). Chikanobu made his artistic reputation in the 1880s with triptychs illustrating political events of the Meiji period, including depictions of the imperial family, customs and manners of a changing Japan, and especially women and children. The painted photographs of the commercial photographers imitated these artworks, offering tourists and foreign residents a realistic compendium of Japanese life. The ukiyo-e images of the women of the pleasure quarters were perhaps the most popular of these Japanese artworks. By the first decade of the twentieth century in the West, the painted photographs would come to represent Japan, as these woodblocks previously had done.

History of Tourist Trade Photography

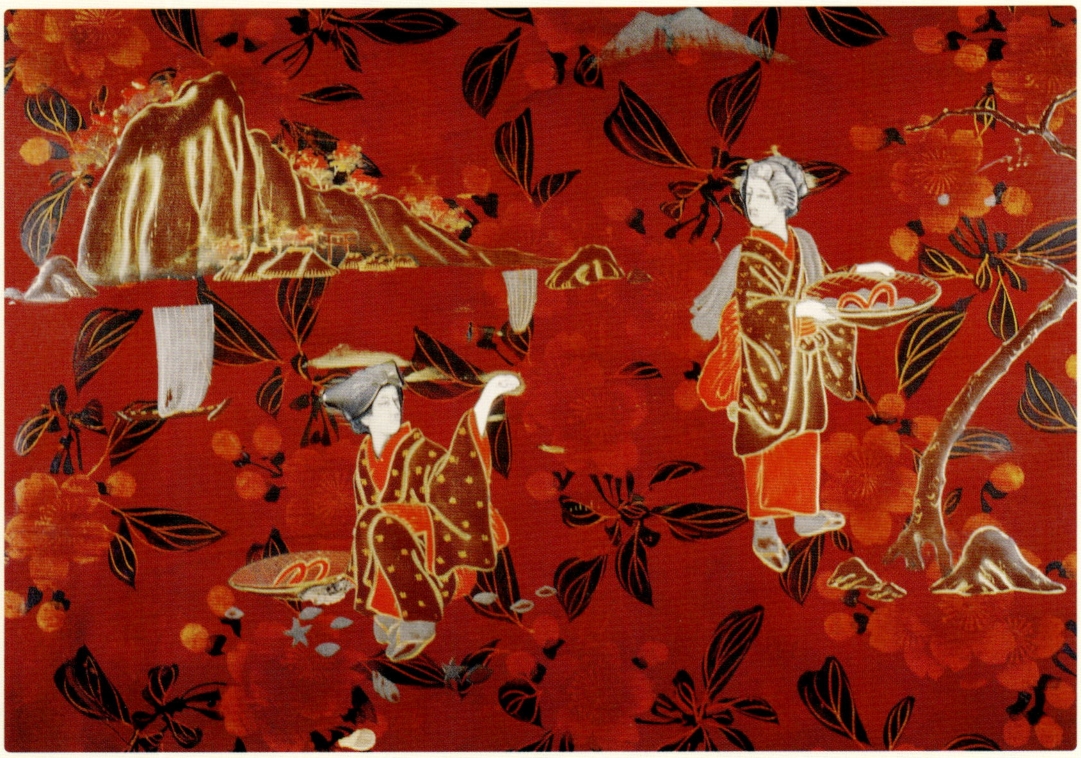

Photograph Album Cover

Typical lacquer cover of a tourist photograph album circa 1895. These covers were inlaid with various materials, usually bone, seashells, or semiprecious materials. They depicted scenes and symbols of Japanese life. The quality varied, much the same as the quality of the painting of the photographs. The earliest albums in the 1860s and early 1870s were cloth covered. Black lacquer albums became popular in the 1880s, followed by red lacquer. During the 1870s and 1880s, the purchaser handpicked the photographs to be placed in the albums, creating their own special souvenir. By the end of the century, studios put many albums together so tourists could simply buy a representative collection right off the shelf. Many of these studio albums were composite and accordion-style, in which the pictures folded out. Albums consisted of pictures of landscapes and shrines in the front and people ("native types") in the back.

The presentation of photography (the daguerreotype) to the world in August 1839 by Parisian Louis J.M. Daguerre was soon followed by worldwide acceptance and use of the medium. Japan's isolation made it the last major country to adopt photography. But once introduced, and to this day, the Japanese were among the most fervent users and appreciators. Japanese photographers and scientists have long been involved in advancing the profession and today are among the leaders of innovations.

Nineteenth-Century Japan and Its Two Main Schools of Photography

Early Japanese photographers can be divided into two different schools. The first were those who learned the art from Europeans and followed their own road to developing the profession for the Japanese. The second offered tourists and foreigners living in Japan souvenir photographs of Japanese culture and landscapes. Many of these images were staged. For about a quarter of a century European photographers were the leaders in tourist trade photography, however by 1890, all the studios had been purchased by the Japanese. The images produced by these photographers were hand-colored albumen prints that were assembled in lacquered albums. These "commercial" photographs are now generally recognized as representative of nineteenth-century Japanese photography.

It is this second group of photographers and their photographs that this text addresses. These photographers catered to the treaty ports' foreign clientele and tourists. They produced what some Japanese have labeled "pictorial Japanalia." Despite the name, the images, for the most part, are accurate representations of the country and culture. They have also been called the "Yokohama" school of photography. The majority of the photographs were taken and sold in Yokohama, primarily with one goal in mind—satisfying the foreigner's taste for the exotic nation and its people.

Photographs of Japanese landmarks were also of interest to the Japanese, who wanted mementos of their native land and of their own sojourns.

The first group of Japanese photographers has been the subject of several significant scholarly studies, including Ann Wilkes-Tucker's *History of Japanese Photography* and the Japan Photographer's Association's *A Century of Japanese Photography*. These works concentrate on the profession as it relates to the Japanese for the Japanese. Tourist photography is not considered a critical part of this aspect of Japanese photographic history, exemplified by the number of tourist images in these texts. For example, Ann Wiles-Tucker's text has 206 plates, of which three are tourist-type portraits, and the Japan Photographer's Association's text has 514 photographs, of which only five are tourist portrait images. Yokohama-style tourist photographs are of the most common surviving nineteenth-century Japanese photographs. They are generally considered representative of Japanese photography because of their beauty, aesthetic, and anthropological interest. The landscape photographs may be accurate examples of indigenous Japanese photography, as they were taken for both markets: foreigner as well as Japanese. The "native type," staged photographs were taken primarily for foreigners.

During the heyday of the hand-colored photograph, 1870 to 1910, the Japanese participated for the first time in numerous world's fairs and expositions. At many of these fairs, extensive exhibitions of Japanese life were offered, including teahouses with geisha. Japanese authorities strictly regulated the perspective of Japan offered to the West, and a quaint feudal culture with beautiful landscapes and shrines was exhibited. It is probable that the photographs shown to the public were censored, as Japanese social and cultural life was rigidly regulated. The most popular "native type" images were of geisha, Kabuki actors, samurai, priests, peasants, and shopkeepers, and the daily life of those groups. Most of these were staged, contrived scenes representing Japanese culture. Tourists also played a significant role in the choice of subject matter, as they preferred photographs of an ancient culture with indigenous peoples. Topics of Japanese life that were otherwise too banal to be the subject of photographs, such as getting dressed or taking a bath, were in demand by Western visitors and European photographers—who were intrigued with all aspects of the exotic. In the last third of the nineteenth century, cultural anthropologists toured the world photographing the world's indigenous peoples, in an effort to establish racial differences and mental traits and to see the diversification of humankind as proposed in Darwin's *Origin of Species*.

Japan, isolated from the Western world for centuries, seemed a perfect laboratory for the adventurous traveler. The exotic photographs they brought home proved it was. Credit belongs to the foreigners for the existence of subject matter the Japanese photographer on his own would not have photographed, thinking the topics too mundane to be recorded. Foreigners' curiosity and ability to pay resulted in an incredibly wide visual spectrum of daily life and occupations. Fascination with Japanese garb and exotic practices dictated their recording. In the 1860s, Western photographers, to supply this audience, created the hand-colored albumen print. These tourist trade commercial photographs were beautiful works of photography and art.

Japan Photographed

The commercial landscape photographs were concentrated around the treaty ports, Nagasaki on Kyushu, the southernmost of the four main islands of Japan; Hakodate on Hokkaido, the largest northern island; and Yokohama on Honshu, the largest and main island of the country. Yokohama became the leading city for commercial photography, and it was here that the majority of albums were produced. Tourists, when visiting the country, usually waited until they got to Yokohama to buy them, as this is where the greatest selection of photographs was available.

Dating of Japanese Tourist Photography

The Japanese Photographer's Association, in their 1980 survey of Japanese photography, stated that, "It is impossible to date many of the earliest photographs precisely, and consequently they are now simply assigned to slices of time peculiar to Japanese history." The first is Bakumatsu, 1853 to 1867, which is the feudal era or time of the Tokugowa shogunate. The next is the Meiji, 1868 to 1912, which is divided into three periods: the early Meiji, 1868 to 1882, the middle Meiji, 1883 to 1897, and late Meiji, 1897 to 1912. During these eras, the greatest numbers of tourist photographs were produced. Since it is unclear when a photograph was taken, in almost all cases, the term "circa" is used to estimate the era.

Models in Japanese Tourist Photography

Japanese commercial "custom and costume" photographs have sparked two great controversies. The first is authorship and the second is discovering who posed for the image. Some photographic historians suggest that models often posed as geisha, while some cultural historians suggest they are actually geisha. Many of the photographs are clearly geisha. The photographs chosen for this compilation, for the most part, appear to be geisha. Geisha and geisha life were revered subjects of photographers, and by the end of the century photography had helped to propel the geisha to national celebrity. The twentieth-century image of the white-faced geisha was not fully established in the nineteenth century. It was *oiran* and other high-class prostitutes that wore white face makeup and elaborate costumes, while geisha were understated so as not compete with them. Geisha who were well off or associated with an important *danna* would not need to pose for photographers, unless perhaps as a celebrity. Other geisha, of which there were thousands, would be available as models. The anthropological mentality of tourists demanded accurate representations. Certainly it would seem reasonable that it was just as easy to hire geisha to pose.

Allen Hockley in *First Encounters—Emerging Stereotypes: Westerners and Geisha in the Late Nineteenth Century*,[5] notes that by the mid-1870s Westerners knew about geisha, and that they were designated singers, dancers, and entertainers. Artist Charles Wrigman, who wrote captions (on the back of the photographs) for Felice Beato in the late 1860s, used these terms, as did others who later photographed geisha. Hockley also notes that, "Western visitors to Yokohama recorded that geisha commonly acted as models in photographic studios." Analysis of hairstyles and other attributes may ultimately result in clearer separation of the models. But accurate nineteenth-century records of geisha dress and life must be the ultimate source, as geisha appearance and social position were evolving in this era. In any case, the photographs, for the most part, accurately portray geisha public and private life in the late nineteenth century. The geisha and *maiko* photographed for twentieth-century postcards were real, as the Japanese public was now a major part of the audience for this imagery and using models would not have been credible, especially since a competitor could offer accurate subjects.

Analysis of early Japanese photographs indicates that, by and large, the individuals posed in the images were in the professions they depicted. Undoubtedly actors were used in the photographs of Kabuki. There is no mistaking sumo wrestlers, *betto* (tattooed grooms), *orian*, Shinto priests, or even trade people in their shops. They are all real and accurate portrayals. The great majority of the numerous photographs that survive of samurai are also certainly of actual samurai. The samurai were outlawed in the early Meiji era (1868), but they fought against their dissolution, which was finally achieved in 1877. But between 1868 and 1877, many samurai had their images taken. They, as well as photographers, wanted to immortalize their glory. The images capture the final moments of the 700 years of their rule. There is no published period evidence stating that the models von Stillfried and others used for soft-core photographs were prostitutes, but they may well have been. Prostitutes were clearly used in hard-core photographs, as the images show detailed sexual acts. Women loosening their kimonos and going topless in hot weather was part of the culture in feudal and early Meiji era Japan, as nudity did not have the same stigma it did in the West. "Teahouse girls," servers and entertainers, are also possible models for some images. Some photographic historians posit that actors modeled in the photographs, but in Meiji Japan all actors were men. Women actors were entertainers: geisha. The question of who posed may be answered in the future. However fires destroyed the majority of the records of Beato, von Stillfried, Farsari, and others—a full and accurate history will most likely never be known.

Staging & Censorship

Most of the portraits of "native types," and "customs and costumes," as the images were designated in period publications, were staged in a studio. The excessive staging that took place in studio photography may be an attempt at recreating the style and format of the ukiyo-e, woodblock print, the predecessor of the hand-colored photograph. On the other hand, it may have been the nature of the Japanese aesthetic.

Outdoor photographs were censored: strict government regulation dictated who, what, and where could be photographed. In 1867, Felice Beato was allowed to take landscape photographs of Lake Biwa near Kyoto, but he was forbidden to take photographs in the city. Also, on January 1, 1872, the new Meiji emperor Mutsu-Hito visited the naval arsenal at Yokosuka. During this tour, Baron von Stillfried surreptitiously photographed the emperor. When the existence of the photograph was discovered a political uproar followed, leading to diplomatic confrontations. The Austrian counsel seized one negative. Marketing photographs of the emperor was forbidden. However since photographs and negatives existed, copies may have been circulated. Therefore it was decided by the government to have an official portrait of the Mikado emperor taken. Uchida Kyuicha (1844–1875) took the first and official images of Mutsu-Hito.

Significance of the Images

The camera records details that writers of the period often neglect, as what they see is so commonplace that they do not feel compelled to describe it. It also depicts subtle nuances in visual composition impossible to express by the written word. These photographs were staged, however they offer a reality that was believed to be representative of their customs by their creators. These photographers show the nineteenth-century world of geisha for us to contemplate. They have given us a vision of geisha from daily life to dinner parties. These images are records of geisha that supplement the written word, and grant us a window in time, a glimpse at their hidden world.

Authorship of Japanese Photographs

Authorship of photographs in the first school of Japanese photography, those taken by Japanese photographers for the Japanese market, is fairly well documented. However a problem exists in attributing authorship of commercial photographs, the images taken for the foreign market. Numerous historians have attempted to document these photographs. The history of photographers, both Japanese and Western, involved in tourist photography is also convoluted. Clarifying these histories has been extremely difficult because of several unfortunate practices and events, among which were the lack of signatures on photographs, negatives, or mattes; the creation of English titles and numbers and routinely changing them; the swapping and sharing of images, especially landscapes and shrines, to enable photographers in different localities a full selection for their clients; the buying of studios and libraries of photographs and re-presentation as products of the new owners; the setting up and taking of photographs by an assistant, not the owner of the studio (just as most of Mathew Brady's Civil War images were found to be taken by Gardner, O'Sullivan, Gibson, and others); and finally the destruction of inventories by fires and earthquakes.

Only five photographic studios are significant in the commercial photography trade, producing over 95 percent of nineteenth-century hand-colored tourist albums. All five studios were located in Yokohama. They were run by Japanese photographers Kusakabe Kimbei and Tamamura Kozaburo, and foreigners Felice Beato, Baron von Stillfried, and Adolfo Farsari. Kusakabe, Farsari, and Tamamura produced the most albums. In Nagasaki, Ueno Hikoma created some tourist albums, but more significantly sold negatives to other photographers. It was for only 27 years, 1863 to 1890, that Western photographers were involved in the tourist photography business.

Several Japanese institutions and Western scholars, including Londoner Terry Bennett, are attempting to reconstruct the lives of photographers working in Japan, and to identify the original artist who produced the photographs attributed to the major studios. John Clark, in his 2001 *Japanese Exchanges in Art 1850s–1930s: with Britain, continental Europe, and the USA*, offers a year-by-year, and in many cases a month-by-month, study of Japanese tourist photographers and others artists. This book is the essential English language source. Not only does it go into explicit detail about their lives, but also gives the location of institutions where their work can be found. At best, perhaps 5 percent of surviving hand-colored Japanese commercial portraiture and costume photographs can be positively identified, as to who snapped the picture. With the current stage of knowledge, it is probably wisest to attribute authorship to a studio rather than a person. The first commercial photographer, Felice Beato, published books and albums in the 1860s: therefore the photographs included therein are clearly his work.

Chronology of Commercial Photography

Selected dates and information on the history of Japanese tourist photography

1854 Commodore Matthew Perry arrives with an American fleet, opening Japan to the West. Accompanying him is daguerreotypist Eliphalet Brown Jr., who takes daguerreotypes of the Japanese.

Prior to 1862 Several foreign photographers, some attached to missions, take images of Japan and teach the Japanese photography.

1862 Ueno Hikoma (1838–1904) opens a small studio in Nagasaki, becoming the master portrait photographer for the wealthy and notable Japanese. His cartes de visite are poignant records of the era. He trades his landscape images with commercial photographers. His studio operates until his death.

Shimooka Renjo (1823–1914), considered by many the father of Japanese photography, opens a studio in Yokohama and practices until the early 1900s.

1863 Felice Beato (1825–1908), a noted war photographer, arrives in Yokohama and creates hand-colored tourist photography. He did not number or sign his images, but vignettes his portraits. It is his work and studio that establish the commercial tourist industry.

1864 Beato partners with artist Charles Wrigman. Beato sells painted photographic albums and Wrigman sells paintings.

1866 In October, a major Yokohama fire destroys many of Beato's negatives and much of his stock.

1867 Beato retires as a tourist photographer, but his studio maintains the photographic commercial business without him. He doesn't give up photography, but continues in an official position for the U.S. in Korea and Japan, documenting conflicts in Asia.

1868 Beato publishes two volumes of photographs.

Baron Raimund von Stillfried-Ratenicz (1839–1911), an Austrian officer, diplomat, artist, and adventurer, arrives in Japan and learns photography.

1871 Von Stillfried opens a studio in the foreign concession area in Yokohama.

1872 Beato visits Europe. John Goddard and H. Woolett run his studio with four Japanese photographers and four artists.

1873–1878 Von Stillfried exhibits his images at various world's fairs, including exhibitions in Vienna, Paris, Berlin, and Amsterdam, as well as America's Centennial Exhibition held in Philadelphia. He brings three geisha to the Vienna exhibition to serve in a teahouse he had had constructed by two Japanese carpenters. At its height, von Stillfried's studio employed 38 full-time assistants to produce his photographs.[6]

1876 Japan passes the "Photography Ordinance," establishing copyrights on photographs with proper fees. Five years of protection is offered.

Tamamura Kozaburo moves his studio, established two years earlier, from Edo (Tokyo) to Yokohama.

1877 Von Stillfried buys Beato's studio with its 15 employees and begins numbering Beato's images. He labels many with English titles. This purchase was perhaps the result of a fire on January 14 that destroyed Stillfried's offices and apparatus. Fortunately, most of his negatives, six years of work, were saved.

1878 Hermann Andersen, von Stillfried's partner, buys the business and keeps the name "Stillfried and Andersen" as well as the impressive title "Japan Photographic Association," that Stillfried had also operated and exhibited under.

1880 The main commercial photographic studios in Yokohama are Andersen's. Stillfrieds brother, Franz, has some of his negatives and attempts to sell albums. About 1,200 foreigners are living in Yokohama alone.

1881 Kusakabe Kimbei (1841–1934) opens his studio in Yokohama. He started his career as Beato's assistant, and subsequently specialized in vividly painted photographs.

1883 The dry plate photographic process is introduced in Japan. It makes photography easier, cheaper, and reduces exposure time. The Yokohama photographs continue to be printed on albumen paper, which was developed in the 1850s, rather than on the modern silver-gelatin based papers, which were developed in the 1880s.

Adolfo Farsari (1841–1898), an Italian American who had arrived in Japan in 1873, learns photography and attempts to create his studio.

Baron Raimund von Stillfried leaves Japan and returns to Austria.

1884 Felice Beato leaves Japan after losing his fortune in the silver futures market.

Andersen partners with Franz von Stillfried and the business continues.

1885 Kusakabe buys some of von Stillfried, Beato, and Hikoma's negatives.

Farsari buys von Stillfried's studio from Andersen, with all the employees. He acquires many of Beato's negatives in the deal. He is now the only Western photographer practicing in Japan.

1886 Fire destroys all of Farsari's negatives and most of his stock. He begins immediately replacing his inventory by taking photographs and acquiring negatives of other photographers. After 1886, Farsari albums no longer contain Stillfried or Beato photos.

1887 A new "Photography Ordinance" is passed, allowing ten years of protection.

1889 Ogawa Kazumasa (1860–1929) opens a photoengraving company, specializing in collotype printing, which he had learned in Boston.

1890 Farsari, the last western commercial photographer, leaves Japan. His studio name continues. By 1891, Fasari's studio has about 20 artists painting photographs. Fasari's best artists paint only two to three detailed photographs a day. Kusakabe and Tamamura, and the Farsari studio, are the leading commercial photographers, producing more photographs and albums in the 1890s than their predecessors.

All commercial photographic studios are now owned and run by Japanese photographers.

1891 Ogawa photographs 100 Tokyo geisha and produces a collotype book with their pictures. He also makes some hand-colored albumen prints, but he concentrates on collotype photographs of *bijin*, beauties.

1892 The Japanese Directory of 1892 lists Kusakabe as offering 2,000 8 by 10 prints at $2 per dozen. Colored lanternslides are offered at $6 per dozen.[7]

1897 Tamamura ships about a half million photographs to Boston for incorporation in the various editions of Francis Brinkley's *Japan: Described and Illustrated by the Japanese*.

1900 Postcards with photographs are authorized in Japan. Many of the commercial photographs become available as postcards. Ogawa's collotype format becomes the foremost process in mass producing picture postcards.

1904/5 Herbert Ponting and other photojournalists are sent to Japan to cover the Russo-Japanese War. They create stereoviews and lantern slides for sale to the public.

1913 Kusakabe Kimbei's studio closes.

1917 Farsari's studio, run by Japanese photographers since 1890, closes.

1923 Tamamura's studio is destroyed in the Great Kanto Earthquake on September 1.

Japanese Postcard Culture

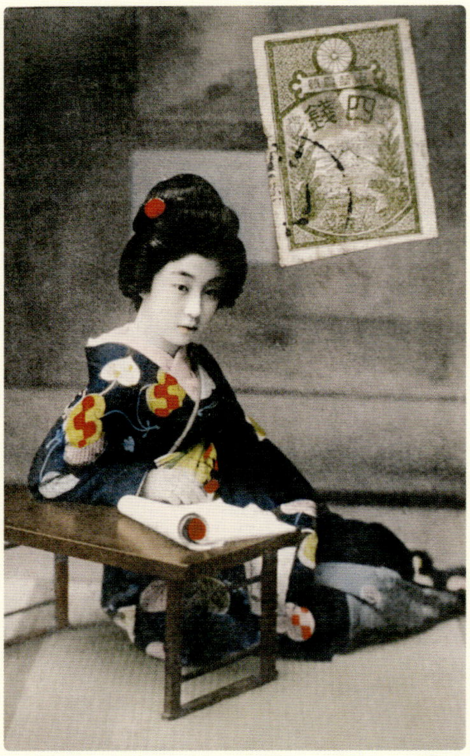

At the turn of the century, two innovations revolutionized the dissemination of photography—the Kodak camera and the picture postcard (*e-hagaki*). During the first three decades of the twentieth century, billions of postcards were created worldwide. With the invention of the easy-to-use Kodak camera, amateur photography spread and all aspects of everyday life were documented. To be developed, the film needed to be sent to a processing plant, and printing the images as postcards was an option. Between the years 1900 and 1910, professional photographers dominated the picture postcard media. In Japan, professional photographers turned to their collection of images and began issuing postcards for travelers and the populace. Many were the same photographs used for souvenir albums. They also created new libraries of images specifically for postcards. One of the most popular topics was geisha. Picture postcards were (and still are) the most numerous and inexpensive photographic images. They offered the public access to images only the wealthy would have previously been able to afford. Blank albums were produced so people could create their own collections of postcards. Professional photographers began offering their classic lacquered souvenir albums with postcard-sized (3.5 by 5.5 inches) photographs instead of the more expensive traditional 8 by 10 inch images.

The defining event propelling the postcard into Japanese public consciousness was the Russo-Japanese War (1904–05). To stir up public pride and support for the war, the government began issuing commemorative postcards documenting the war effort and Japanese victories. Postcard collecting became a national craze, and exchange meetings were popular social events. People would line up overnight at post offices to get newly issued cards. When the war was won and war fever dissipated, photographers turned their camera lenses to topographical imagery of Japan, and its beautiful women and geisha. Before 1910, the only means of producing color images was to hand-color the postcard, as had been done with the large souvenir prints. However in 1910, a collotype coloring printing process was introduced. During the Russo-Japanese war, the Japanese soldiers viewed the postcard geisha in much the same way as the American World War II servicemen viewed the pin-up girl. The Tokyo geisha postcards were akin to Betty Grable posters, the most notable of WWII pin-ups, and were reproduced in the collotype process by Ogawa Kazura. Hand-colored photographic postcards (*te-saishiki e-hagaki*) of geisha became a symbol of national pride. They can be considered a continuation of the traditional wood block (ukiyo-e) imagery into the twentieth century.

Postal & Postcard History

Japanese postal history began in the 1870s. Postal service was established in March 1871 and the first stamps were issued in April. In December 1873, the first postcards were issued, and consisted of two cards folded together. They were replaced in May 1875 with the single-card style used to this day. During the next 25 years, various combinations of postcards from simple single cards to special double cards were issued. One style featured a return card to be mailed back to the sender. In 1894, the Japanese postal service released its first commemorative stamps and in 1902, the first commemorative picture postcard.

In 1900, a new law allowed private (non governmental) postcards to be made, and they were called *shisei hagaki*. This change of regulations attracted artists and photographers, and picture postcards became very popular. Many noted artists created cards, which are now quite valuable as original works of art. The picture postcard had a photograph, print, or drawing on one side, and the other side, by law, was for the address (and could not contain a message). As a result the pictures were often written over, however some cards were produced with small images, leaving space for the message.

The new picture cards gave rise to a postcard culture and a new era in Japanese postal history. In July 1905, a revised postal act allowed the privately issued postcards to have postal information in foreign languages. In 1906, the instructions "write only name and address," which were on the "front" of the card, were deleted. (In this era, the "front" of the postcard was the side with the address.) On March 28, 1907 the modern style of postal card was created, when a dividing line was printed on the "front" of the card and a message could be written on one side. Initially the line was not in the center, but divided the card into thirds: two-thirds for the address and one-third for a message. In March 1918, the dividing line was moved to the center, where it has remained to this day.

Dating Postcards

It is easy to date a postcard if it has a stamp or cancellation mark. If it has no postal marks, examination of the front of the card helps in determining the era in which it was produced. A printed front with no dividing line means that the card was issued between 1900 and March 1907. Cards with a one-third dividing line were produced from 1907 to 1918. While postcards with drawings, prints, or other such artwork were made in every time period, the age of photographic postcards can be roughly estimated by the format and coloring of the image. There were several photographic formats. Initially, in 1900, hand-colored photographs, *te-saishiki e-hagaki*, were produced, followed by collotype prints, and, by 1910, colored collotypes had appeared. The collotype was a mechanical photograph produced by a special printing press. They were a permanent image that did not fade. Sepia-toned silver-gelatin photographs but were produced from 1900 onwards, but became stylish in 1908. By the end first decade of the twentieth century, they were the most popular format. These "real photo" postcards have become a desired collectible worldwide.

Geisha Chronology

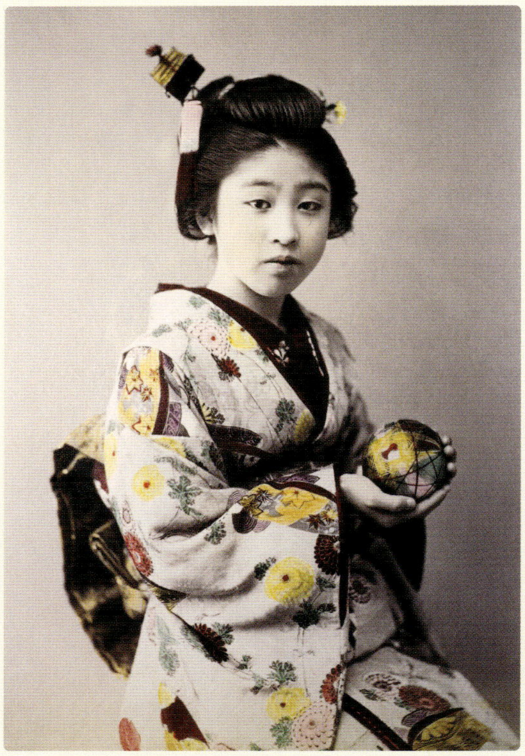

Geisha with a Thread Ball (attributed Adolfo Farsari, c. 1890)

A thread ball was a prop used by some geisha in performances, as well as in games such *temari asobi*, bouncing a thread ball. This beautifully painted photograph is from the studio of Adolfo Farsari (1841–1898), the last Western tourist market photographer in Japan. Farsari prided himself on the quality of his photographs. In a very competitive market, he did not compromise his ideals and charged the highest prices in Yokohama. He offered technically perfect images with extremely detailed painting in bright and accurate colors. His best colorists could paint only two to three photographs a day.

Geisha are artists preserving the traditional music, dance, and literature of feudal Japan. The literal translation of the word "geisha" is "arts person." Since Japan opened to the West, the vision of the painted, kimono-clad exotic woman has warranted fascination. Her singular appearance and esoteric lifestyle are unlike any other. To the nineteenth-century Victorian mind, the geisha was possibly the most intriguing aspect of a newly encountered country. To this day, the concept and the art of the geisha remain great mysteries of Japanese culture. The idea of a mistress or prostitute was well ingrained in Western society, but the notion of a woman dedicating her life to learning various and sophisticated cultural practices, and using them for the sole purpose of entertaining and pleasuring a man (without sex), was hard to fathom. Geisha came to epitomize the exotic East.

By the end of the 1870s, Western travelers in Japan recognized the primary roles of women in society: the wife, the prostitute, and the geisha. Once married, a woman's domain was the home. She was not expected to go out with her husband, to socialize, or to entertain. A wife did not accompany her husband to dinner parties or any other social activities. Marriages were arranged and sex was for procreation, certainly not recreation. It would be considered shocking for a wife to enjoy sex with her husband. Promiscuity was the norm, and recreational sex was to be found outside the home. In Heian and Edo Japan (794–1867), homosexuality was simply part of the sexual experience. A fundamental aspect of samurai life, similar to the ancient Greeks, was a sexual relationship between a young apprentice and seasoned warrior. This love was revered and had many names, including *bi-do*, the beautiful way, and *wakashudo*, the way of youth. Western moral concepts changed the nature of Japanese sexuality.

Prostitution was legal in Japan until 1958. During the early Edo period, licensed pleasure quarters were created and the districts became essential parts of all cities. The areas became known as the "floating world," *ukiyo*, where reality was to be left behind and one could indulge in worldly pleasures. Various levels of prostitute, as well as entertainments, were available. For centuries the *tayu*, courtesans to royalty and the highest members of society, were revered and respected. They dressed in the latest fashions, with elaborate hairstyles and makeup. They were entertainers, who sang, danced, and recited poetry. They were well educated and often members of the upper class. Their company was so desired that some were booked months in advance. It was not easy to arrange an assignation with a *tayu*, and she had the right to refuse any man. The age of the *tayu* ended in 1761, but the tradition was continued by the *oiran*. These women, dressed in a similar manner, were skilled performers. By the early nineteenth century, *oiran* concentrated on sexual practices and geisha took their place as entertainers.

The "flower and willow world," *karyukai*, the term used to describe geisha society, had, like the rest of Japan, its own codes of behavior. Even to their own countrymen, geisha have always maintained a level of secrecy about their culture. Their world is an intriguing, exotic, alternative universe. Each large city had its own geisha community, called *hanamachi*, "flower towns." They were usually incorporated into the pleasure quarters of a municipality. The *hanamachi* was a community within a community. It is essentially composed of *okiya*, houses where geisha lived, *ochaya*, teahouses, and *ryotei*, restaurants, where they worked. It also included the educators, stylists, and artisans that provided services for geisha. Every community has its own dialect and entertainment specialty. Pontocho, Gion, Shimbara, and Kamishichiken in Kyoto and Shinbashi, Akasaka, Kagurazaka, and Yoshicho in Edo were noted geisha flower towns. Other large groups of geisha existed in communities in Osaka, Nagasaki, and Kobe.

Becoming a geisha involved a lengthy and rigorous apprenticeship, the cost of which bound a girl to a geisha house. In the nineteenth century, it traditionally began at age six. Some acolytes were children or relatives of geisha, but many were sold by impoverished families to *zegen*, procurers who searched the countryside looking for beautiful children. The girls' general education included various traditional arts. They had to learn the distinctive slang of their district, which was seductive to clients and served to identify girls who ran away. A geisha had to study the shamisen, a stringed instrument, singing, dancing, writing, literature, poetry, calligraphy, flower arranging, and traditional ceremonies, such as tea and incense. She also needed to be a master of the art of conversation. It was considered a privilege for a man to converse with an educated woman. The art of the geisha lies in her ability to charm, seduce, and pleasure men.

Maiko or *akaeri*, apprentice geisha, were always required, when going outside the *okiya*, to appear in full dress—wearing a kimono with their hair and face made up. For a *maiko* to become a geisha, she was required to have a *mizuage*, a ritual deflowering. The honor was given to the highest bidder. The money paid for the *mizuage* went toward repaying the *maiko*'s debt to the geisha house, which was considerable and included about a decade of room and board, lessons, clothing, and training. Once a geisha, she would hopefully find a *danna*, a male patron who supported her and usually took her as a lover. She was expected to accompany him to social events, as a wife did in Western society. Geisha never married, but they did have children. Girls were trained to carry on the name and tradition of their mother, and boys generally became attendants or filled other ancillary roles. Geisha names were stage names that were associated with a geisha house or noted geisha. For the title "geisha" to pass on to the *maiko*, she must have perfected the arts of her predecessor. Various *hanamachi* have developed geisha names that have passed down for generations. Geisha, because they are talented entertainers, could expect to work until late in life. Eighty-year-old geisha are not uncommon —if no longer performing they remain a part of the *hanamachi*, either teaching or operating an aspect of geisha business.

Since 1872, geisha have performed in groups at public festivals, however their main vocation is still to be hired as a hostess and entertainer. They are living works of art, evoking the majesty of feudal Japan. Their special role in men's society is unparalleled. They create for their clients a world of dreams and fantasy. Cross-cultural studies indicate there is no equivalent to geisha in any other society. Many aspects of their profession are found in various cultures throughout history, but none mimic their distinct place. For over 250 years, geisha have mystified and entertained.

CHRONOLOGY

680 *Saburuko*, "ones who serve," were the predecessors to geisha. They were women of all classes who, as a result of conflict, were displaced from their prior station. They lived by trading for sexual favors. Some came from the educated classes and were talented singers and dancers who performed for the victors' courts.

794 Kyoto is established as the capital of Japan with the founding of the Heian dynasty. The independent cultural style of the fledgling nation is created during three centuries of peace. Performers and courtesans are an integral part of the Heian court scene.

900 A class of cultured, talented courtesans is established and becomes an important aspect of the society.

1100 The exotic Shirabyoshi dancers become noted courtesans and concubines to noblemen. The Shirabyoshi wear white, Shinto-style outfits that make them visually recognizable as a new class of entertainers. They are expert musicians specializing in playing various drums and the fife. Dancing and reciting ballads based on Buddhist prayers make them valued entertainers for the educated classes.

1160 Shizuka Gozen, a noted Shirabyoshi dancer and concubine of a nobleman, creates a dance that is still emulated today. She and Kamagiku, concubine to Emperor Gotoba, are regarded as honored predecessors of the geisha.

1192 With the establishment of the Kamakura Shogunate (1192–1333), a new hierarchy of Japanese society is created: the shogun; *daimyo* (regional princes); samurai; farmers and peasants; artisans and craftsman; and shopkeepers and merchants. Below this recognized order are servers, entertainers, and *hinin* (nonhumans): beggars and those doing the dirty work of society. It is impossible to move from one level to another. Marriage must be within the social strata. The shogun controls every aspect of life.

1400s The shogun begins confiscating the property of merchants who become too wealthy. Showing wealth by building a fine home or outfitting it with expensive items is very risky. It becomes the norm to spend one's wealth while one still has it. Personal, hedonistic outlets are sought.

1560s The shamisen is introduced into Japan. Its three strings make it easy to play and entertainers use the instrument to accompany popular songs. It becomes the instrument of the courtesan. Over the next half-century however, the courtesans begin using professionals accompanists. *Odoriko*, professional dancers, become part of the performance—they continue the tradition of the Shirabyoshi.

1589 Hara Saburozaemon starts to build the first walled-in pleasure quarter in Japan. Saburozaemon is granted permission from his master, Hideyoshi, to open up a brothel. He builds a walled-in quarter in Kyoto, basing the design on the noted (Chinese) Ming Dynasty pleasure quarters.

1603 Okuni of Izumo sets up a stage along the Kamo River in Kyoto. Along with her fellow dancers, she put on a spectacular performance that results in similar shows put on all over the country. The spectacles were wild and raucous events. A new term, Kabuki, arose as a result of Okuni's dancing.

1606 The Tokugawa shogunate is established, creating stricter laws throughout the country.

1617 The first official pleasure district is licensed, opening in 1618 in the Yoshiwara district of Edo. Brothel owner Shoji Jin'emon convinces officials it would be better to have all brothels within one area so that they could be regulated, business could be controlled, and taxes could be collected more easily. He is appointed *Keisei-machi Nanushi*, director of the prostitute quarter. The district is completed in 1626. Prostitutes are forbidden to work outside the district.

1628 The start of a series of laws, which finally pass between 1647 and 1652, that prohibit women from performing in public, especially in the outrageous Kabuki performances. Teenage male prostitutes also were part of Kabuki entertainment, and they were also banned. Adult men became the only actors allowed to perform in public.

1640 The Kyoto pleasure quarters move to the suburb of Suzakuno. The area becomes known as the Shimabara because the area resembles the Shimbara Fortress in Kyushu.

1650 The pleasure quarters in Edo, Kyoto, and Osaka develop independent customs, manners, and traditions. Each area becomes known for particular arts and specialties that represent the district for centuries. Unregulated, smaller "pleasure quarters" emerge around shrines, hot springs, and other areas along travelers' routes.

1652 Kabuki theater, with only male actors playing all roles, becomes popular.

1661 Asai Ryoi pens *Ukiyo monogatari*, or *Tales of the Floating World*, idealizing the hedonistic world and the live-for-the-moment attitude pervading the Yoshiwara in Edo, Shimbara in Kyoto, Shinmachi in Osaka, and Maruyama in Nagasaki. The term "floating world" becomes the euphemistic term of this demimonde.

1670 The predecessor of the modern female geisha, men called *taiko-mochi* or *houkin*, entertain clients for prostitutes.

1680 Trained teenage female dancers, *odoriko*, become a popular entertainment for the households of royalty and rich samurai. Eventually sex is added to their repertoire and they become another class of prostitute.

1712–20 Laws pass allowing for establishment of teahouses, *ochaya*, in Kyoto's *hanamachi*. The *ochaya* sell sake and liquor, not tea—hence the necessity to be licensed.

1740 Most women entertainers at this time have sex with their clients. Those without musical skills can only offer sex. They are called *gei nashi*, meaning "no geisha" or "geisha without an art." A *senryuu*, poem, of the era, *Shamisen no heta wa, korobu ga jouzu nari*, translates as "Those who are bad at the shamisen, become good at falling down." [8]

1750 Each pleasure quarter has distinct social classes of prostitutes with different names. In this time period, the teenage dancers, *odoriko*, are rounded up and sent to the pleasure quarters. By the end of the century, most of the prostitutes are no longer noted for their artistic skills. Associate entertainers become important parts of pleasure quarter entertainment. Kabuki and Sumo wrestling become significant activities of the quarters.

1751 The geisha arise as a new class of entertainer. In Kyoto they are called *geiko*, even to this day. The first woman to proclaim herself a geisha was a prostitute named Kikuya, who declared she would offer herself for hire only as a musician and dancer.

1761 The last *tayu* is recorded in the Yoshiwara. After her departure the rank of *tayu* is closed forever. To this day, the elegance, extravagance, and demeanor of the *tayu* is emulated—first by the *oiran*, who were the highest class of prostitute in the nineteenth century, and now by entertainers who play the role at festivals.

1762 The Yoshiwara district begins to recognize the geisha, who are now expected to entertain clients of *oiran* and other prostitutes.

1779 Geisha is officially acknowledged as a distinct profession and female geisha now outnumber male geisha. A former brothel owner in the Yoshiwara, Daikokuya Shoroku, comes up with the idea to register geisha to control them and collect taxes. The *kenban*, the official registration office of the pleasure quarters for geisha, is established. It defines the profession and forbids them from having sex with clients, a practice reserved by law for prostitutes. The regulations include several other restrictions, including not wearing extravagant and brightly-colored kimonos and wearing only the *shimida* hairstyle with three ornaments. The look of the geisha becomes uniform.

1780s *Niwaka,* parades, floats, and entertainments, become annual events in Edo's Yoshiwara district. *Niwaka* provide geisha with a forum for public performances, leading to further development of the profession.

1790 As a result of the *niwaka* events, geisha become renowned performers and rise to prominence. The restrictions imposed by the Yoshiwara *kenban* become established country-wide in the pleasure districts. The geisha profession is enhanced by the rules, which has clearly defined who they are, how they dress, and what they do. Also in this year, licenses are issued for brothels.

1800 Geisha are now generally recognized as female, non-prostitute entertainers of the pleasure quarters.

1840s Geisha communities become firmly established during the first half of the nineteenth century. They have created their own sisterhood society. A community of geisha houses, teahouses, restaurants, and educational facilities make the flower and willow world of the geisha an integral part of Japanese culture.

1842 The Tempo reforms are passed, addressing public morality. In Kyoto, many brothels are closed in geisha districts. Prostitution is permitted only in the Shimbara. In Edo, thousands of prostitutes, functioning outside the Yoshiwara, are rounded up and placed inside the licensed, walled quarters. In the 1850s, restrictions were relaxed for behavior inside the pleasure quarters.

1854 United States commodore Matthew Perry forces the opening of Japan to the world.

1860s Officials become lax in enforcing regulations and geisha begin wearing the latest and most fashionable dress—becoming trendsetters.

1868 The Meiji Restoration begins. Tokyo is declared the new capital of Japan. Geisha enter their golden era. As a result of protecting samurai, politicians and noblemen who were successful in overthrowing the shogunate, geisha have elevated their status in society. Many geisha are adopted symbolically by noted families to qualify socially for marriage to various revolutionaries, who are now among the leaders of the country. By the mid-1870s, many geisha are revered heroines and hold significant positions in society. Geisha, as a social class, becomes respectable.

1872 Japan is accused of keeping women as slaves. The government addresses the concerns of Western nations in an attempt to enter the global stage as a modern country. In October, Japan issues an emancipation act that abolishes obligatory terms of service for women. Under the act, geisha (entertainer) and *oiran* are placed in the same category. Debts to brothels and geisha houses are cancelled. Contracts of indenture are limited to seven years. Also in the same year, public appearances of geisha begin—with the first public dances performances held by three *hamanachi* as part of the 1872 Kyoto Exposition.

1873 Photographer Baron Raimund von Stillfried exhibits his soft-core photographs of Japanese women at slide lectures throughout Europe, helping to establish misconceptions about the profession of geisha.

1874 The emancipation edicts of 1872 are modified so that geisha can work as entertainers, but must also be taught a trade such as weaving cloth, spinning silk, or making clothes. Classes are mandatory. Also, *Japan and the Japanese Illustrated*, penned by Aimé Humbert, becomes the first text presented to Westerners clearly portraying the geisha as a distinct class of entertainer.

1875 In Kyoto, the mayor officially establishes a yearly spring festival containing dances by geisha and *maiko* from various *hanamachi*, the Miyako Odori of Gion, the Kamogawa Odori, and the Kyo Odori. The dances become a major attraction, not only for foreign visitors but for the Japanese as well.

1881 The mandatory classes to learn trades are made voluntary, and geisha return to their profession full time.

1885 Gilbert and Sullivan produce the light opera *The Mikado*. Its portrayal of Japanese women influences generations. Misconceptions about geisha are reinforced by this work, but there are no geisha portrayed in the production.

1886 Standardization fees for geisha services are established and regulated pricing exists to this day.

1887 Julien Viaud, writing as Pierre Loti, publishes several novels about his life in Japan, including his experiences with a "temporary wife." His *Madame Chrysanthème* is a worldwide best seller and helps shape European concepts about Japanese women. He writes about women of easy virtue and, unfortunately, they were assumed by Western readers to be geisha.

1891 The photographic exhibition of Tokyo geisha by Ogawa Kazumasa is voted on by the Japanese public. The five winners receive prizes. Geisha in this era become celebrities.

1895 The patriotic spirit of geisha becomes established with the Sino-Chinese War.

1897	Thousands of copies of Captain Francis Brinkley's *Japan Described and Illustrated by the Japanese* are distributed throughout the United States. The book contains tipped-in, hand-colored tourist photographs—expanding America's knowledge of the geisha.
1898	Some 25,000 geisha now work in Japan.
1899	J.E. De Becker's *Yoshiwara: The Nightless City* gives an accurate account of geisha, *orian*, *yujo*, and most aspects of Japanese life as reflected in Tokyo's entertainment district. Also the former geisha Sadayakko, also known as Sada, begins her noted career of theatrical performances in the West. Her tragic portrayals of ritual suicide and love affairs enthrall audiences and provide Westerners with a flamboyant geisha star.
1900	Photographic postcards are introduced. Portrait images of beautiful geisha and images of geisha in various settings are now inexpensively produced. They are sold to the Japanese public, which begins a collecting craze. Also this year, American David Belasco writes *Madame Butterfly*—adding to the misunderstanding of geisha in the West. It tells a story of a temporary wife, based on the common practice of Japan's supplying women to foreign diplomats for the duration of their stay in the country. Temporary wives were considered a special class of prostitute who sacrificed themselves for the benefit of the country. They were never geisha.
1902	J.P. Morgan's nephew George Morgan falls in love with Oyuki, a geisha, and marries her in 1904. She is not accepted into New York society, so they move back to Japan, where their union was also not socially approved. They finally settle in Paris. After his death in 1915, it is said that she returned to New York and was accepted in New York society, amusing guests with piano recitals.
1904	Giacomo Puccini creates an operatic version of *Madame Butterfly*, furthering the confusion surrounding the geisha's role in society.
1904–1905	Geisha become the "pin-up girls" of the Russo-Japanese War. Soldiers carry postcards of geisha into battle. Japanese *hanamachi* form organizations supporting the war, such as The Conference of the Confederation of Geisha Houses.
1908	Collecting postcards of geisha becomes popular and fan clubs develop.
1910–1920	The geisha become "advertising models" to promote a wide range of products. Their pictures now appear on posters and in periodicals.
1912	The end of the Meiji era.
1915	The start of Japan's infatuation with Western entertainment begins as a ballroom dance craze sweeps the country.
1920s	A periodical, *The Geisha Reader*, is published, offering advice and comments on geisha life.
1925	The number of geisha in Japan is now about 80,000.
1927	The beginning of reevaluation of the role of the geisha in Japanese society.
1930s	Competition from café and bar girls as well as nightclub performers convinces geisha organizations to abandon modernization and emphasize traditional dress and entertainment. They become curators of the arts of the past.
1942–1945	During World War II there are no geisha. They are forced to find other work in the war effort.
1946–1952	"Geisha girl" becomes the colloquial term used by American GI's in Japan for common prostitutes.
1948	Thousands of geisha return to the arts and entertainment world, reestablishing their role as those who preserve Japanese feudal traditions.
1958	Prostitution is outlawed and the pleasure quarters are disbanded, a landmark year in Japanese culture. Compulsory education is mandated for all children until age fifteen. This changes the entire geisha world, as fifteen is now the earliest age a girl can begin training as a geisha. Study now lasts about five years.
1960–present	Hiring geisha shows reverence and support for traditional Japanese arts and culture.

Photographers & Artists

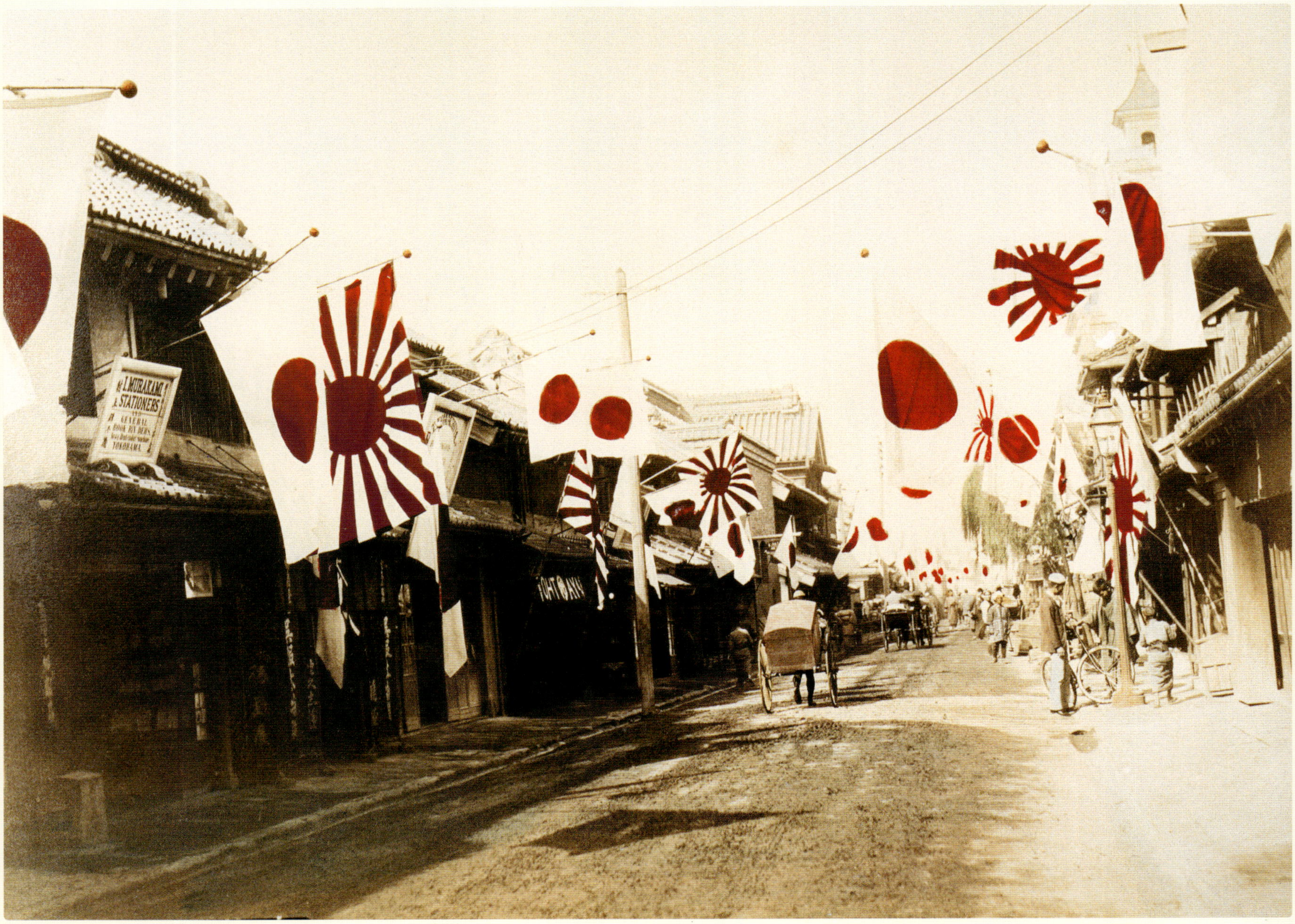

Benten Dori, Yokohama (B35)
(attributed Tamamura Kozaburo, c. 1895)

Many noted photographers' studios were located on this street in Yokohama. In 1881, Kusakabe Kimbei opened first his studio at N° 27 Benten Dori Ichome, then moved to N° 36, and he left the street in 1889. Tamamura Kozaburo had a renowned studio at N° 2. Many albums have a photograph of Benten Dori, as it was a popular shopping area where tourists and foreign residents went to buy provisions, antiques, and Japanese goods. The typical image shows holiday lanterns adorning the shops. This previously unpublished photograph has two types of Japanese flags—both with a *hinomaru*, a circle symbolizing the sun. The flag with the radiant sun represented the imperial household. (In the twentieth century, it became the flag of the army and navy, with the circle slightly off center.) The red circle sitting on a white background became, as of 1870 at the start of the Meiji government, the official flag of Japan. The flags were most likely displayed to show patriotic pride, possibly for the Sino-Japanese War of 1894–5, or the Russo-Japanese War of 1904–5. Another possibility is the visit of an important foreign dignitary.

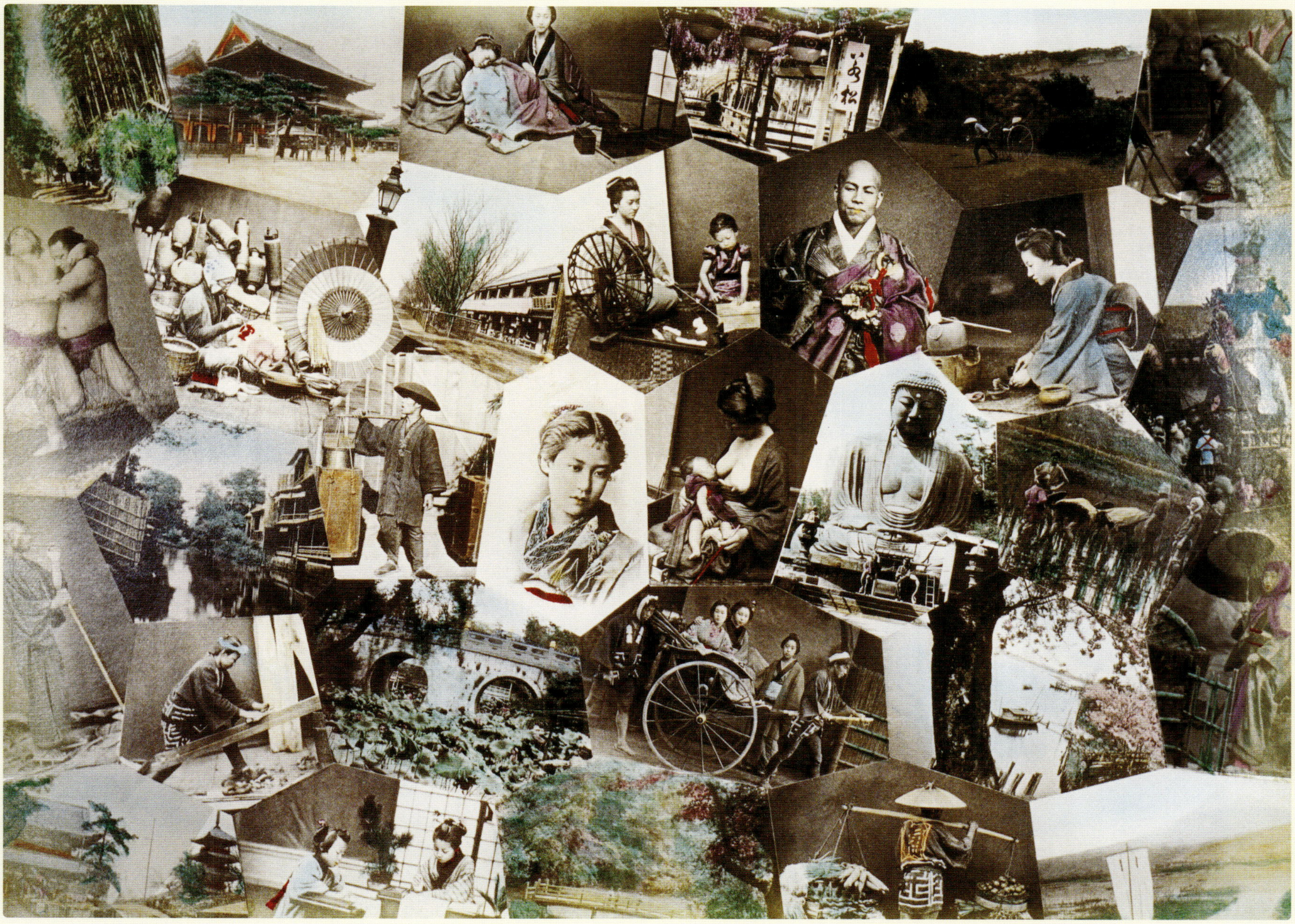

Studio Composite Photograph (unattributed, c. 1880)

Composite collages were created to exhibit images available from a photographer's studio. Several historians have attributed the woman in the center of this compilation to Adolfo Farsari. However this photograph seems to consist of some early images from the 1860s through the 1870s. If it was created by Farsari, then it must have been produced before 1886, when his studio, which contained negatives by Beato and von Stillfried, was destroyed in a fire.

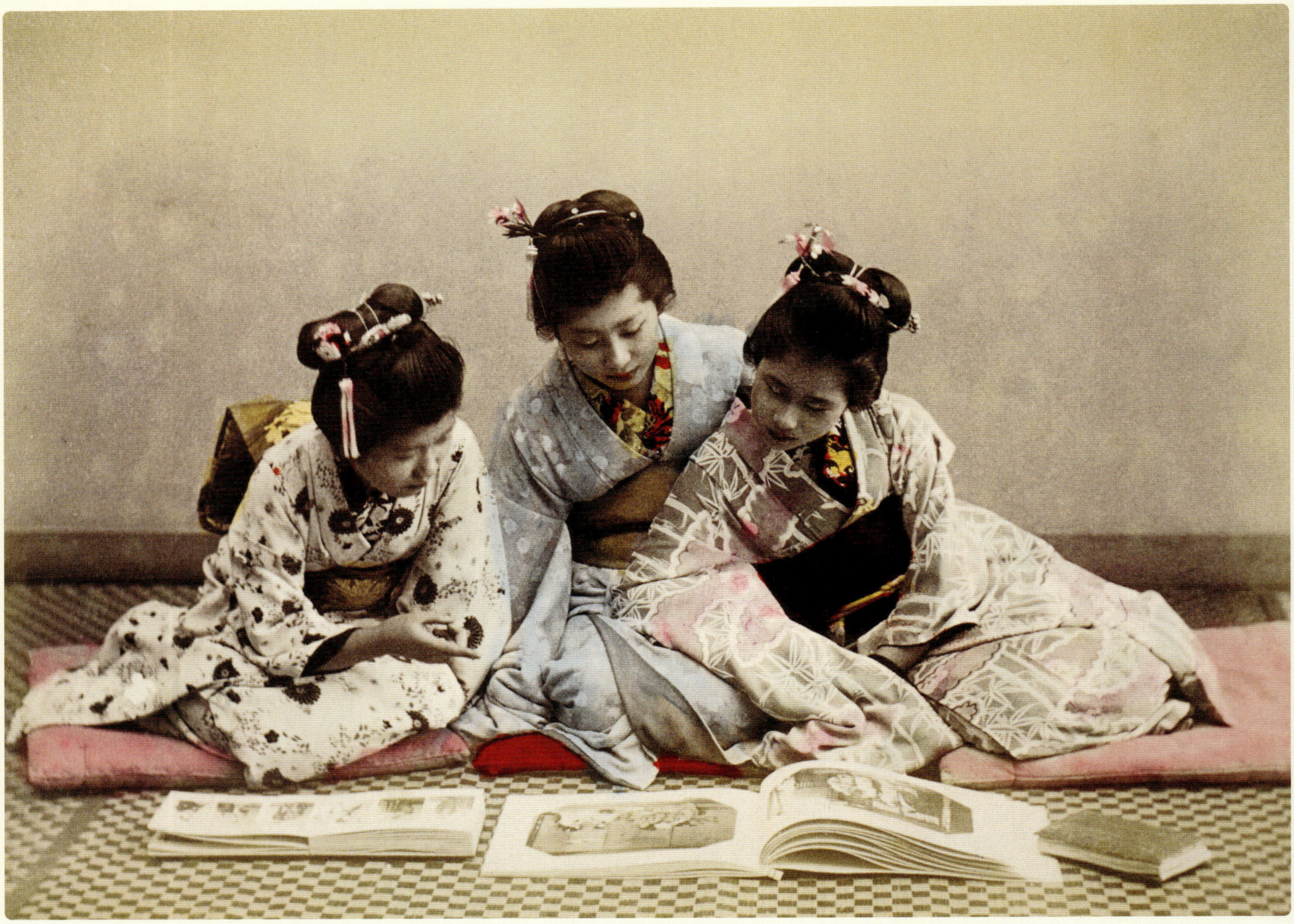

Looking at Photographs (attributed Adolfo Farsari, c. 1890)

These geisha are poring over a group of photograph albums. They are posed to show their interest and approval in the artists' work.

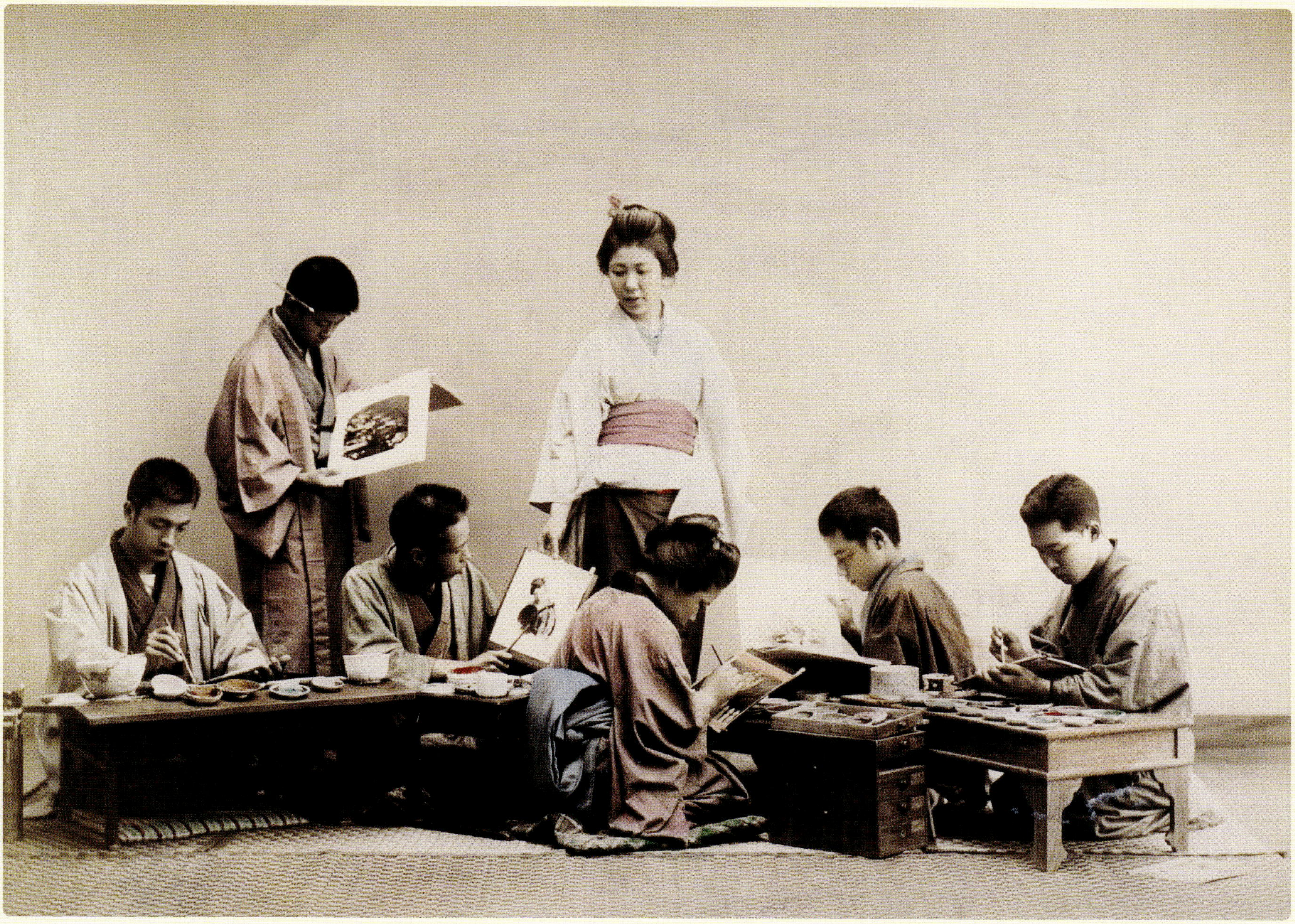

Painting Photographs (unattributed c. 1885)

It is unknown who initiated the painting of photographs in Japan. In Western countries, it was available by special order from about 1845 on. In England, several photographers specialized in painted daguerreotypes and albumen prints. It has been suggested that the process was introduced in Japan by Englishman William Sauders during his three-month stay in 1862. Or it was conceivably artist Charles Wirgman, Felice Beato's studio partner, who recommended painting the images. But it was Beato who recognized the commercial potential of painted images and became its leading proponent. Photographers hired artists to paint the images, and this is perhaps the only known photograph of a group of photographic painters at work. Photographers "auditioned" painters, assessing the quality of their work and the time it took them to paint a photograph. Some claim that artists could only paint about three photographs during a 12-hour workday. Adolfo Farsari was particularly critical in choosing his painters. He and Kusakabe Kimbei's artists produced the largest number of delicate, finely painted images. Their photographs challenge modern color photography sensibilities.

The Oiran & The No 9 Girls

Oiran and Shinzo in Full Regalia (unattributed, c. 1890)

This rare photograph documents an *oiran*, her two attendants called *shinzo*, and her male umbrella carrier. The umbrella displays the symbol of the pleasure house in which she is employed. *Oiran* are usually depicted with *kamuro*, their young child attendants, not with their *shinzo*, who are older and most likely already in the trade. These *shinzo* are wearing high shoes and matching outfits, and carrying gifts. (whereas *kamuro* who are in the following photograph wear low shoes, denoting their rank). The *orian* wears a beautiful, brightly colored kimono and no *tabi*, split-toed socks. She is barefoot, as was the tradition for prostitutes. The feet of the *shinzo* can't be seen, which also designates their ancillary role. The obi of the *oiran* is tied in the front, making it much easier to remove. She would never be mistaken for a geisha, whose obi is always tied in the back. Geisha often performed the entertainment for courtesans and their clients. The styles of music and dance of the *oiran* were different from that of the geisha. There were laws that forbade geisha from having sex and the pleasure quarters were well regulated with significant fines and punishment.

In the nineteenth century, *oiran* were courtesans, the highest class of prostitute. They dressed and mimicked the flavor and attitudes of the famous seventeenth century royal courtesans, the *tayu*. *Tayu* were true royal courtesans. They were women of exceptional qualities and often came from noble families. They were the concubines of imperial princes and others of rank. *Tayu* wore multilayered, flamboyant kimonos tied in the front, which cascaded as they walked on high shoes called *geta*. *Tayu* did not wear *geta*, exposing bare feet, which were considered sexually provocative, indicating a real woman was beneath the robes. Their highly styled hair was festooned with numerous decorations and ornaments. *Tayu* were usually well educated, and talented performers, singers, and dancers. The last *tayu* was written of in 1761, although in modern-day Japan there are entertainers who dress as *tayu* to carry on the tradition.

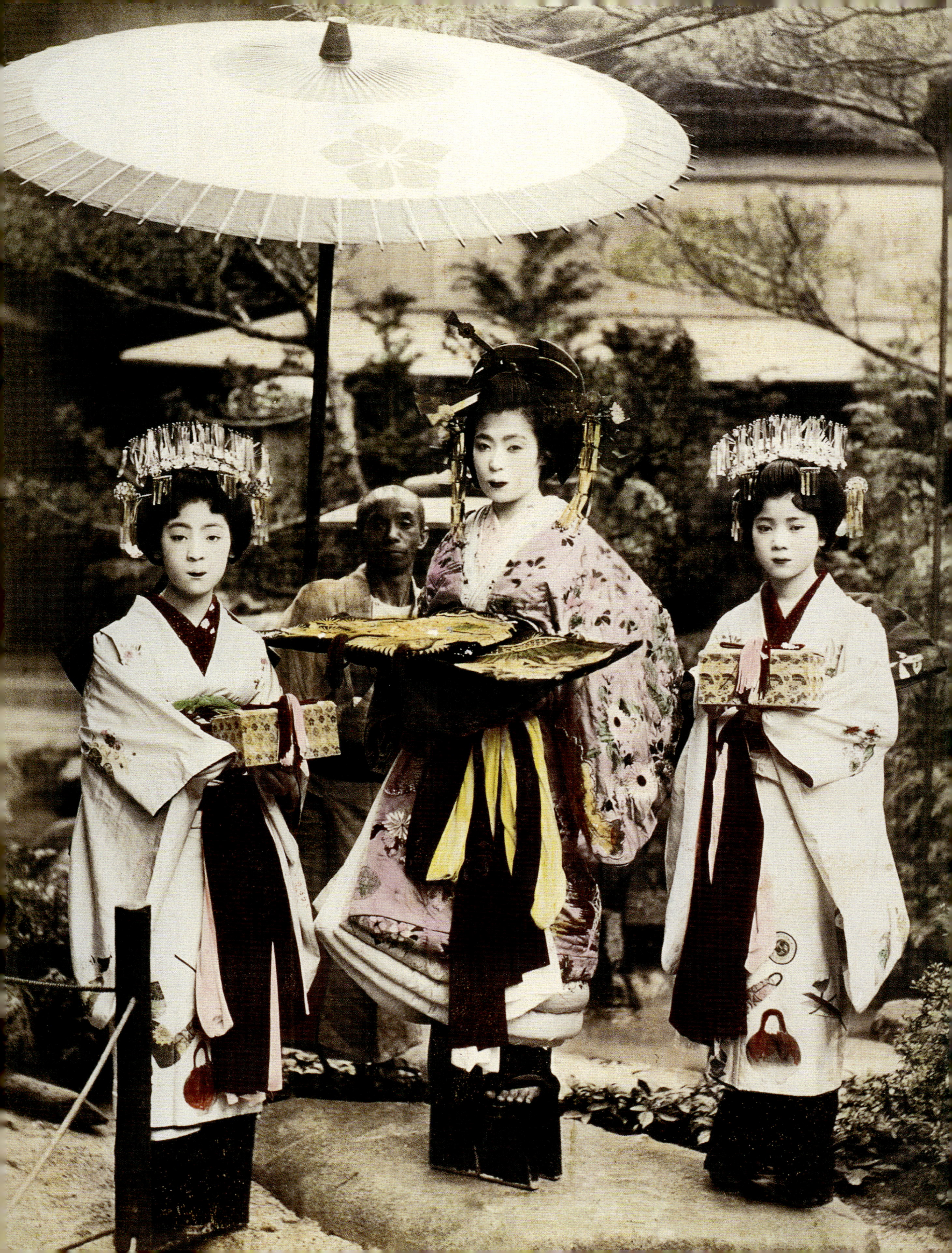

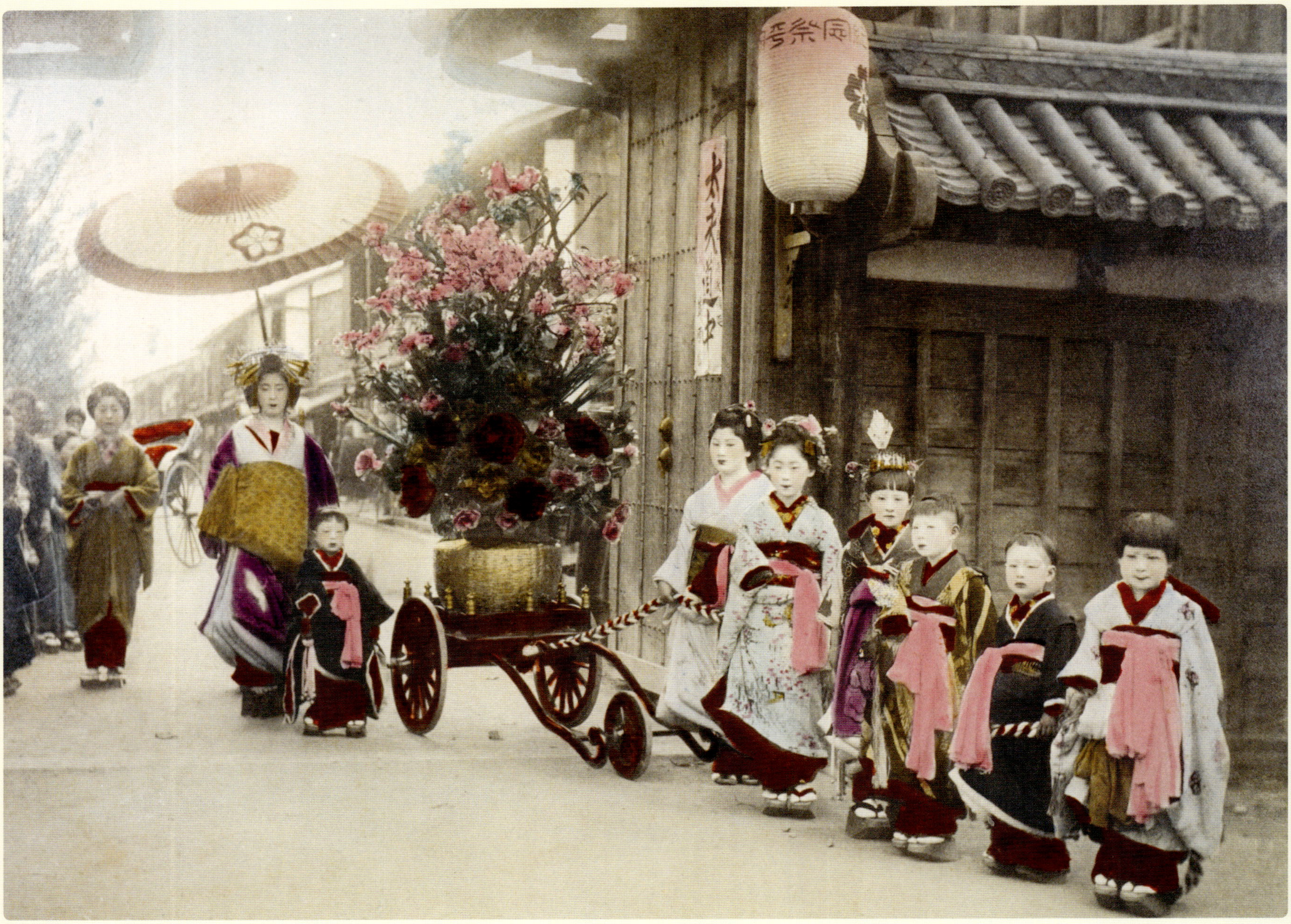

Oiran Procession (unattributed, c. 1890)

In the tradition of the *tayu*, this *oiran* is attending Kyoto's Shimbara spring flower basket festival, *hanakago*, with her entourage. The number of acolytes and attendants a *tayu* or *oiran* had designated her importance and status. Meeting a *tayu* in the seventeenth century was not easy, nor was it easy to arrange an assignation, as they were the stars of the pleasure world. Because of her status she could turn down any client at any time. To see a *tayu* one had to apply at a special house, *ageya*, for permission. A letter for a meeting would then be presented to the house where she lived. It could take months to get a meeting with a celebrated *tayu*. When an arrangement was finally made, she came in a procession: a slow moving flotilla that displayed her importance. The evening was spent drinking, singing, dancing, and performing various ceremonies, such as tea and incense. This was very costly for the patron. It took at least three such engagements for a sexual encounter, usually more. Her value increased the more elusive and unobtainable she became. Retaining a *tayu* was an expensive and time consuming proposition.

Child attendants were an important part of the *tayu* experience. The children, usually age six or seven, were recruited from poor families who sold them to *zegen*, procurers who traveled the countryside looking for beautiful children. (To this day this remains a social problem in some Asian countries.) They were sold to pleasure houses in the various districts and were the property of the house until they paid off their debt. This not only included their purchase price but their clothing, lessons, and room and board as well. The children were first used as maids, and as they learned the language and dialect of the district, they were taught the various ways to lure and entertain men. They accompanied the *tayu* on her various meetings, and by age 14 were ready to enter the profession as a full-fledged prostitute. They were deflowered in an official *mizuage*, a ceremonial procedure in which a patron pays for the honor. Hopefully much of the girl's debt and expenses were met by *mizuage*. *Yujo* was the general term used for sex professionals, of which there were many classes.

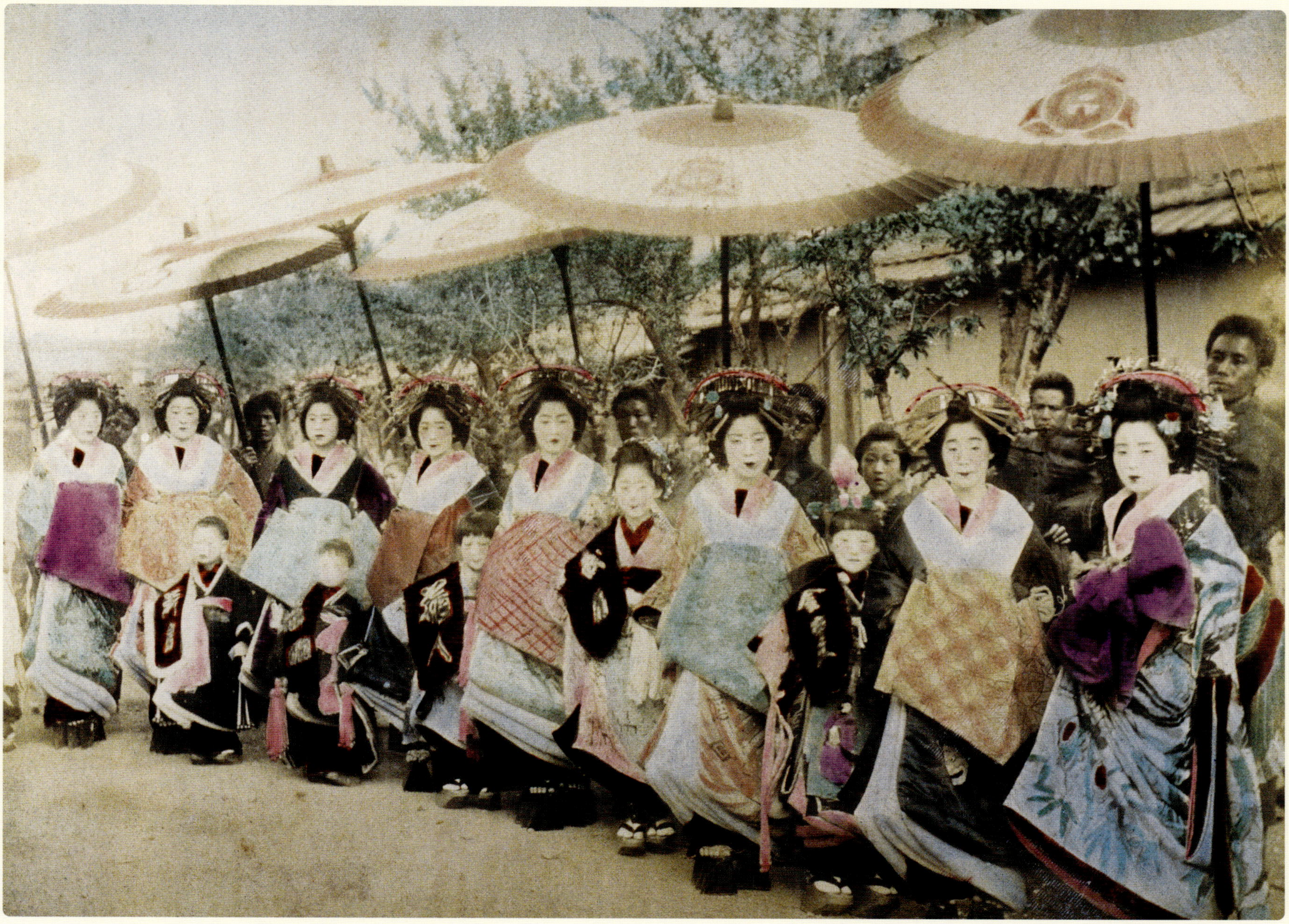

Parade of Oiran and Kamuro (unattributed, c. 1890)

This procession of *oiran* was not put together for an occasion, such as the noted cherry blossom festival, in which the staff of all the pleasure houses paraded. This procession was simply advertising. Each day, to attract clients, brothels would send some of their finest *oiran*, all decked out, into the streets of the quarter for display. It was a beautiful, slow moving sight that foreign visitors would come to view and photographers would record. The *oiran* would walk with each hand supported at the tips of her fingers by an attendant for balance. Her high shoes shaped her slow deliberate step, called *hachimonji ni aruku*, figure of eight walking. This group includes umbrella carriers and *kamuro*. The red sash placed about the child attendants' shoulders carries the name of the "older sister" with whom they are training. It's a subtle way of advertising the name of the *oiran*. The quality of the painting on this photograph has not stood the test of time, however the print is excellent, as can be evaluated by the sharpness of the faces of the men holding the umbrellas.

Oiran and Shinzo (unattributed, c. 1890)

This appears at first glance to be a closer view of the *oiran* and a *shinzo* depicted in a previous photograph. However it is not, but it does serve to demonstrate the nature of Japanese commercial photography. Photographers took several images at a session and then sold or traded the negatives with others of their profession. This is quite unusual in photographic history. In general, photographers copyright their images, want recognition for their work, and to offer their unique vision to the public. In Japan, because of the commercial tourist trade, photographs were unsigned and shared. Thus most studios could offer a wide selection of imagery.

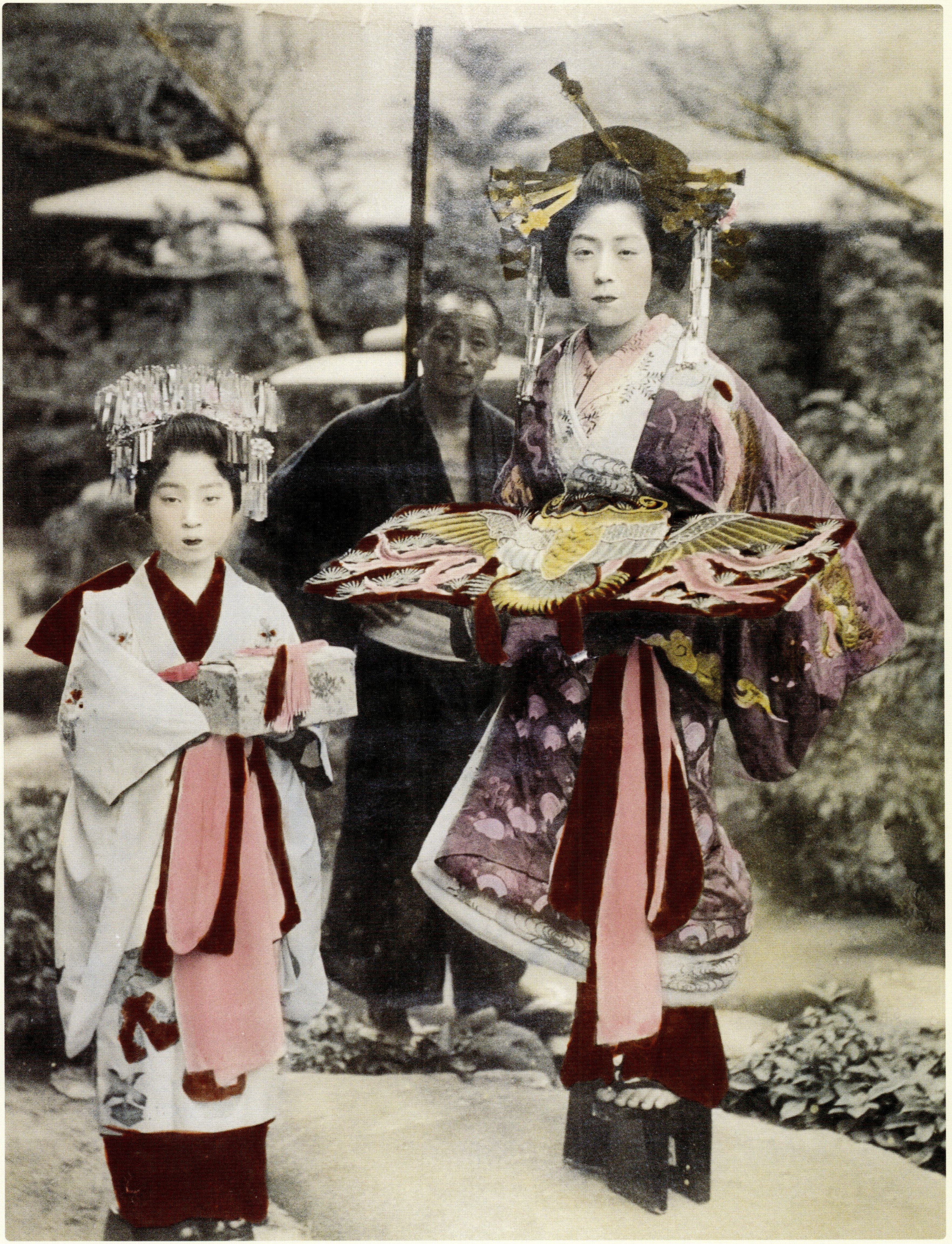

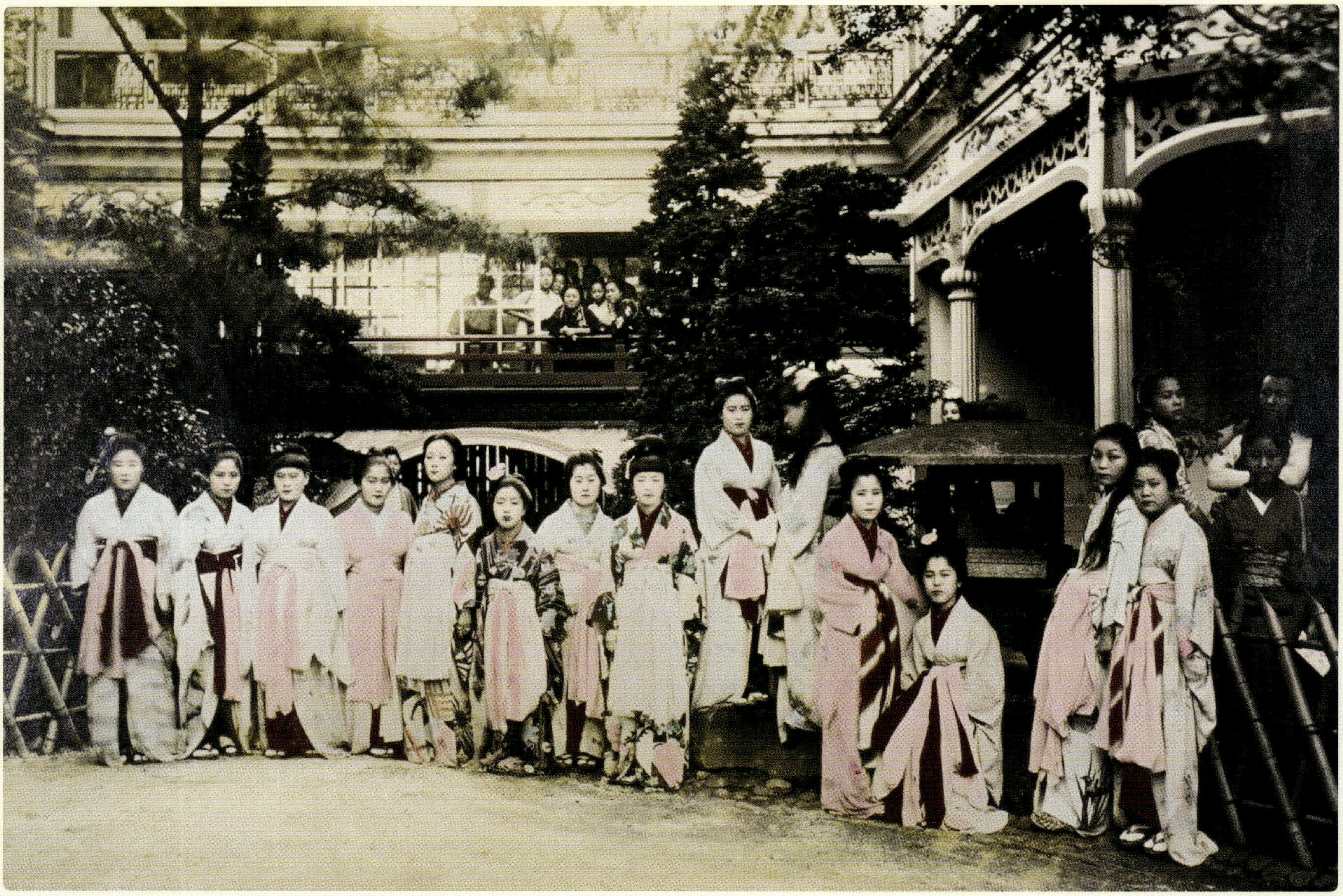

New No. 9 Girls, Kanagawa (P5) (unattributed, c. 1880)

Many histories recognize N° 9 girls as prostitutes. However no explanation has ever been proffered. Researching photographs of licensed prostitution houses shows that each one, no matter what city it was in, or what street it was on, was frequently designated N° 9. It is not clear when this practice started, or when the phrase "N° 9" girl became a euphemistic term for prostitute. The group of women in this photograph are from Kanagawa, an area south of Tokyo. It was there, on March 31, 1854, that the first treaty between Japan and the United States was signed, opening Japan to the West.

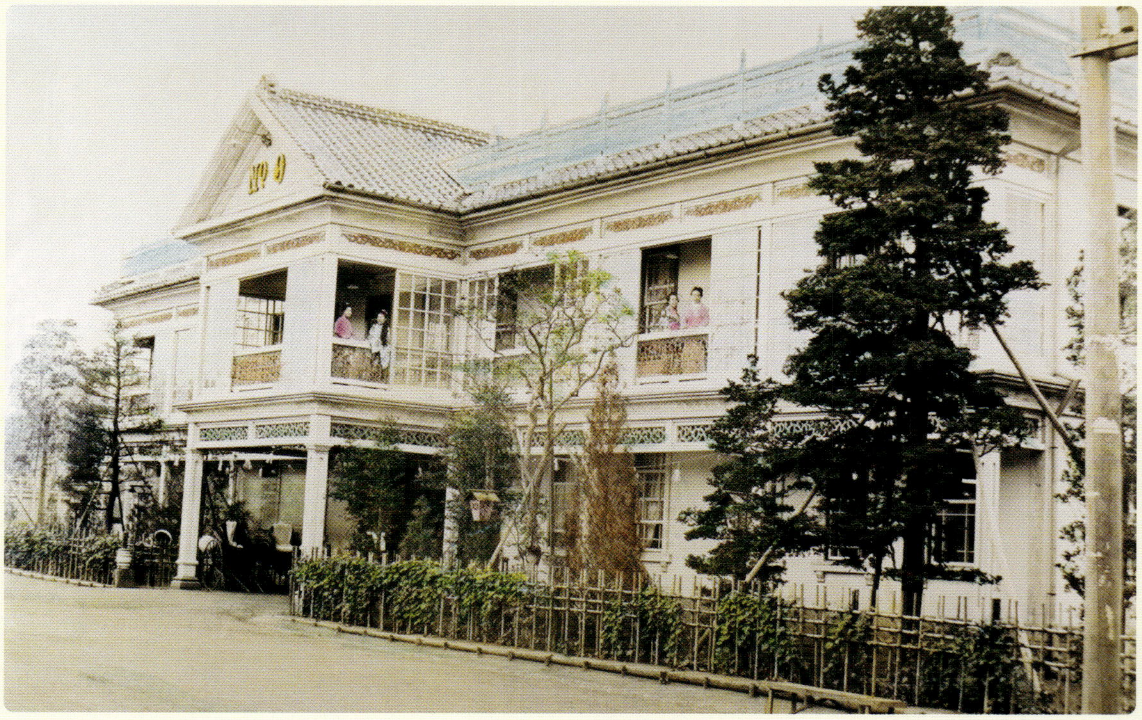

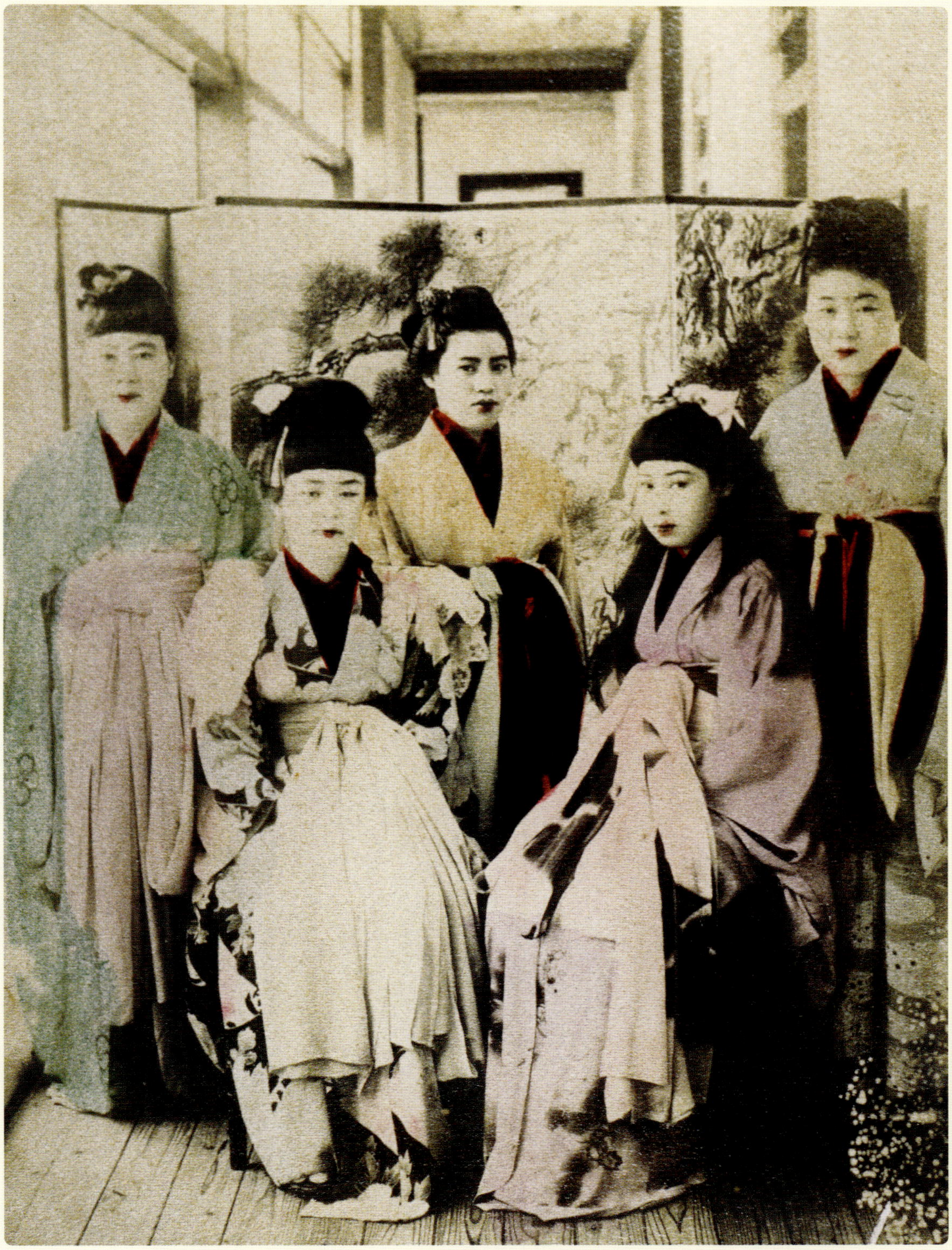

New No. 9 Girls (P16) (unattributed, c. 1880)

Clearly identified as N° 9 girls, these women's obis are tied in front, the typical form and insignia of a prostitute. For centuries, Japanese society and tradition dictated specific modes of dress for all classes. With just a glance, status, occupation, and geographical origin were apparent. Every article of clothing, as well as the style, type, and quality were regulated. This photograph also serves as a key to identification. It was taken in the hallway of a N° 9 house and is the setting for other images of women who are not identified as N° 9 girls. It was found in the album of a German sailor.

Number 9 House (unattributed, c. 1880)

This building is a house of prostitution. It is apparent not only by the "N° 9," but by the presence of women. Typical advertising has the girls standing in all the walkways, windows, and balconies. In 1895 alone, 40 war ships with thousands of sailors from the treaty nations that visited Japanese ports. Sailors and others looking for a house of prostitution could easily find one in any city, as the buildings were labeled N° 9.

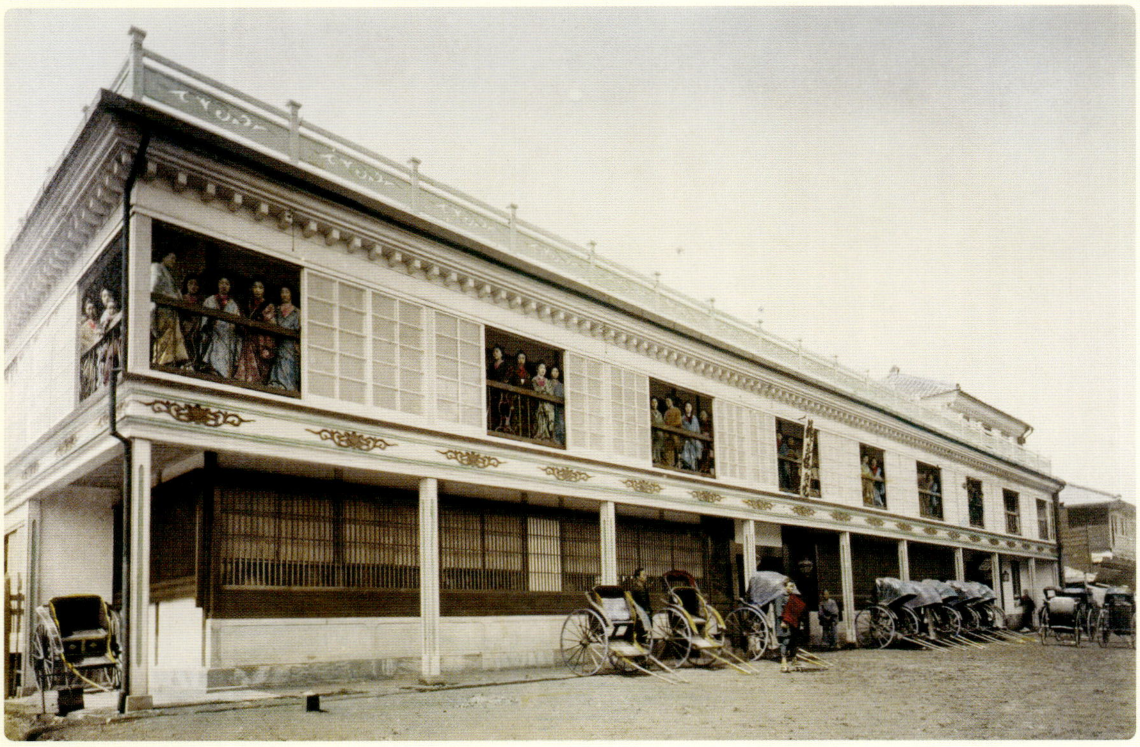

Nectarine, Yokohama (122) (Kusakabe Kimbei, c. 1890)

Spectacular overview of the Nectarine N° 9 licensed pleasure house. This beautifully painted image from a Kusakabe album shows the quality of his studio's production. All of the women, about 25, that are gathered in the walkways and windows are individually and exquisitely painted. The sex industry aspect of the floating world is called the water trade, *mizu shobai*. The social and moral issues with many of the houses of prostitution included the fact that girls were bought at a very young age (four to six) and were essentially bound to the house until they paid of their debt, which could take a lifetime. Freelance prostitutes, "riverbed people", were usually poverty-stricken young women and widows. At hot springs and other resorts, rural *onsen* geisha offered sex. They were not trained in the arts: these "pillow geisha" were a different breed of entertainer. In the twentieth century, some bar girls and hostesses became another class of sex worker with the ascendancy of café and nightclub life. It was not until 1958 that prostitutes were released from the bondage of their employers.

No. 23 Maganecho, Yokohama (C19) (unattributed, c. 1880)

The women in this photograph at the Maganecho pleasure house in Yokohama are displayed in the window in the typical arrangement, with the front row sitting and the back row standing. The design of the bars and other architectural items help determine which house is represented. Fortunately this photograph is labeled. The vertical bars of this house are more typical than the crossed lattice windows of the unidentified Yokohama house (N° 12).

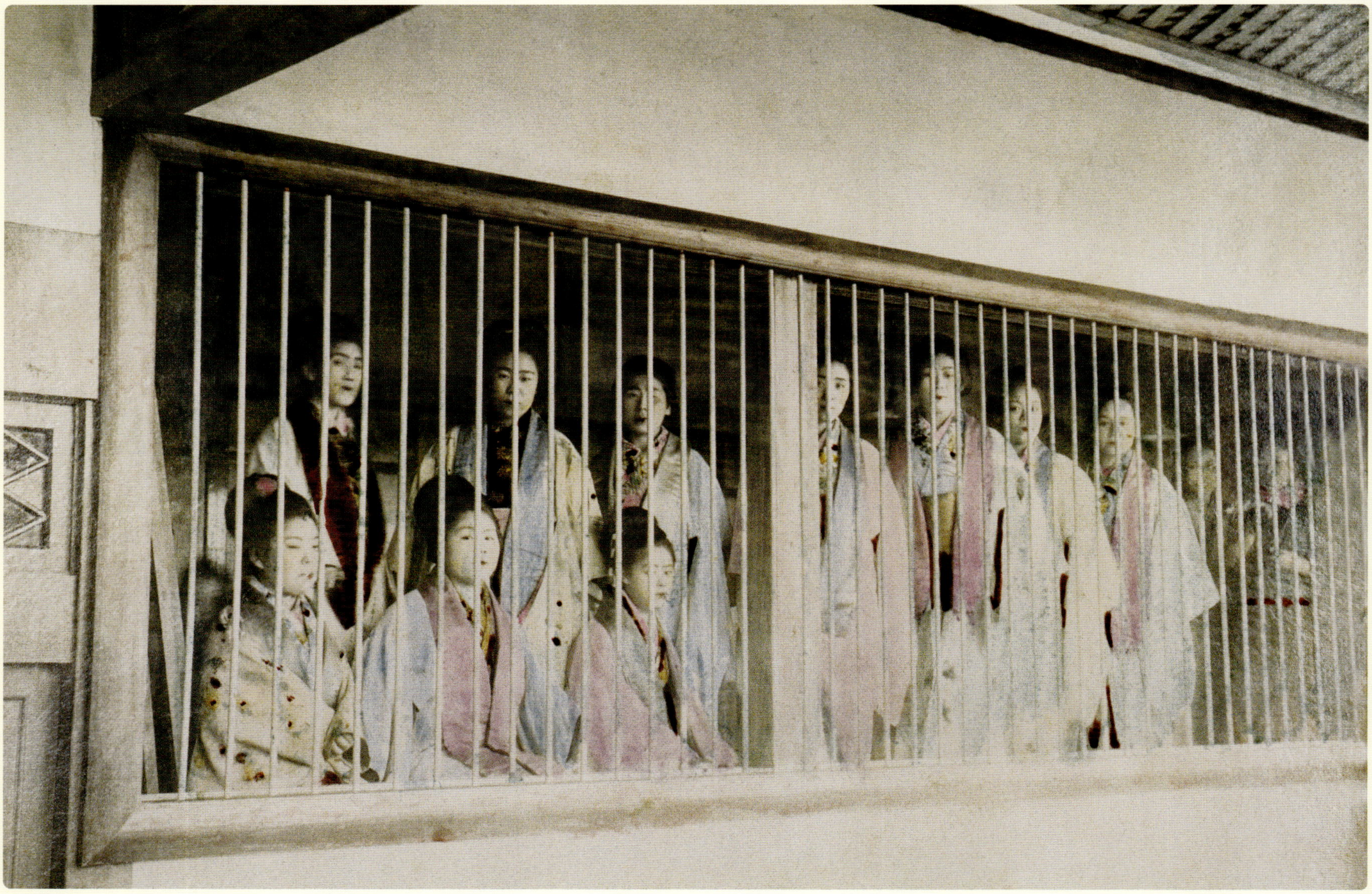

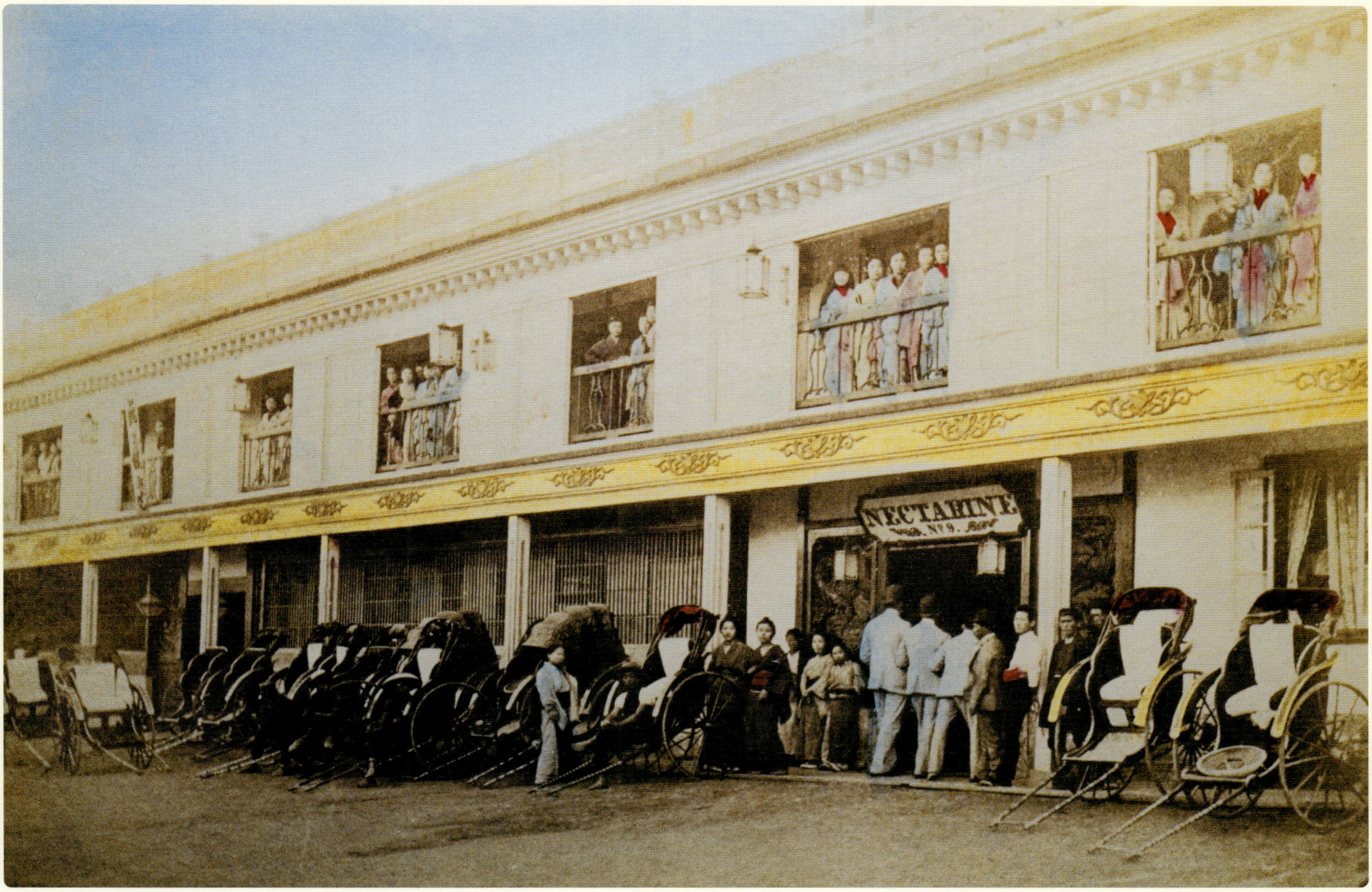

Entrance of Nectarine No. 9 (unattributed, c. 1880)

The image would certainly be the highlight of an adventurer's photographic souvenir album. Not only does it have the name of the house, Nectarine, clearly visible, and prostitutes in their typical positions in the walkways and windows, but also three men in western suits are walking in the entrance, perfectly placed by the photographer. No other tourist photograph documents clients entering a house of prostitution.

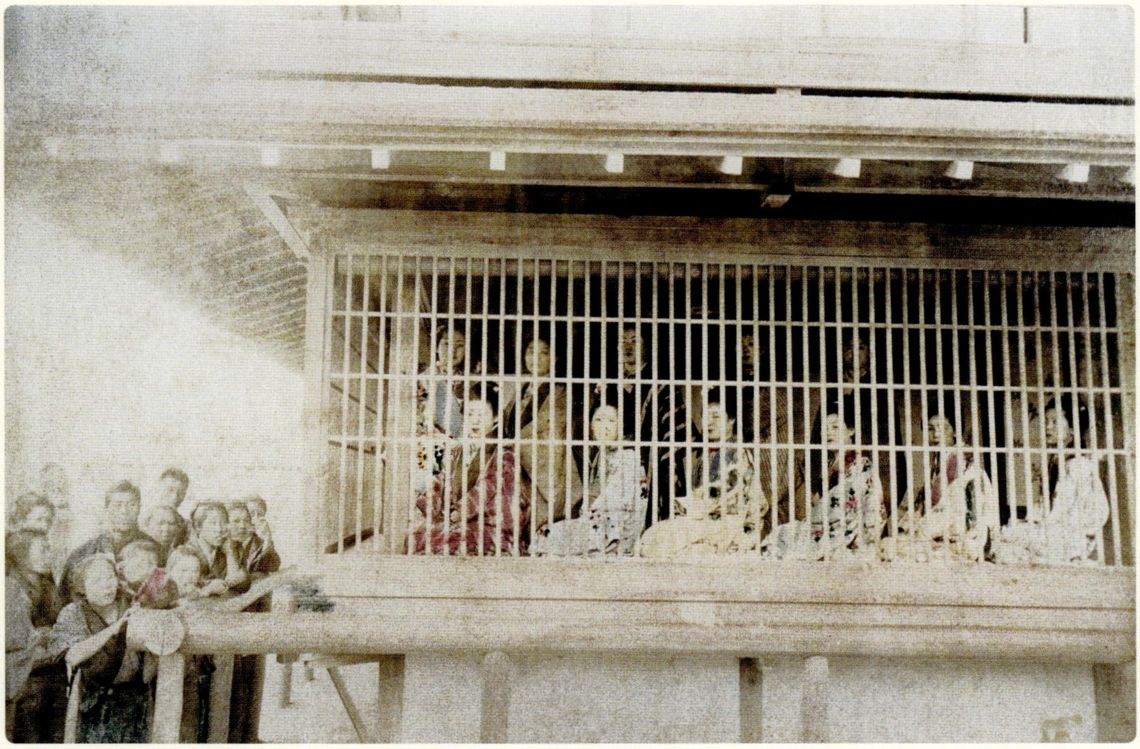

The Girls At Yokohama (U18)
(attributed Kusakabe Kimbei, c. 1890)

This image is of low-level prostitutes behind the barred windows of a licensed house of prostitution. That customers could walk up to the windows and pick out a woman was offensive to missionaries and others with "Western" ideas of sexuality. The outlook of the Japanese was very different from the West. Sex, love, and marriage were clearly defined in Japanese society. Marriages were arranged, a bond between families, and individual love was not considered. Husbands and wives led separate lives. Women ran the household and men went to work. Sex in marriage was for procreation not recreation, and men were expected to go outside the house to get it. Licensed prostitution was available throughout Japan until 1958. A Japanese couple did not socialize or entertain together. Men went out with business associates and, if they could afford it, their mistresses or geisha. A Japanese saying goes, "There's no personality below the naval"—in other words one's private business has nothing to do with nor represents one's public, family, or traditional life.

New No. 9 Girls, Kanagawa (An Eurasian) (P11)
(unattributed, c. 1890)

This woman is dressed as a geisha, with her obi tied in back, but she is actually a prostitute. She is doubtlessly special, as she is photographed close up like a celebrated geisha. But she is clearly identified as a N° 9 girl, the euphemistic term for prostitute, so there is no question of her occupation. She is "Eurasian," perhaps making her more attractive. The image appears in many later albums.

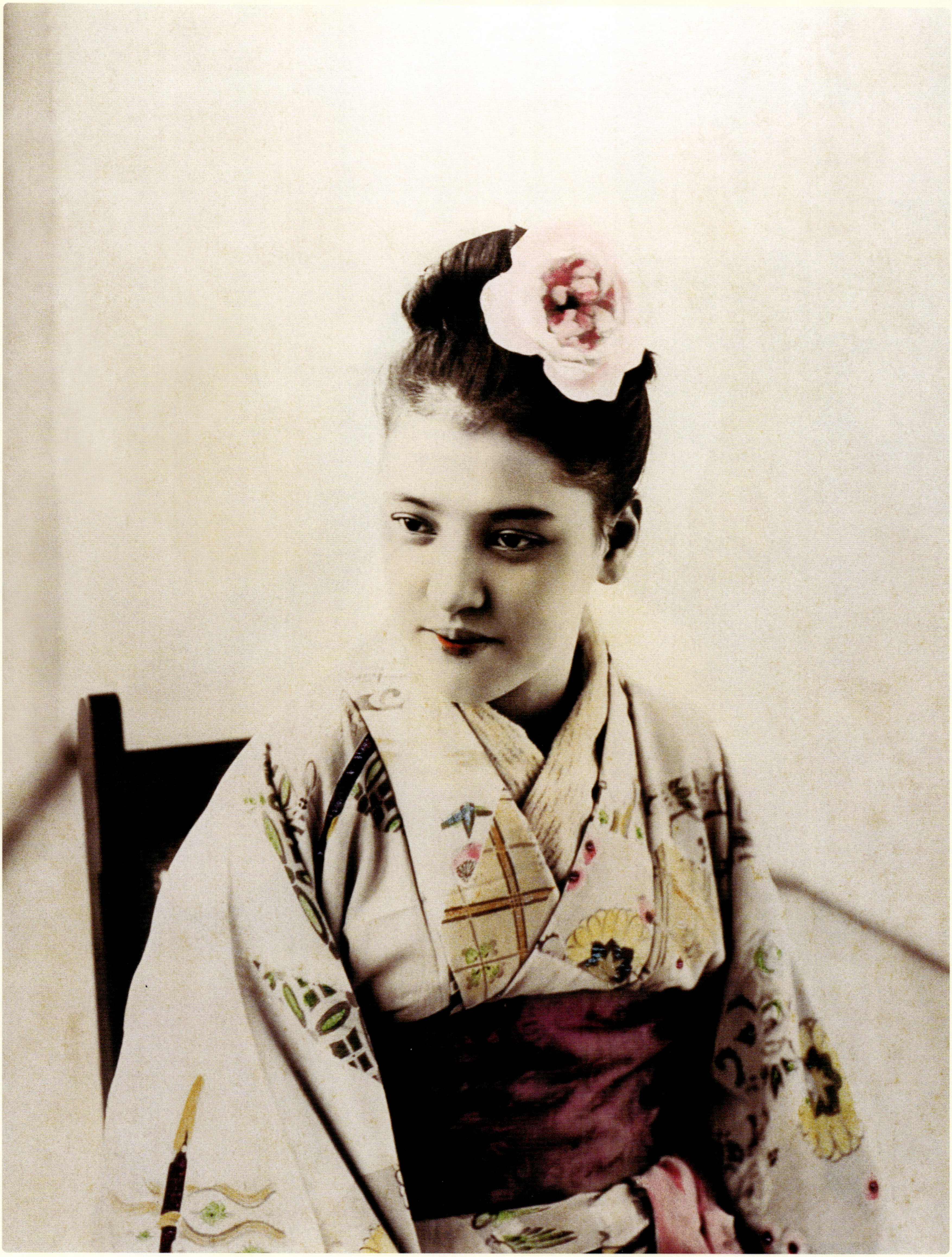

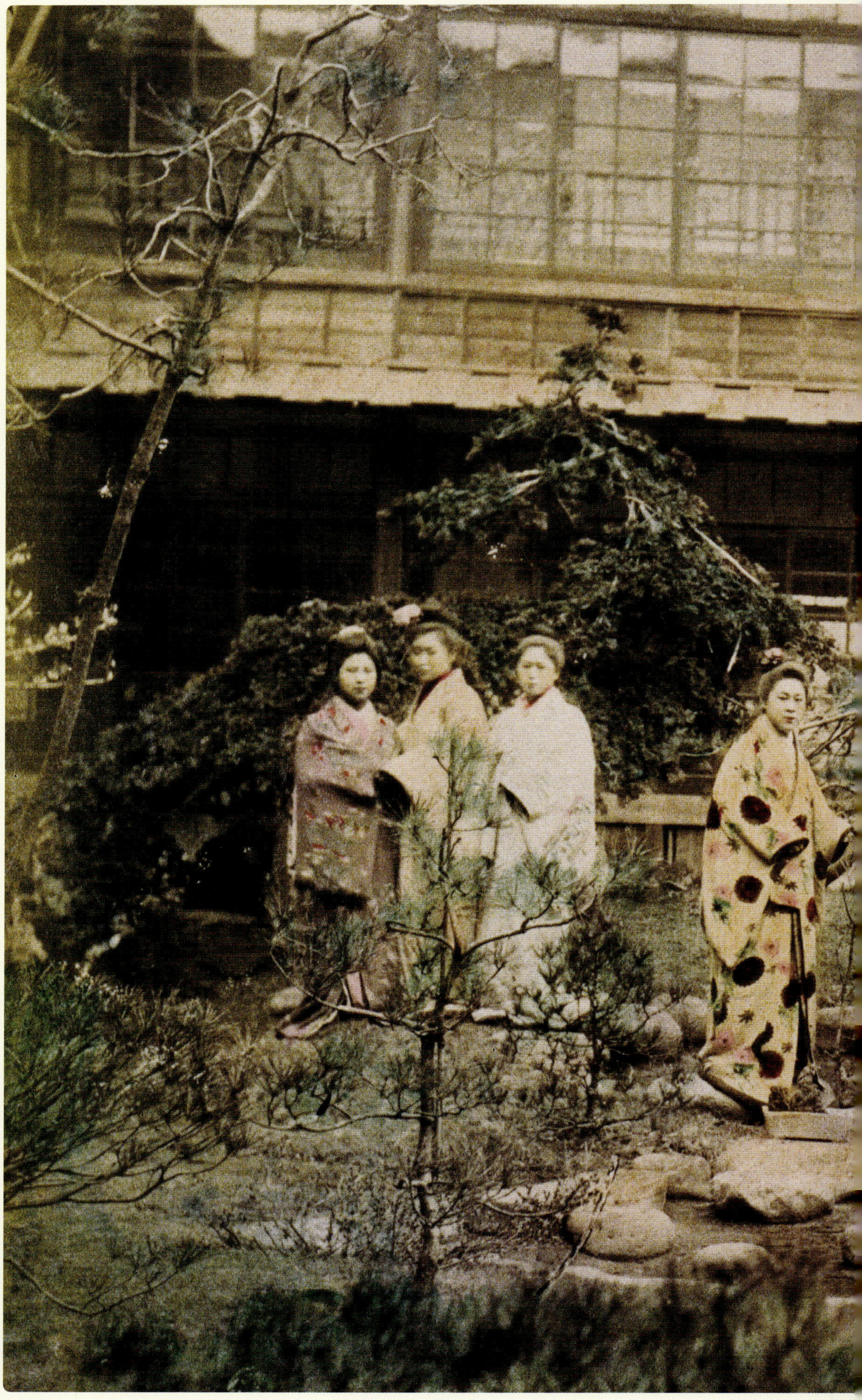

No. 9 Girls, (F53) (unattributed, c. 1885)

The Yoshiwara in Edo (Tokyo) was established in 1617 as a licensed pleasure district. In 1657, it was relocated to the Akasaka area of the city. The Meiji restoration of 1868 made Edo the capital of Japan. Politicians and a prosperous mercantile class swelled the city and the Yoshiwara became the cultural center of Edo. Restaurants, theatres, teahouses, geisha houses, courtesan houses, and especially licensed houses of prostitution were popular attractions. In 1900, a law was issued allowing free movement of licensed prostitutes, and many courtesans who were freed of their obligation to special houses set up shop in other parts of Edo. In 1958, the Yoshiwara was formally disbanded with the passage of an anti-prostitution law. This image was taken in Yoshiwara and the prostitutes in this photograph are typical of the lowest level of licensed pleasure woman. They are posed in their garden, some with their hair down and kimonos open.

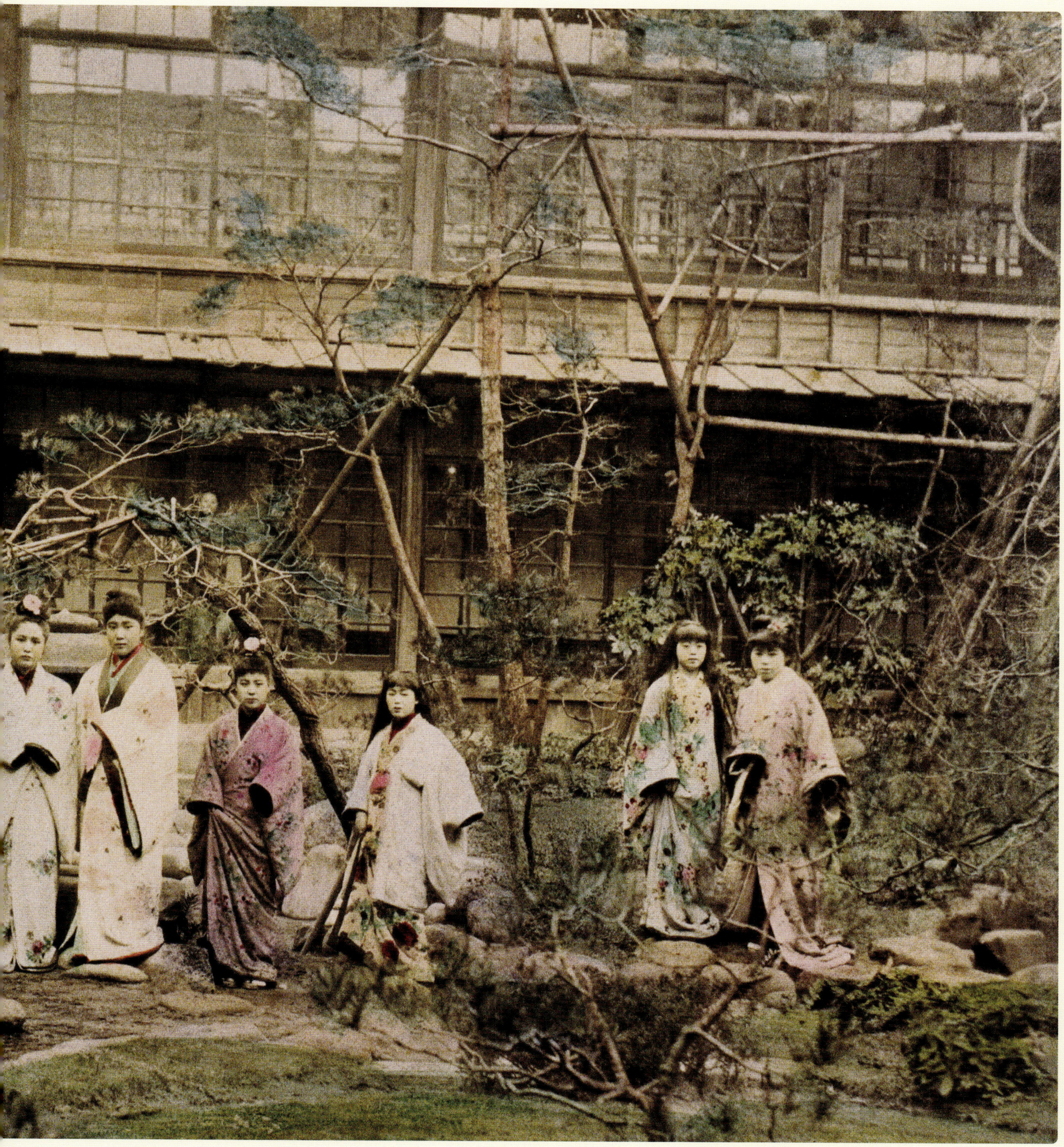

The Geisha

The Geishas (396) (Baron Raimund von Stillfried, c. 1880)

This studio photograph by von Stillfried captures the essence of the geisha. The aristocratic pose of these geisha in an empty setting, wearing exquisite kimonos, magnifies their beauty. At one time, geisha were the living symbols of modernity and high style. They were expected to be the height of fashion, wearing the latest dress, accessories, and hairstyles, becoming walking visions of desire and aspiration. During the twentieth century, that vision reversed. Geisha began to represent tradition and feudal Japan. Along with Kabuki actors, they were to become living legends of a past age. Their duty is to preserve and present old Japan, to glorify the past in dress, manners, ethics, and lifestyle.

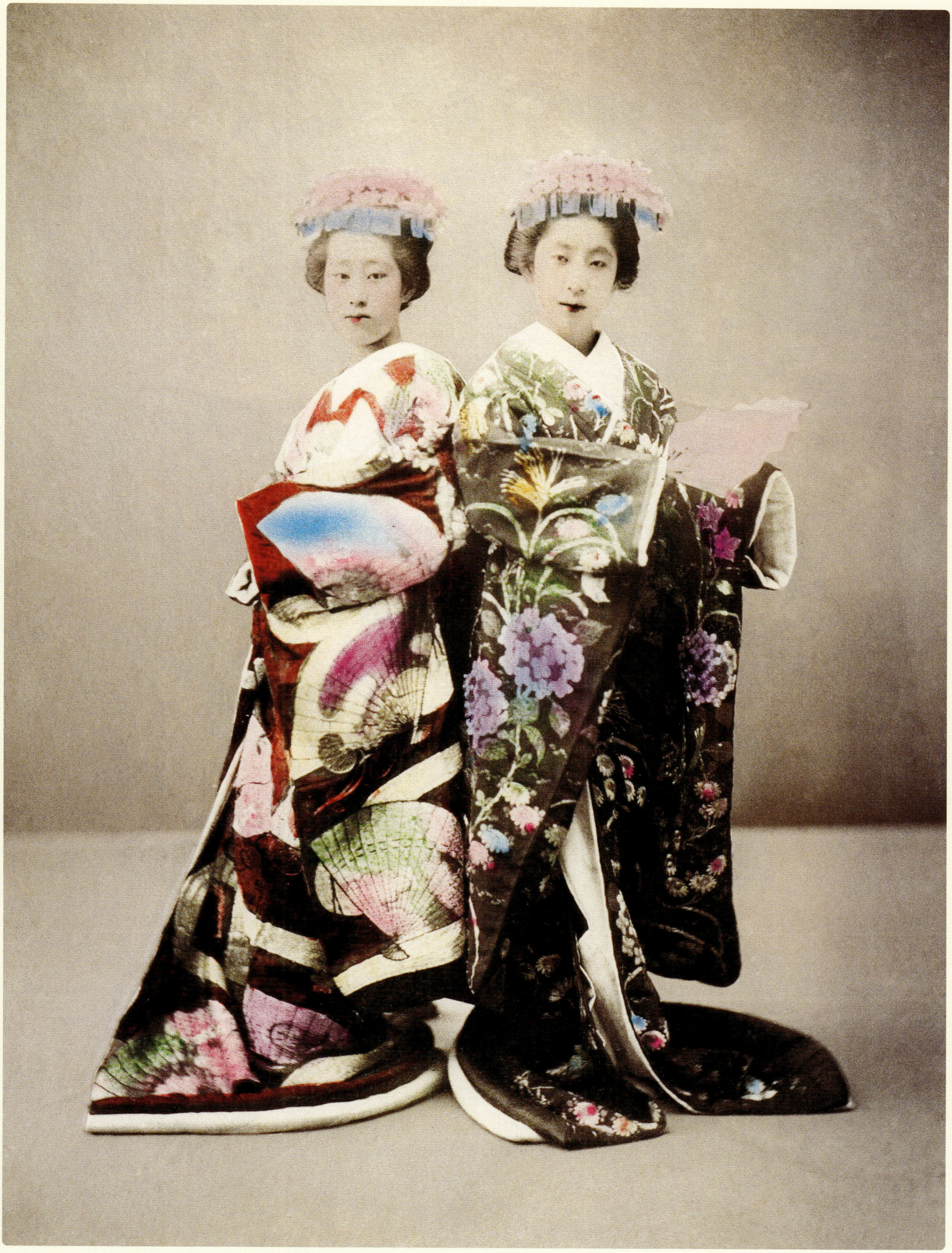

Dressing Obi (211) (Kusakabe Kimbei, c. 1890)

The kimono is tied with a broad sash called an obi. The knot is shaped and enhanced with a pillow called a *makura*. It is then wrapped with a long piece of silk, the *obi-age*. It is finished off with an *obi-jime*, a decorative cord. The large obi of the geisha's kimono, as it had to be tied in back, required an attendant. Japanese dress and other aspects of appearance allowed observers to instantly know the social class, position, and occupation of the person. Every aspect of dress was a part of identification. Cloth for *maiko*, for example, had specific designs to be worn at different ages. Obi material, size, and pattern had to be chosen in accordance with the season and occasion. The large tie and bulkiness of the obi precluded sitting in a Western-style chair, but held the body upright when sitting on one's legs Japanese-style. The protruding, bustled dress popular in Western culture around the turn of the century bears a resemblance to the obi. Perhaps the numerous appearances of geisha at American and European expositions influenced the design. "Japonisme" certainly influenced other forms of design, such as furniture and décor.

Playing Koto & Shamisen (212)
(attributed Kusakabe Kimbei, c. 1885)

These geisha are posed with two instruments of their trade, the shamisen and the koto. The shamisen, introduced in 1561 from Korea, is the trademark of geisha, and they affectionately call it *o-shami*. The shamisen is a long-necked, banjo-like instrument with three strings that are plucked with a large spatula-shaped plectrum, usually made of ivory. The frame of the body of is covered with cat skin in the more expensive models and dog skin in the cheaper models. Geisha were nicknamed *neko*, cat, because of this instrument. The koto is a large, thirteen-stringed, harp-like instrument that was introduced from China in the 7th or 8th century. It has a subtler sound than the shamisen. Geisha had to become proficient in at least one instrument to accompany other geisha in their performances. They needed to memorize hundreds of songs, as part of their entertainment repertoire, so as to match the song to the situation or event.

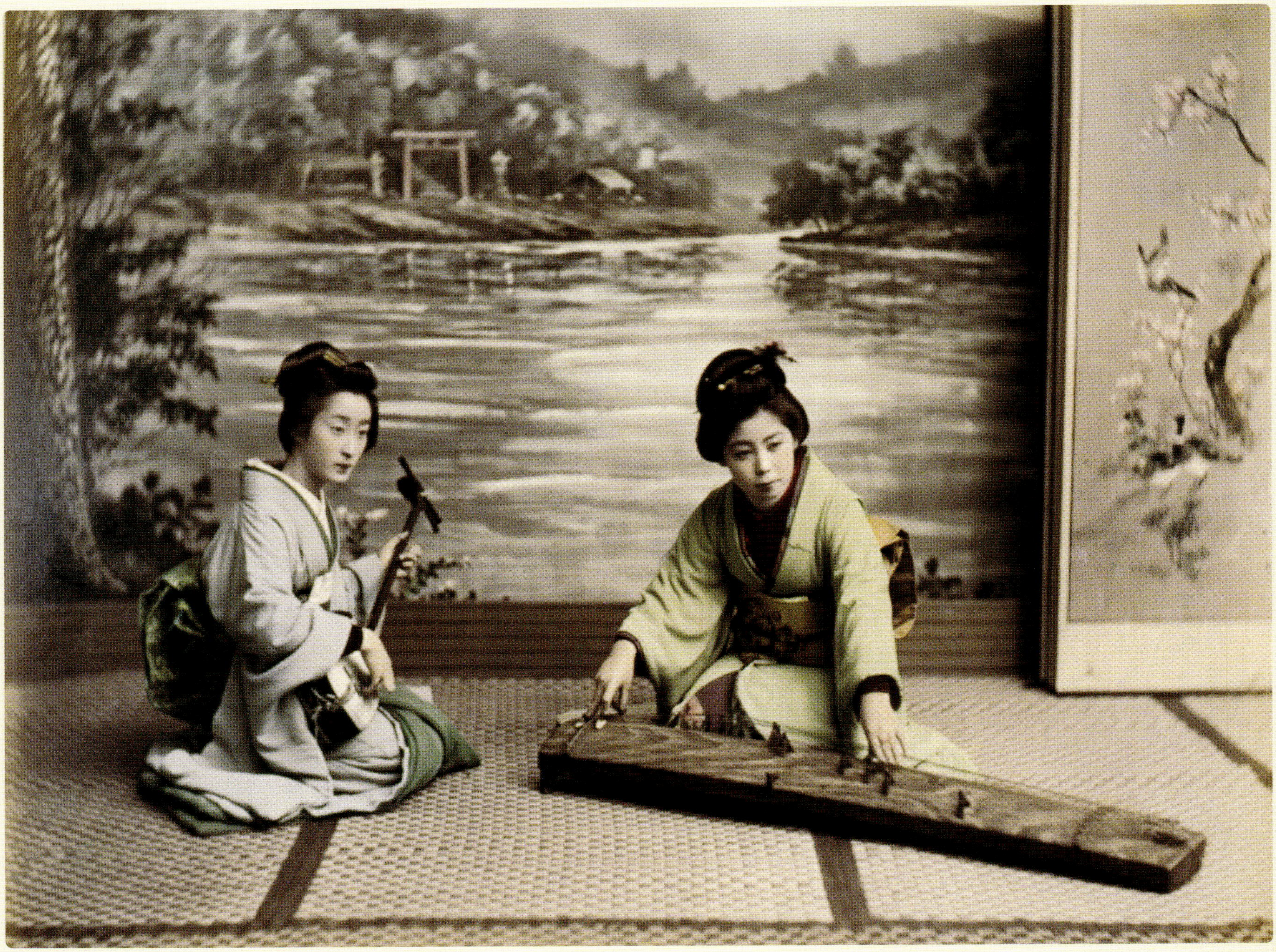

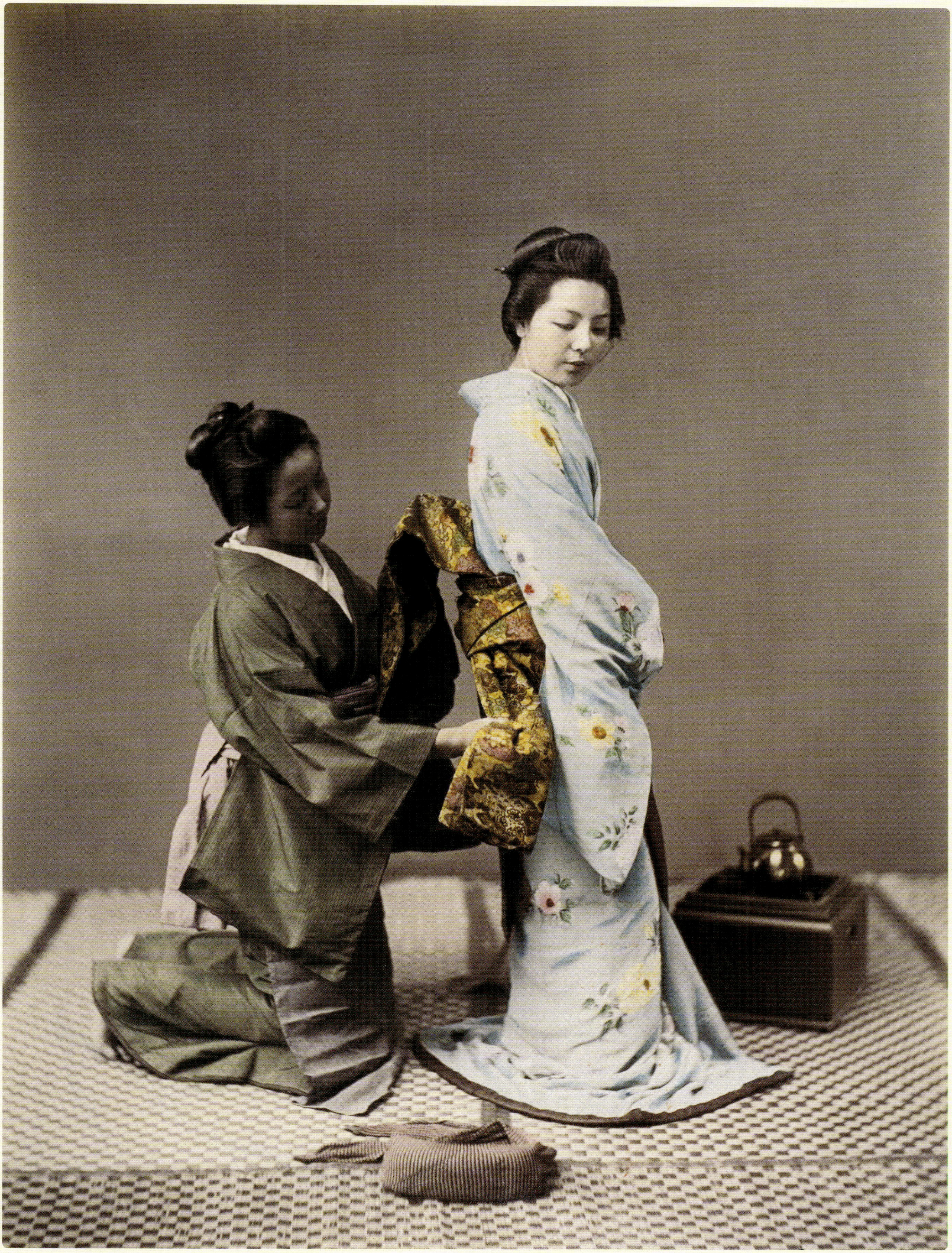

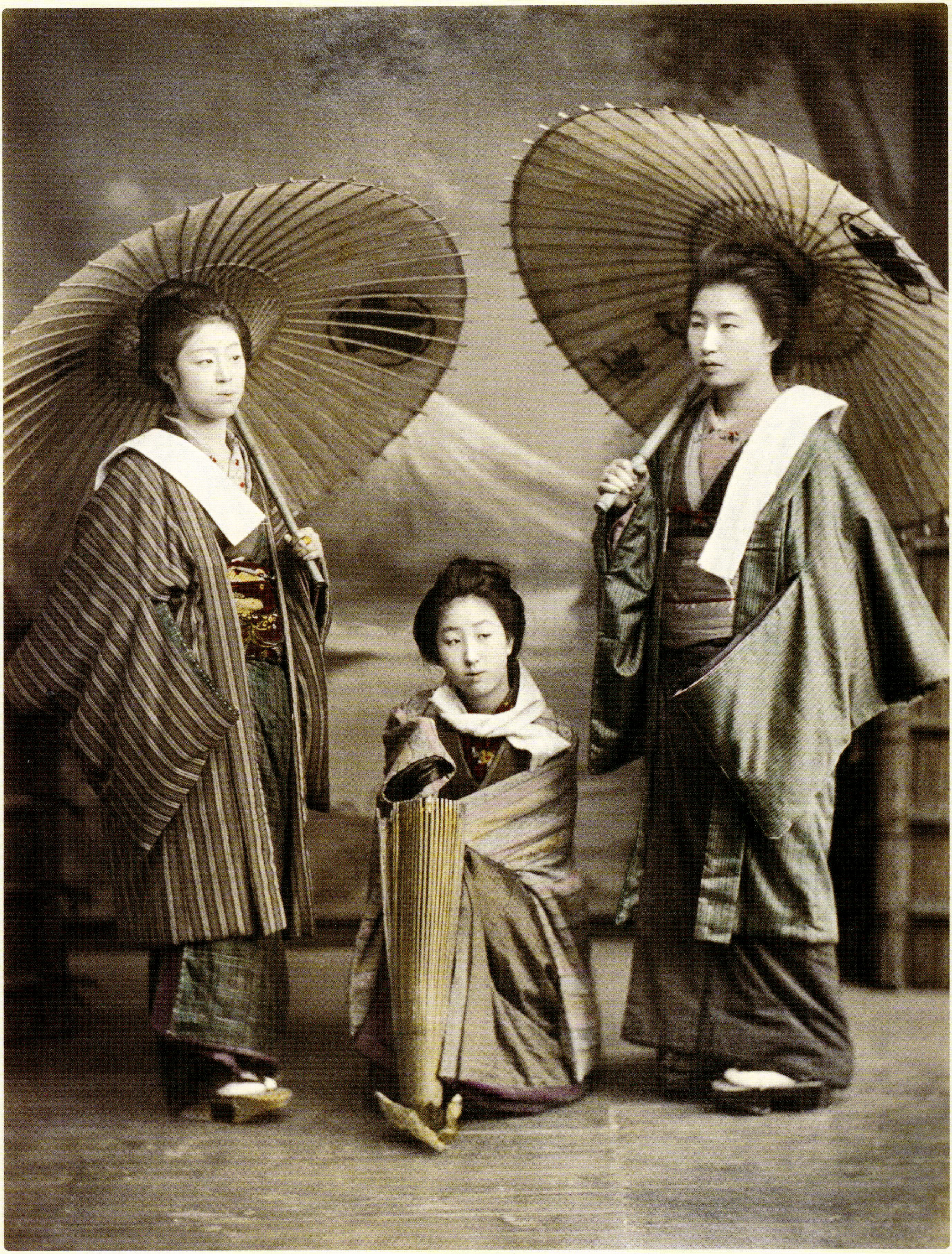

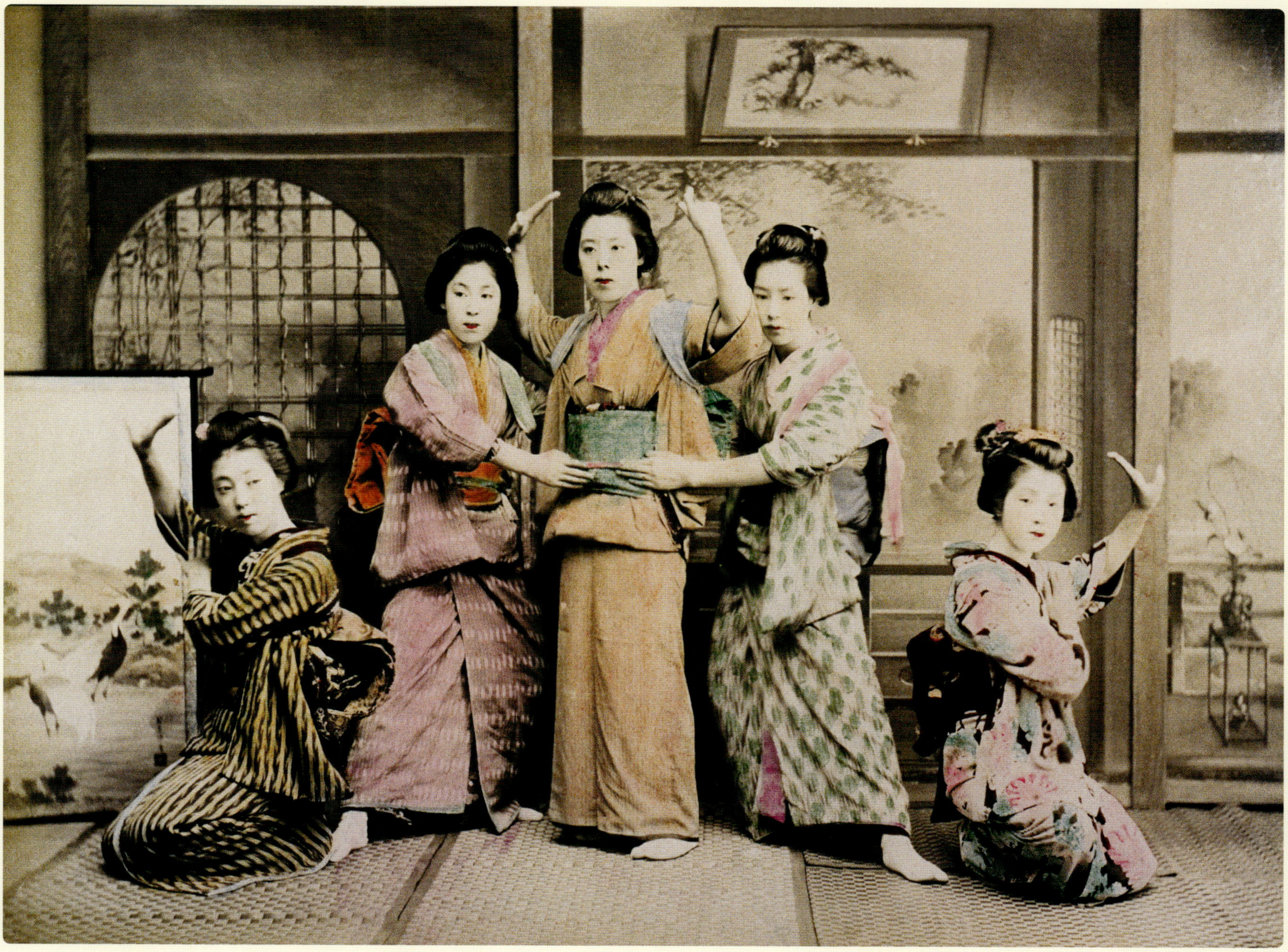

Dancing Party (P44) (unattributed, c. 1890)

Dancing is another essential geisha entertainment. A geisha's height effects her participation as a dancer. Tall women are expected to be accompanists, *jikata*, "seated ones." *Tachikata*, "standing ones," is the term used for dancers, who were originally known as *odikoro*, or "dancing girls." The kimono and obi restrict movement of the legs and body so that dance steps are small and measured. Because of the long sleeves, arm movements are concise and sometimes performed with a fan to exaggerate motion. Traditional dances told a story or complemented the lyrics of a song. In the spring of 1872, the first public performance by geisha was held in Kyoto: the cherry blossom dance. It has been held every year since and has become an attraction for tourists as well as the Japanese.

Yokohama Singers (C18) (Kusakabe Kimbei, c.1885)

Geisha had to be skilled in all aspects of entertainment. She had to be a good musician, dancer, and singer. But she had to excel in one of these fields to become a desired companion and star. Just like today, if a great singer, dancer, or musician was highly desired, they were quite costly. It was the same for geisha. Specific *hanamachi*, flower towns, and *okiya*, geisha houses, specialized in the diverse arts. Being a *maiko* to an especially accomplished geisha was comparable to apprenticing a master craftsman. Geisha became noted and wealthy when they were among the leading performers. In Yokohama, the singers were especially renown, and this photograph places three acclaimed performers in front of a backdrop of Mount Fujiyama, the most recognizable landmark of Japan.

Clowning Geisha
(attributed Baron Raimund von Stillfried, c. 1880)

The rarest images of geisha depict them in their role as jester and comedian. Since their job was to relax, alleviate stress, and ease tension, laughter was (and is) one of the best medicines. Comedic, clever entertainment was part of what a geisha offered. *Kabuku* means to frolic and be wild and outrageous. These women are certainly playing that role. The word "kabuki" is derived from the word *kabuku*. Kabuki, which is now generally recognized as traditional Japanese theatre, was originally part of the entertainment of the floating world. A woman, Okuni, around 1603, set up a performance on a dry riverbed and she danced with her all-female troupe. They were an instant success and there soon were many imitators: other groups of courtesans and prostitutes began public performances. The shows were erotic and electrifying, and riots often followed, as there was much fighting over the actresses. In 1628, the first law was passed that forbade women from the public stage. The law was repeatedly passed until finally in 1647 it stuck. For the next 250 years only men performed public Japanese theatre. Women took up entertainments that led to the development of the geisha a century later. This photograph is one of the few images that conjure up the seventeenth-century image of women frolicking.

Dancing Party (186) (attributed Kusakabe Kimbei, c. 1885)

The serene or contemplative facial expression typical of geisha is gone from these dancers as they joyously are asked to pose in a dance position.

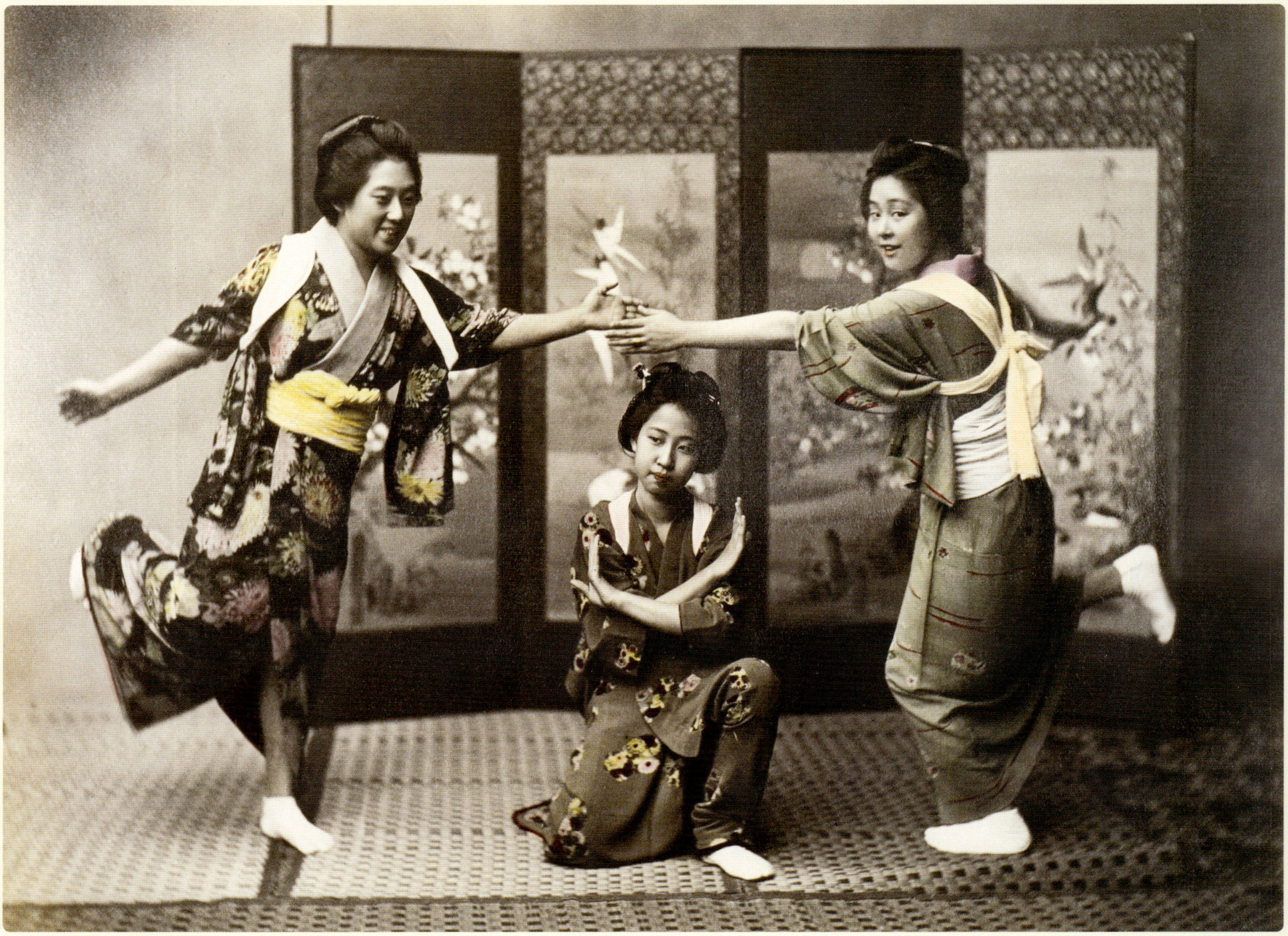

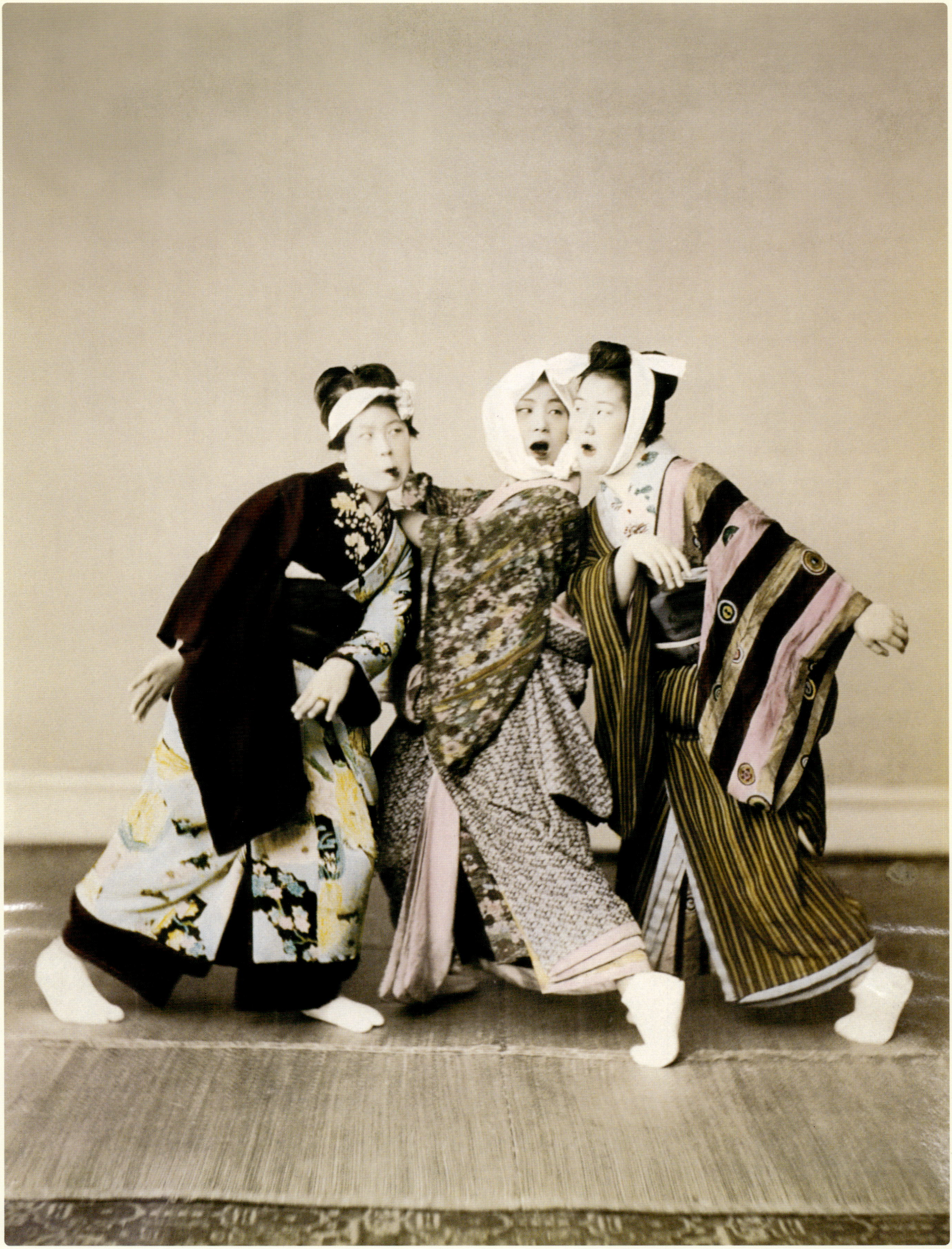

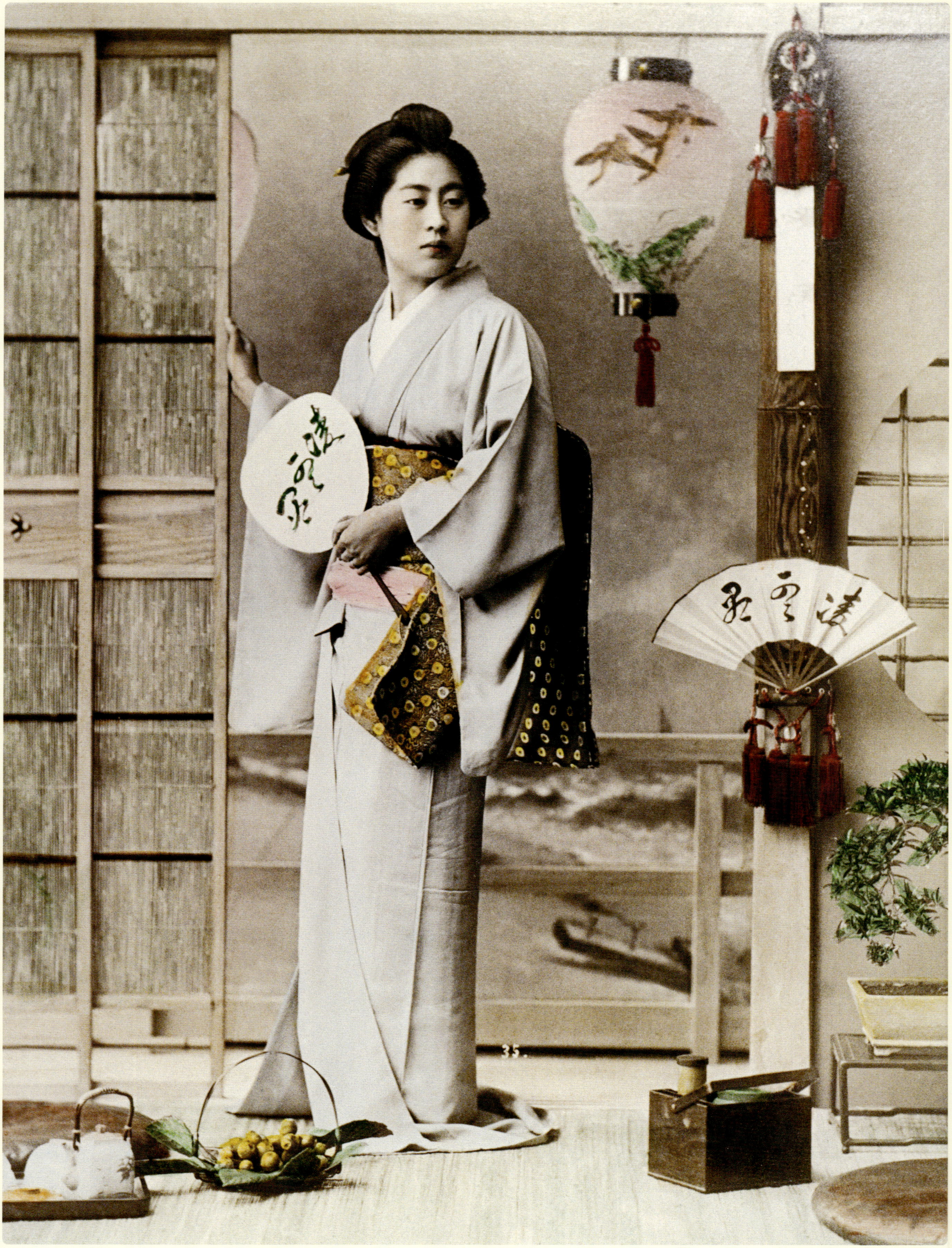
35.

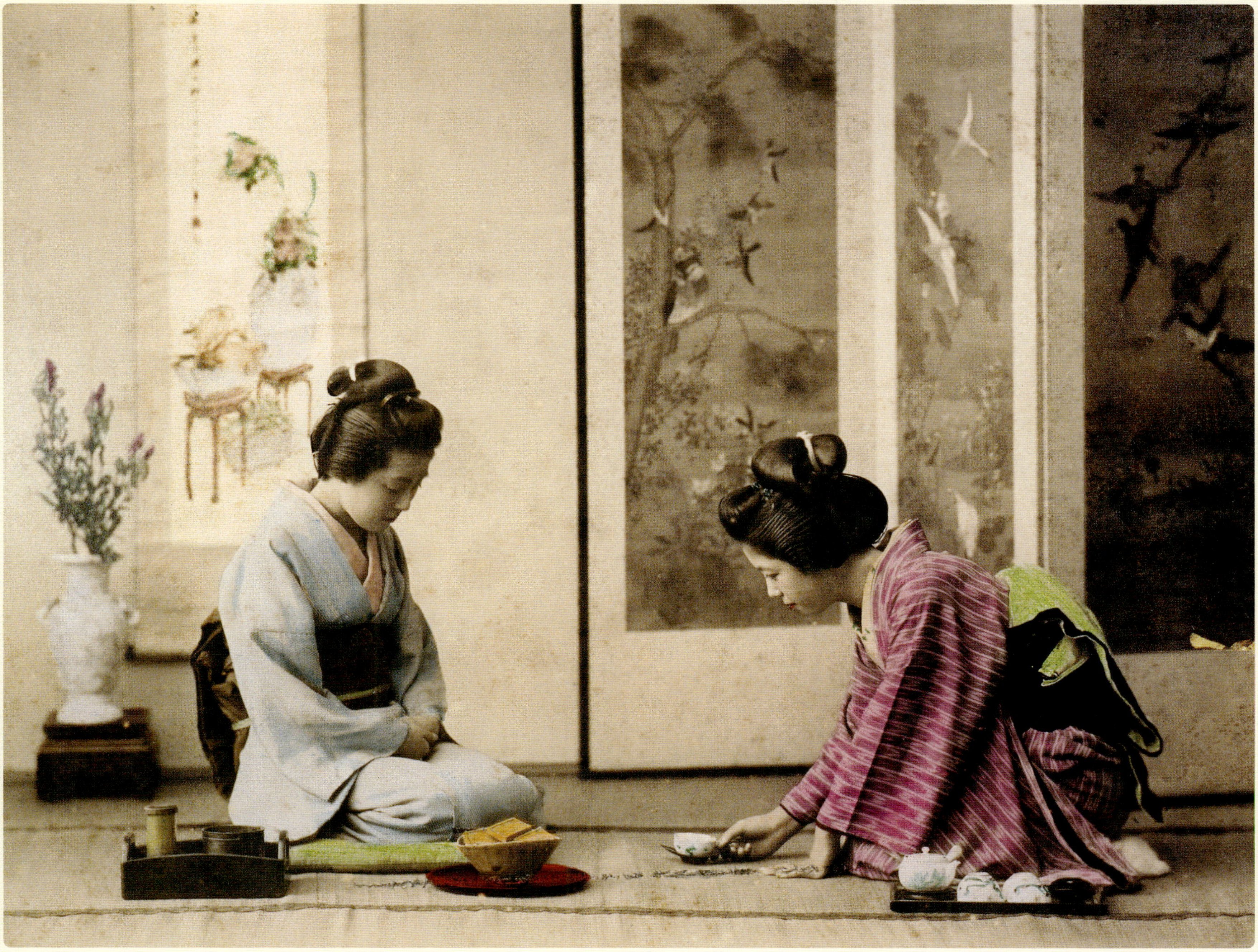

Performing Tea Ceremony (Kusakabe Kimbei, c.1890)

Tea ceremony is a revered part of Japanese culture. Geisha need to excel at the intricacies and etiquette. Traditional tea ceremony takes place in a special room, a *chashitsu*, with appropriate furniture arrangement and floor coverings. The room must have a central alcove for the host to hang a *kakemono*, or scroll painting, revealing the theme of ceremony. Every aspect and movement is choreographed. There are many nuances and particulars, including type of tea, water, kettle, cups, pouring bottle, straining cloth, sweets, and especially the order of preparation and serving. Tea ceremony is so involved that there are books and periodicals devoted to its variations and performance.

Tokyo Geisha: Prize-Winning Beauty (P46)
(Ogawa Kazumasa, 1891)

In 1891, an exhibition was held at the newly opened Ryounkaku, known as the Twelve-Story Tower, in Asakusa, Tokyo. The building was designed by Scottish engineer William Kinninmond Burton and was the largest Western-style edifice in Meiji Japan. (Burton also aided in ridding Japan of cholera by overseeing the establishment of sewage and fresh water systems across the country.) The main event at Ryounkaku was the presentation of an exhibition of 100 portraits of geisha from Tokyo's various pleasure quarters. The images taken by Ogawa Kazumasa were produced as a book. Visitors to the exhibit were asked to vote on their favorite geisha. The top five chosen got prizes. The winner was 19-year-old O-Tama. She not only won the contest, but also attracted a *danna*. The word *danna* means patron, and it was a mark of a man's prestige and wealth to keep a geisha. A *danna* is like a husband to a geisha in that he supports her financially, however he usually already had a wife. This man paid for O-Tama's release from her Tamagawaya geisha house in Shimbashi. Geisha were bound to their house until the expense of all their years of training, clothing, and living were paid. It was usually a *danna* who freed a geisha, supported her, and became her only lover. O-Tama carries a flat, rounded fan called *uchiwa*, which typically carries the name or crest of the geisha.

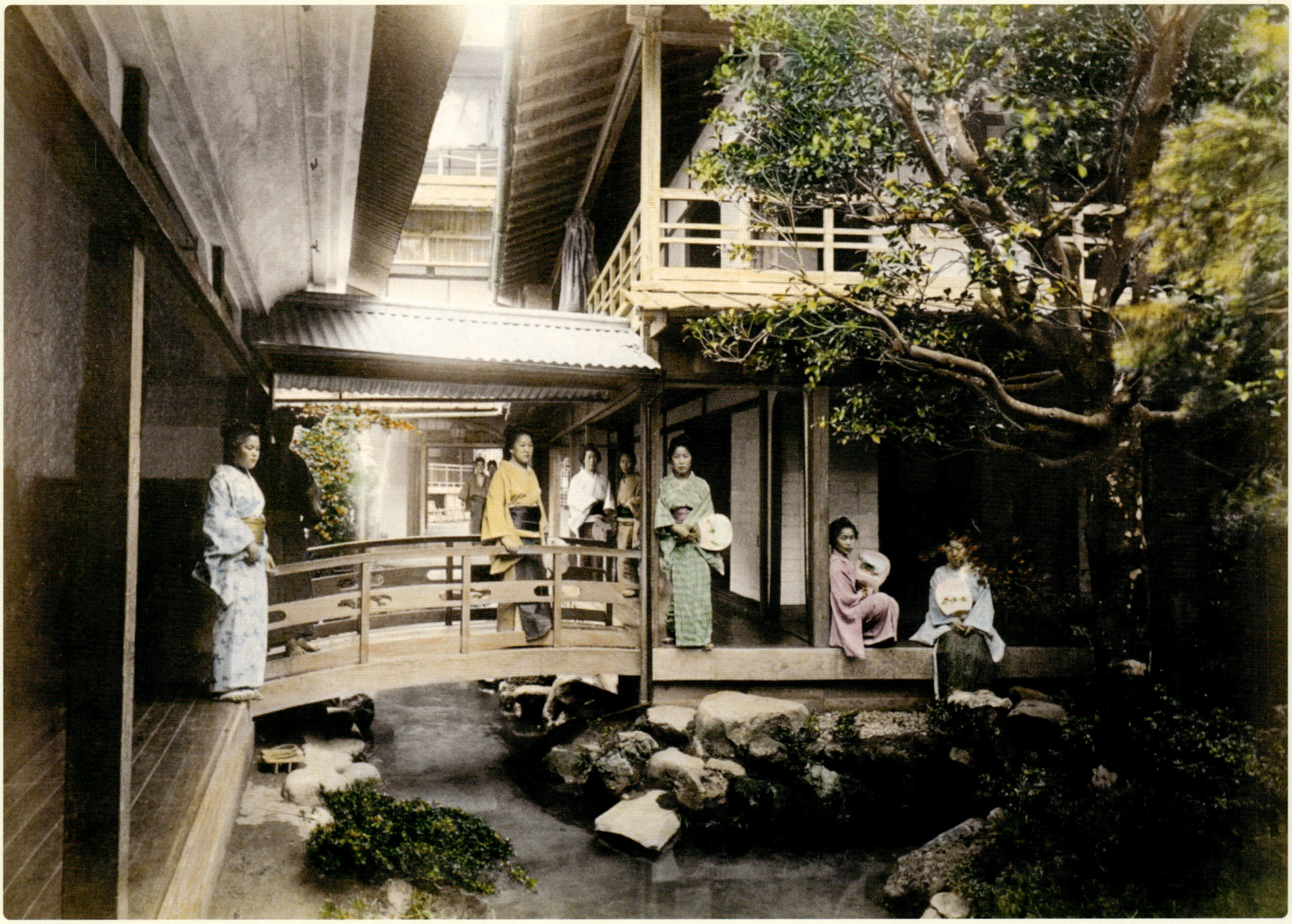

Inside Tea House Tonosawa (961) (unattributed, c. 1890)

This overview of a classic teahouse illustrates the fantasy atmosphere of the domain of the geisha. The kimono-clad geisha pose serenely in this garden setting. Gardens with waterways were typical of the best establishments. At the entrance to the geisha quarters, a willow tree was often planted, announcing the entrance to this special world. Gardens are an absolutely essential part of Japanese life. The intricate mosaic of stones, ponds, waterfalls, trees, and plants create a sublime, religious, calming experience. The Japanese word for garden, *niwa*, derives from the Shinto term *yuniwa*, denoting the sacred inner ground of shrines and palaces. Japanese gardens exude an aura of sanctity and otherworldliness, when combined with the geisha and courtesan experience, it is, as many writers suggest, as close to heaven as one gets. Supporting this concept, the Japanese exported it. Temporary teahouses with gardens, trees, and waterways staffed with geisha were set up at various expositions and world fairs so that the Western world could experience the atmosphere, ambience, and hospitality of the Japanese. Japan became the desired destination for seasoned travelers, and the geisha an icon of the nation.

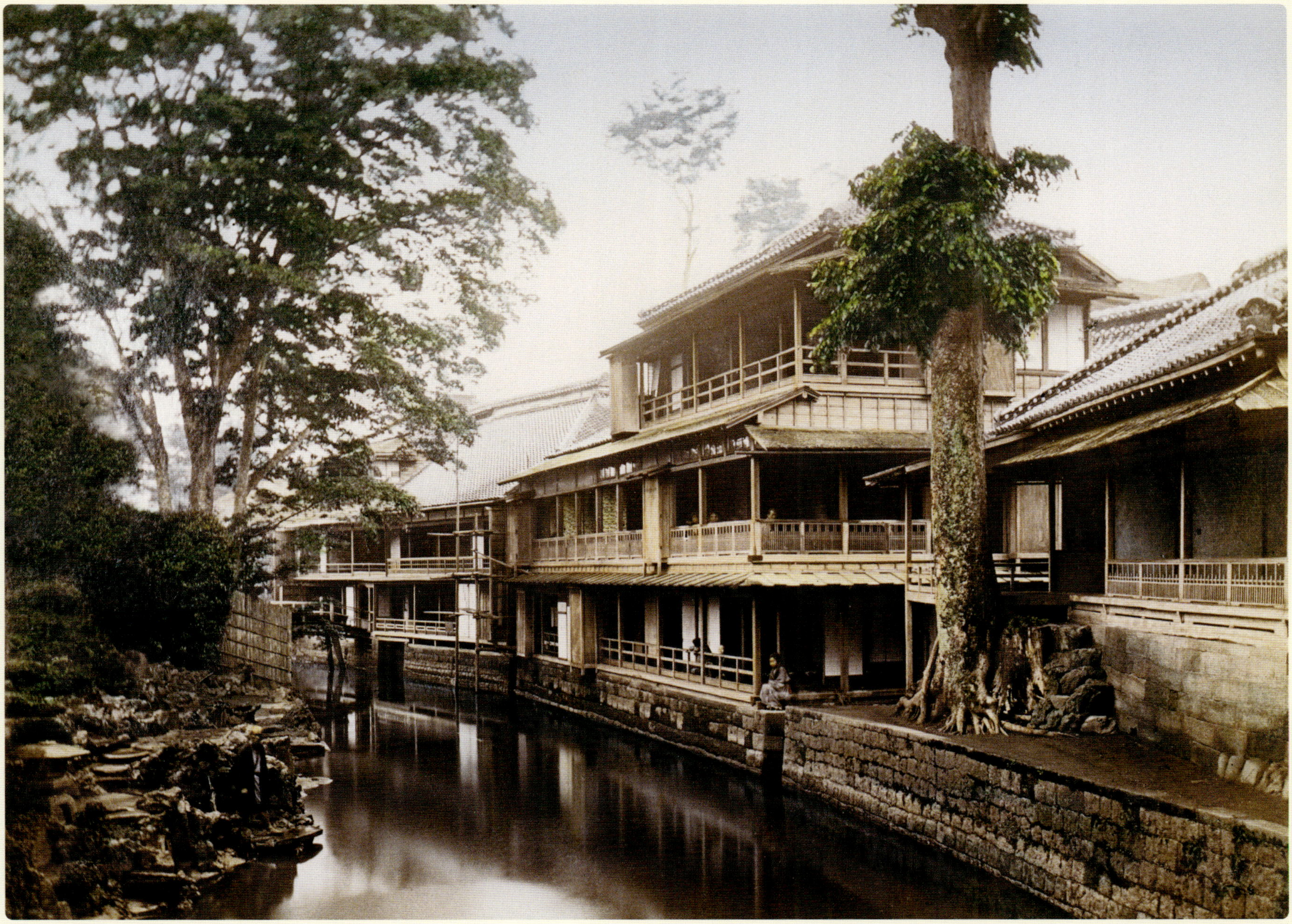

Oji Tea House Tokyo (652) (unattributed, c.1885)

The teahouses, *ochaya*, and elegant restaurants, *ryotei*, were the central places where geisha entertained in the flower and willow world. This photograph of the Oji Teahouse also shows an array of other establishments along a canal. The gated communities Shimbashi and Yoshiwara were the leading licensed pleasure districts in Tokyo. The elegant geisha teahouses were in these licensed quarters. In some areas, clients were ferried by boats to the geisha and courtesan establishments. Teahouses initially built for tea ceremony became the backbone of the pleasure quarters, and functioned more like a special café or nightclub. In these districts, the main beverage served was not tea but sake or other liquor. While tea ceremony could be performed as part of a dinner party, it was the party that was the central event. Geisha would perform and at times, courtesans would end the evening's festivities. Teahouses were generally not restaurants and for parties meals were ordered in. Attendants served the food and cleared the dishes. Geisha never ate, but entertained, poured drinks, and drank with the guests during the meals. It was their job to keep the sake cups filled and the conversation flowing.

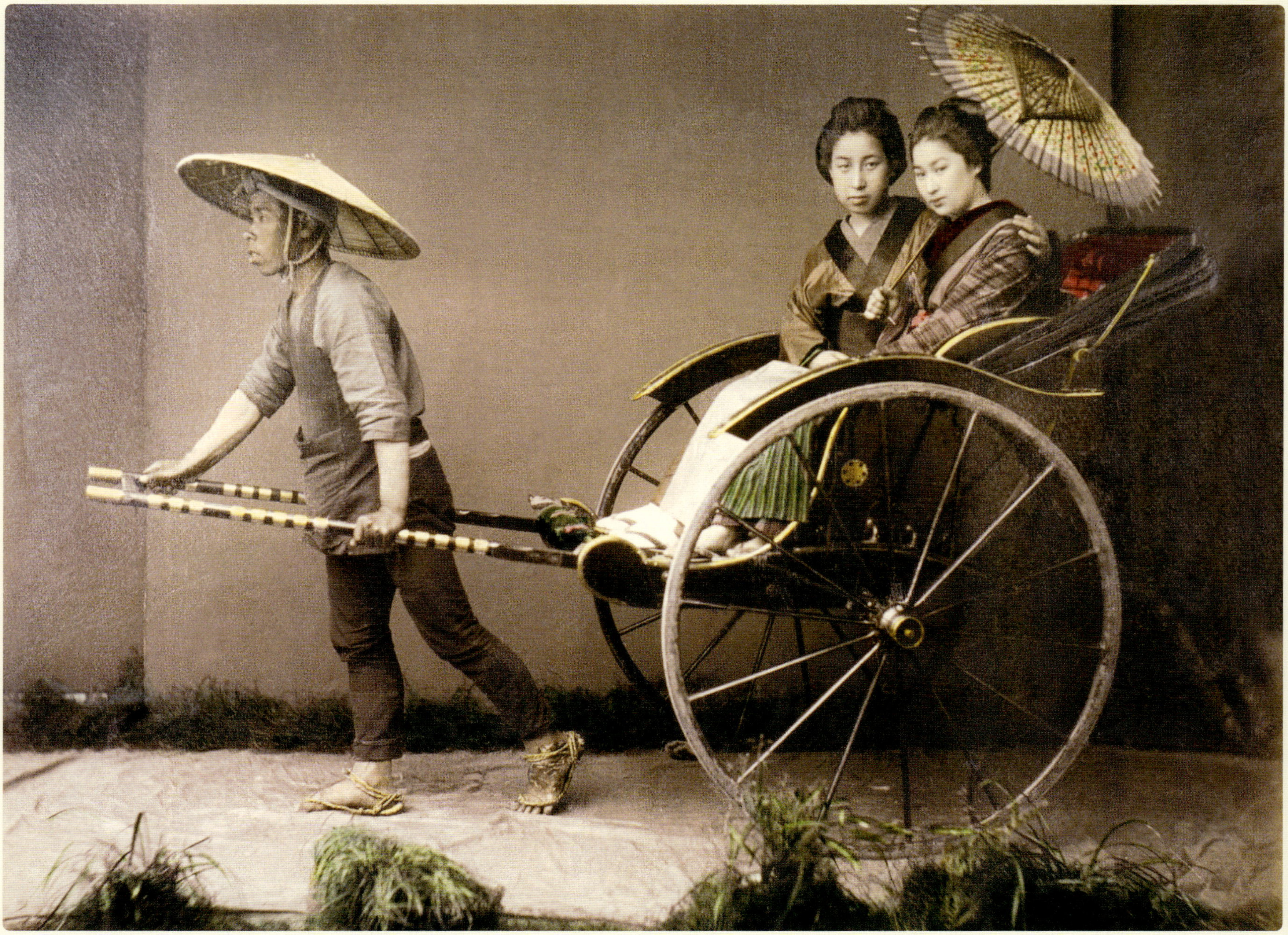

Jinrikisha (7) (Kusakabe Kimbei, c. 1885)

The rickshaw is the traditional mode of transportation of the geisha. They survived in Kyoto up until the end of the twentieth century, but for geisha use only. Geisha travel first class and stay at the best hotels, an essential part of the image. *Jinrikisha*, in Japanese, means "human powered vehicle." The rickshaw is a light, two-wheeled cart on springs, pulled by one man. They replaced the *kago* chair, a two-man version of the ancient sedan chair. Several claims to their invention and introduction into Japan abound. The Japanese credit Izumi Yosuke, Suzuki Tokujiro, and Takayama Kosuke are said to have invented them in 1868. Rickshaws were supposedly inspired by the horse-drawn carriages that were introduced to the streets of Edo. Most credit a New England missionary who in 1869 designed the cart to carry his invalid wife around Yokohama. In 1870, the three Japanese "inventors" were granted licenses to build rickshaws. By the end of 1871, over 15,000 were in operation, and by 1872, 40,000 rickshaws were in Edo alone. They had become the principle means of land transport in Japan. The average speed of a good rickshaw runner with a light person in the cart was 5 miles per hour. Twenty to 30 miles per day was expected.

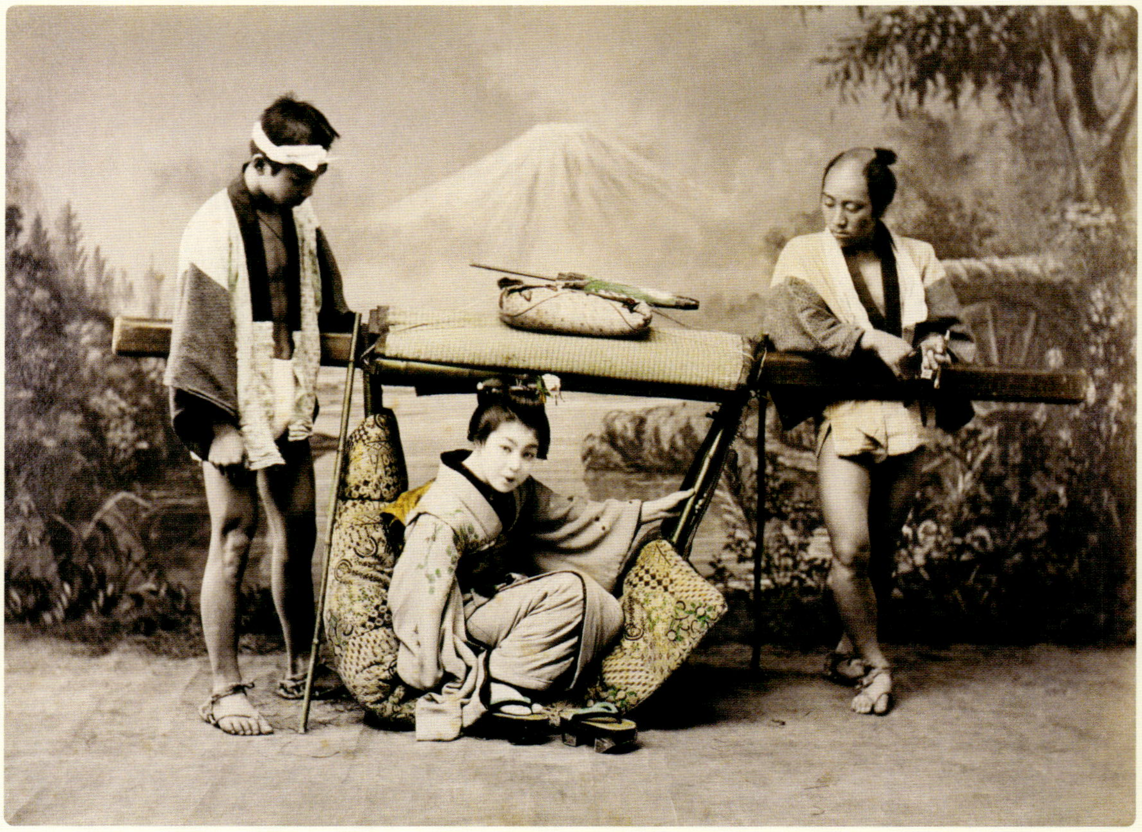

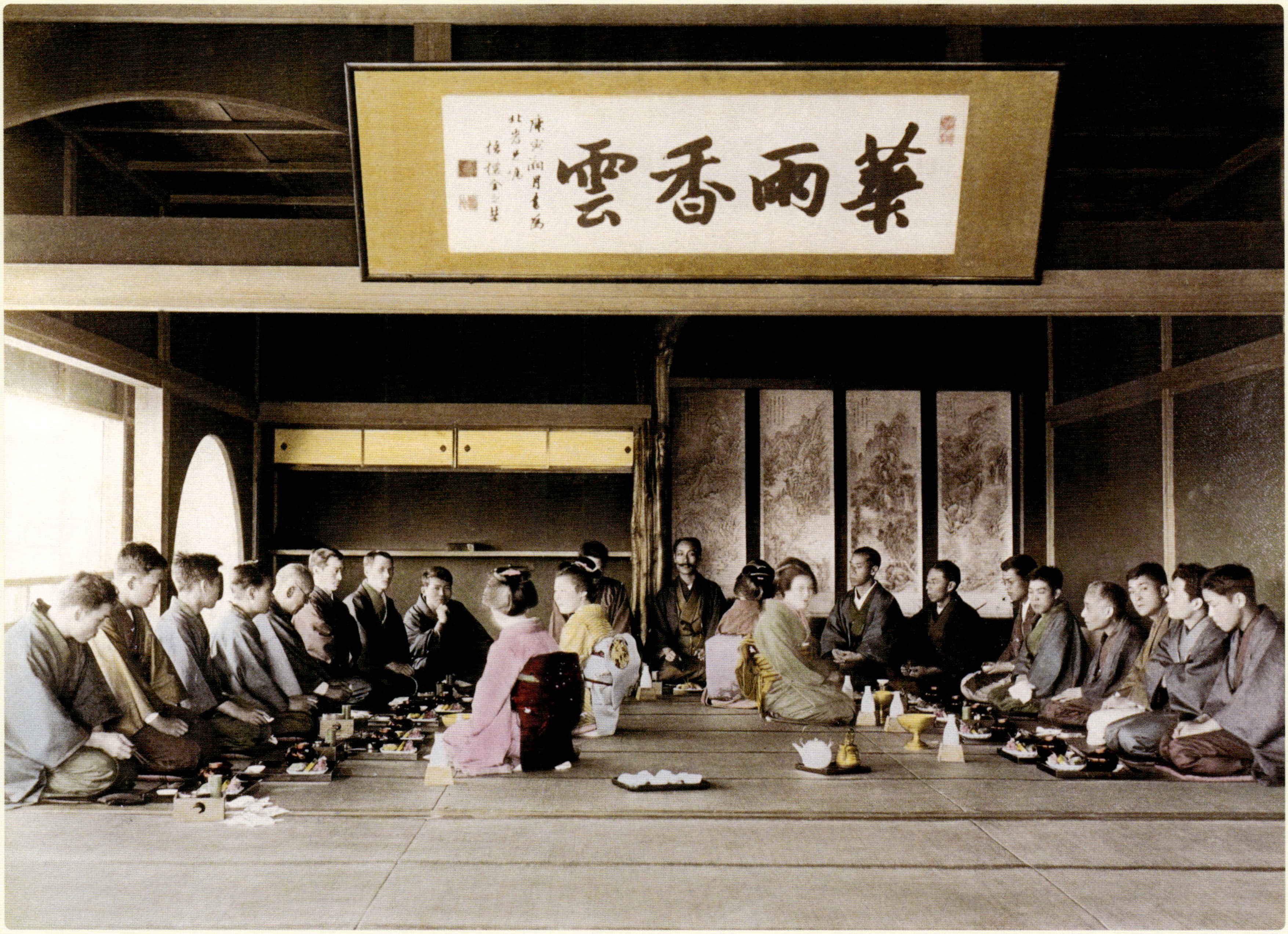

Dinner Party (unattributed, c. 1900)

This is one of the few photographs documenting the typical seating arrangement at a dinner party. Geisha can only attend dinners at *ryotei*, approved restaurants: high-class establishments that were not only elegant, but also served the finest food. The U-shaped table arrangement was traditional for geisha banquets. The open central space allowed the geisha to kneel in front of each guest as she poured drinks or entertains. Placement of the guest depended on importance. At the center of the U was the guest of honor, and then the guests were seated in descending order, the least important persons at the ends. Guests could leave their seats and enter the center area to sit opposite a person they wanted to talk to or toast.

Girl Taking a Ride on a Kago (Traveling Chair) (B1156) (unattributed, c. 1875)

Geisha were typically carried to events. Before the introduction of the rickshaw during the Edo period, the kago, or "palanquin," was a standard means of transportation. It is a typical sedan chair, used and developed in Africa and Asia. The kago was a bamboo chair suspended from a stout pole carried by two men. It was uncomfortable and unstable, as it depended on the smooth operation of two men walking in sync. The front and back were always covered to prevent dust and other particles from hitting the person carried. The sides were open, but could be covered with a cloth in bad weather or for privacy.

Geisha Private Life

[Whispering] Singing Girls (P22)
(attributed Baron Raimund von Stillfried, c. 1880)

The secrets of the flower and willow world are emphasized by numerous photographs of geisha or *maiko* whispering to each other. Here one geisha, standing near a painted screen, whispers her secrets. All hold a piece of their outer kimono to their mouths to shield the viewer from reading their lips. The photographs taken by the commercial photographers were created to reveal geisha and their world for foreigners. This photograph is labeled "P-22 Singing Girls" but von Stillfried, as well as others who used this image, created several other names—including the correct title, "Whispering." In another version, the same two seated geisha are depicted in the exact pose, painted in the same colors, but without the pink flowers and the standing geisha. That image is titled "P-35 Whispering." Terry Bennet, Japanese scholars, and others are working on identifying and classifying Japanese commercial photographs to create a catalogue of known images to ascertain authorship and other associations. These "whispering" images are examples of the confusion initiated by commercial photographers randomly naming and sharing their images.

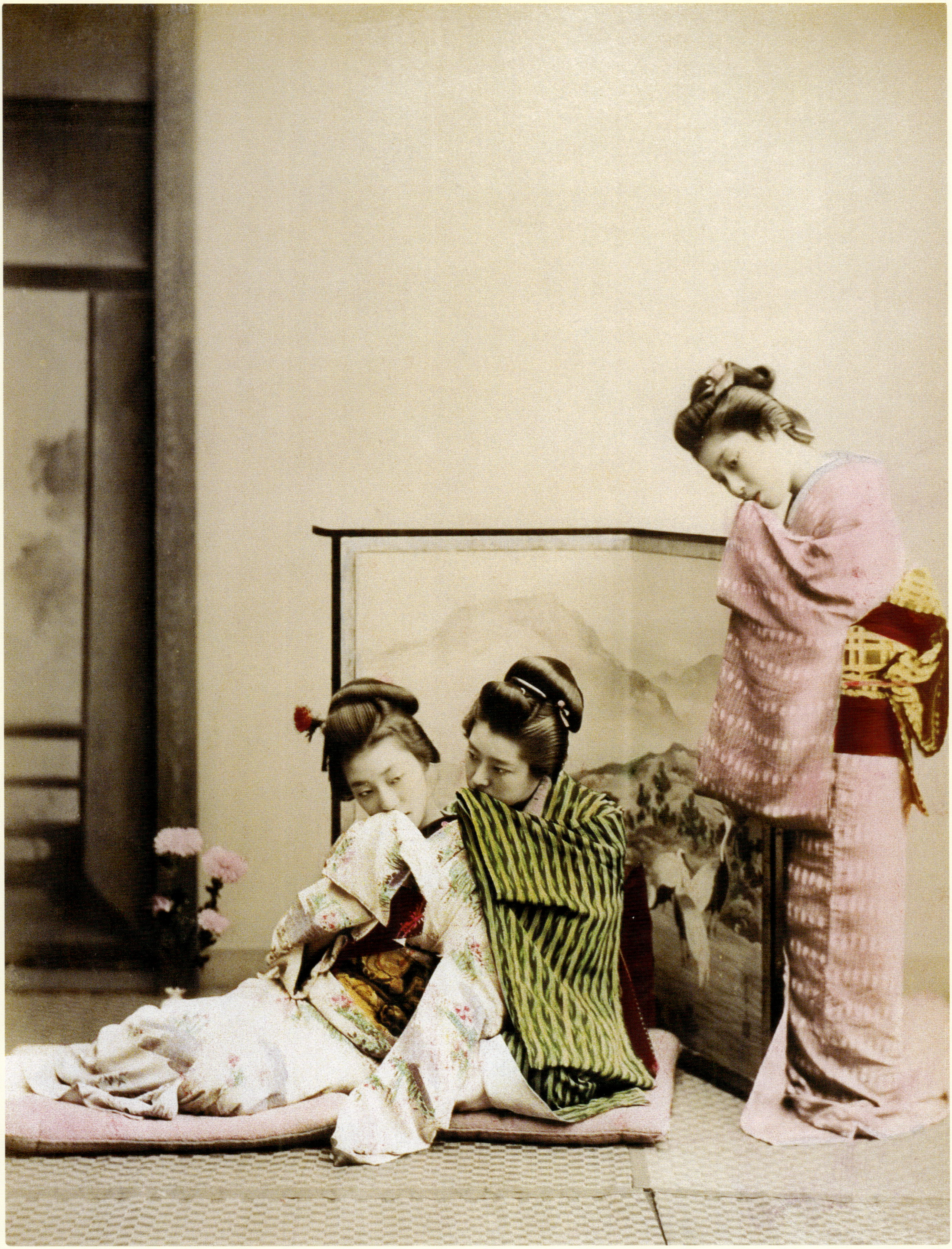

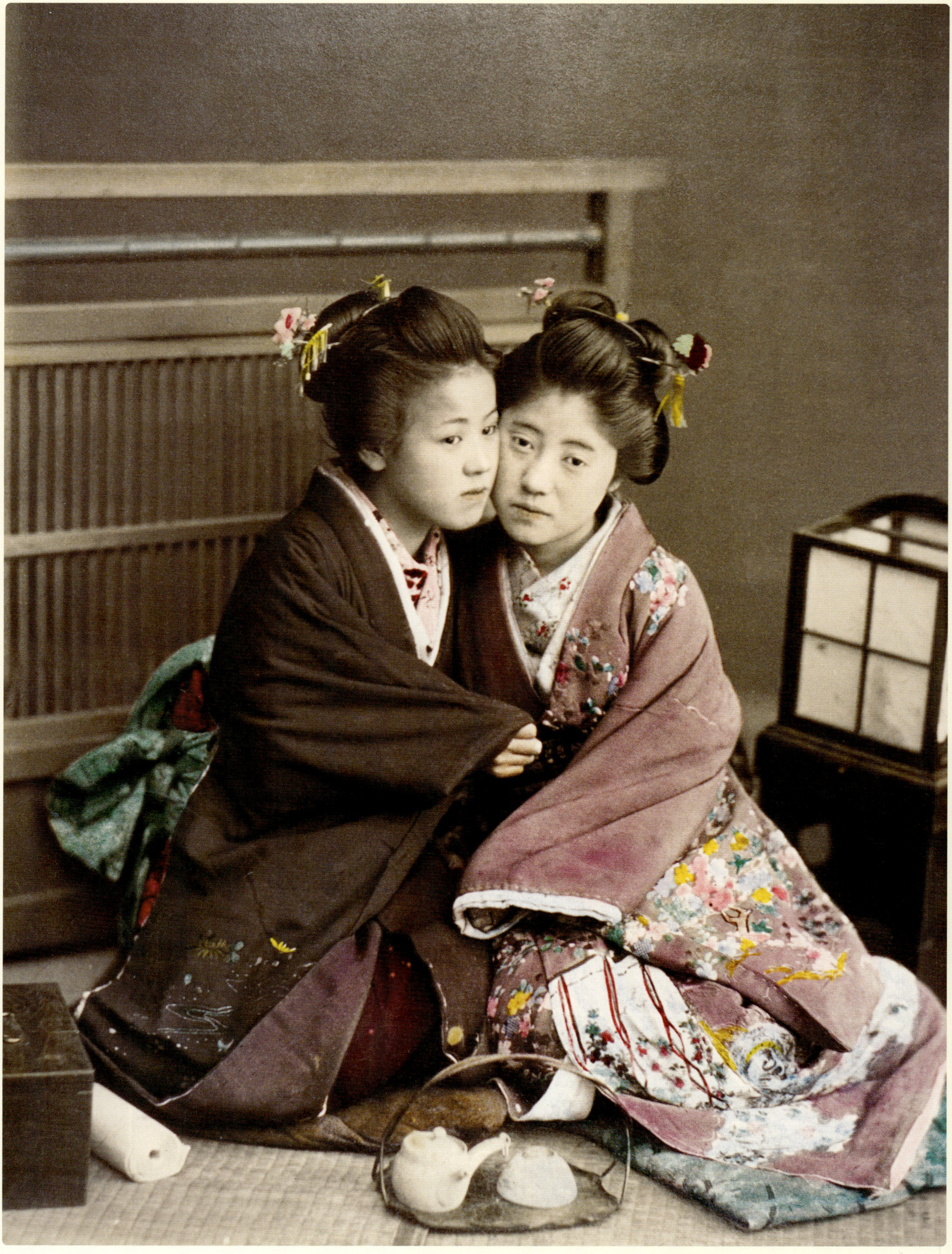

Maiko and Onesan Huddled Together (attributed Kusakabe Kimbei, c. 1885)

The sisterhood of the geisha profession is essential to its function and survival. A special kinship is established to guide the apprentice through her trials and tribulations. The geisha, or senior *maiko*, *oyabun*, "one in the role of the parent," can have several students. In Kyoto, the central area of geisha training, the tying together of destinies is achieved symbolically with a variation of the marriage ceremony, *sansan-kudo*. The participants drink ritual wine and exchange cups. At first impression, this image appears as a photo of two *maiko*, but the age difference and dress indicates that the relationship is most likely that of either a geisha and her trainee, or that of an older *maiko* and a young apprentice. An older sister, *onesan*, relationship is critical to a *maiko*'s development. Kimono design and patterning are related to age and stage of development. The flowered kimono of the older girl is that of a more advanced *maiko*, or geisha. The young girl wears a simple kimono. The red underkimono and pink/red collar are also indicative of *maiko* status in the younger girl. This image was most likely taken to convey the close relationship of Japanese geisha. Images such as this in Victorian times, in Western countries, were considered part of the soft-core eroticism inherent in photographs of women in other cultures.

Girls in Bed Room (89) (Kusakabe Kimbei, c. 1885)

This image is part of a series that seems to offer a peek at the private world of the geisha. The raised wooden pillow was an essential item in the life and training of a geisha. It preserved their hair for the next day. Since hairstyling was a time-consuming and costly endeavor it was critical that it stay perfect. A hair out of place was not acceptable, especially in a trainee, or *maiko*. Like boot camp for the military, the rigors and expectations of the trainee experience were harsh and unforgiving. To make sure that the *maiko* didn't accidentally or otherwise let her hair touch the floor, the *okamisan*, geisha house mother, or *onesan*, older sister, would spread sticky-wet rice on the floor about the pillow. The rice would adhere to the hair like glue if any part of the head touched the floor. In the Meiji and previous eras, geisha training started at age six. In a time when options for survival were few, the discipline necessary to finish the long training is easier to comprehend. Today geisha training is started in the mid to late teens after compulsory schooling is finished. Most quit after a few months or stop right before becoming a geisha. University attendance seems a better choice to many. In the 1920s there were over 80,000 geisha in Japan, today there are only a few thousand.

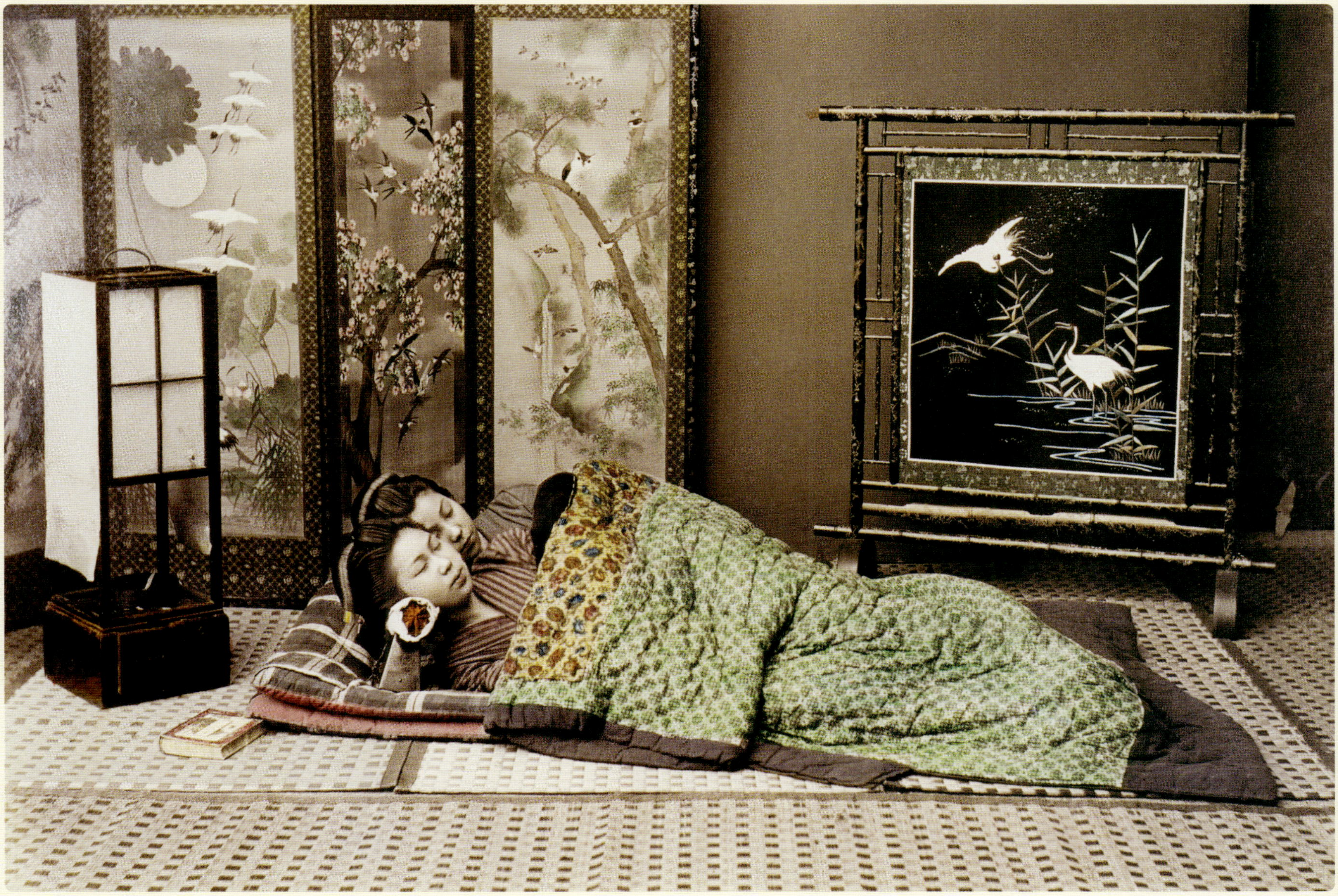

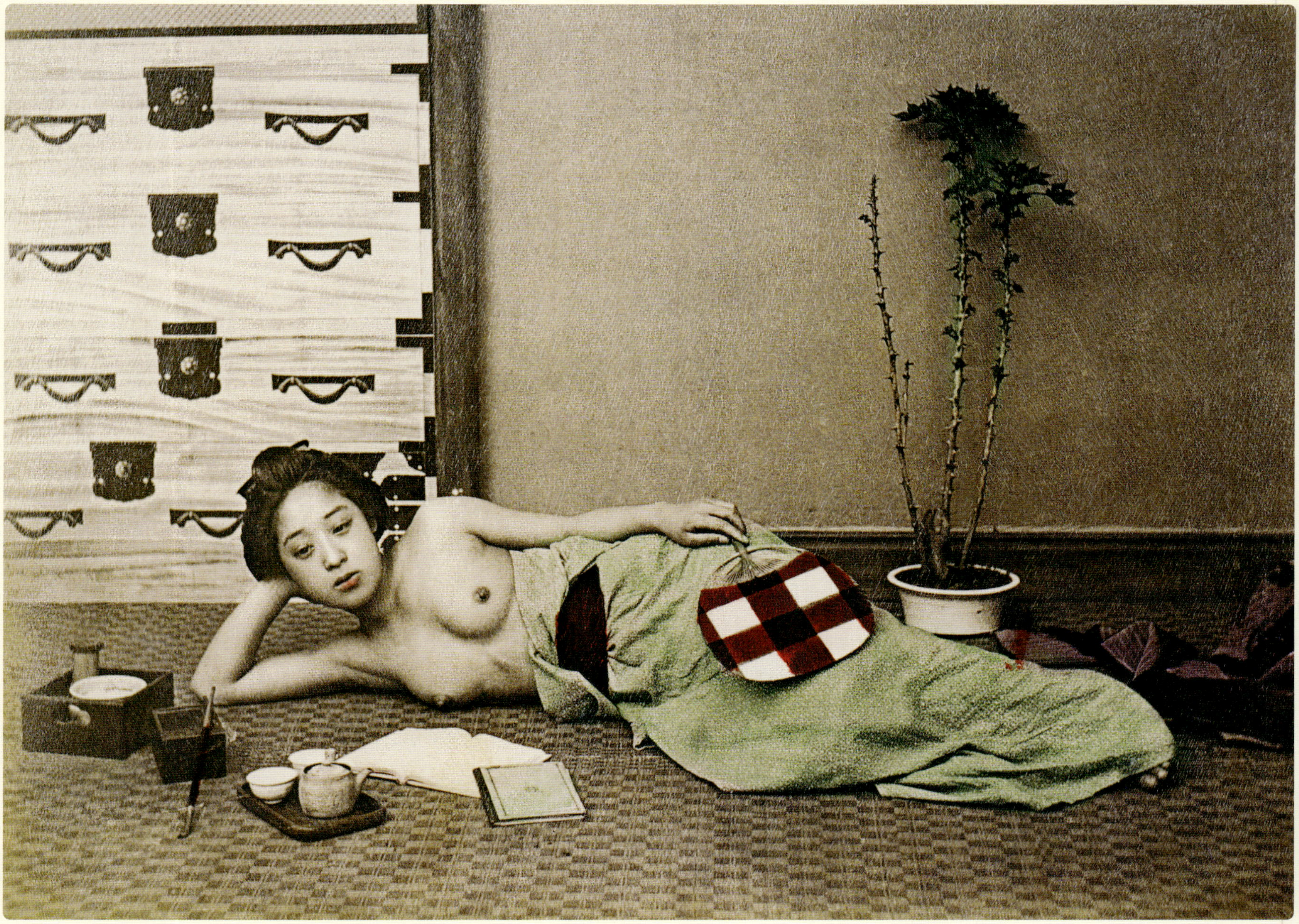

Reclining Nude (Baron Raimund von Stillfried, c. 1880)

In the Victorian era, peering into the private life of an exotic culture warranted images of nudity. Nudity was not shameful in Japanese society: men and women routinely bathed together, especially in the hundreds of resort hot springs. It took hard work by Christian missionaries and the puritanical ideology of others to change Japanese customs. In very warm weather, it was not uncommon for the Japanese woman to undo the top of her kimono and let it fall to her waist, bearing her breasts. While Kusakabe and other photographers may have photographed women in private poses, it was Baron Raimund von Stillfried-Ratenicz who exploited the communal and everyday nudity of Japanese women. Von Stillfried specialized in creating an extensive series of photographs of women in various activities with their breasts exposed. It was he, through his photographs, which he exhibited in Europe at expositions and in slide lectures, that helped develop a soft-core Japanese pornographic culture in the West. The last decades of the nineteenth century were the high water mark of cultural and physical anthropology. Anthropologists traveled the world photographing indigenous peoples. In many primitive cultures the women were nude or topless. These "scientific" photographs circulated in proper Victorian society as studies of race and culture. Von Stillfried exploited this interest. His photographs were also an inducement for Westerners to think of the Japanese as a more primitive society, as they were often lumped with images of primitive undeveloped cultures. By the late 1880s, the Japanese government, in an effort to appear favorably in Western eyes, placed some restrictions on nudity in bathhouses as well as other activities.

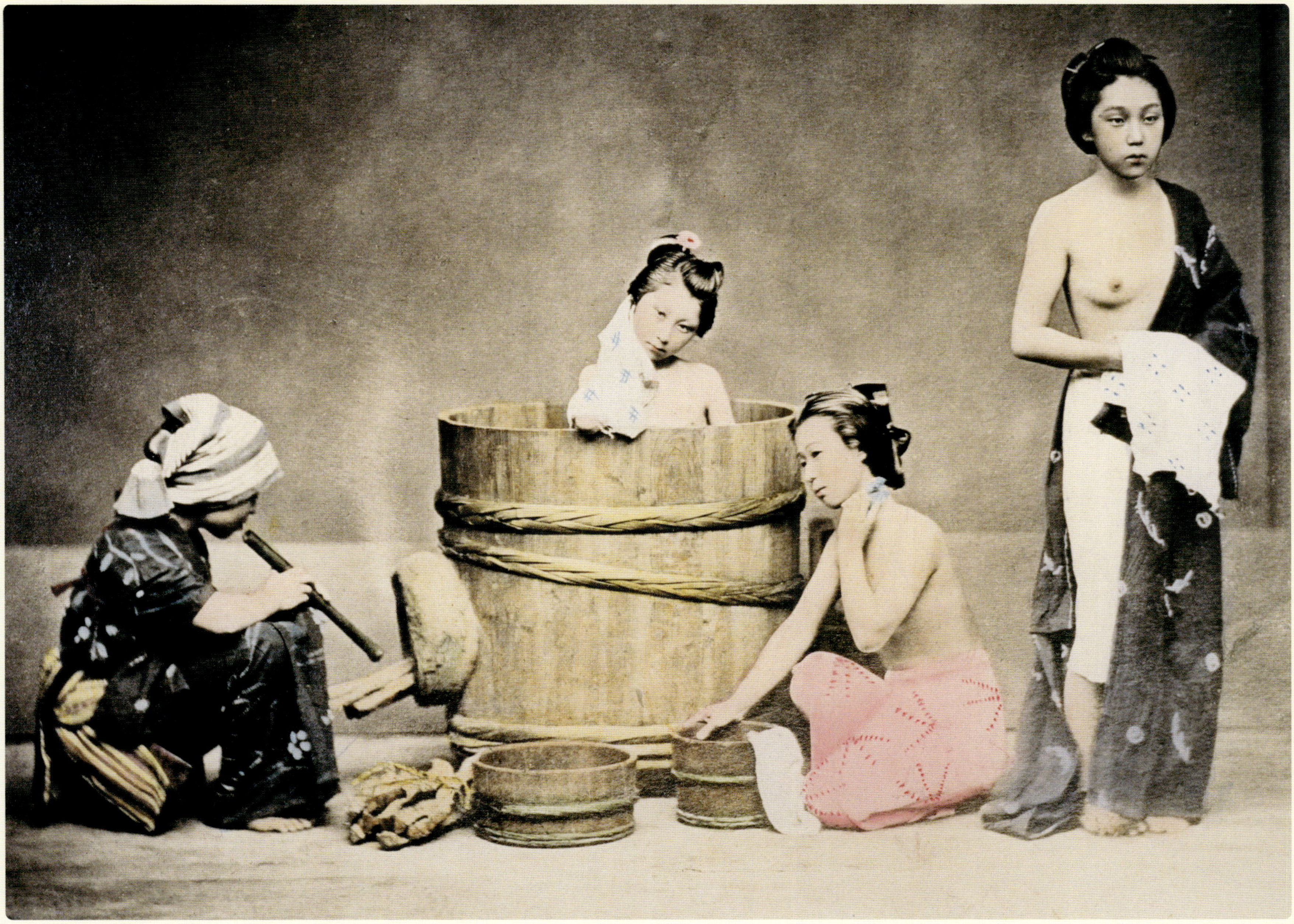

Home Bathing (67 & B1099)
(attributed Baron Raimund von Stillfried, c. 1880)

There are numerous versions of the bathing scene genre of which these photographs are typical. All are quite similar in composition. An elderly woman usually attends to the stove that heats the water. There is always one person in the tub washing, and one or more women drying themselves. To the Victorian mind, this would be a very titillating view of one of life's private moments.

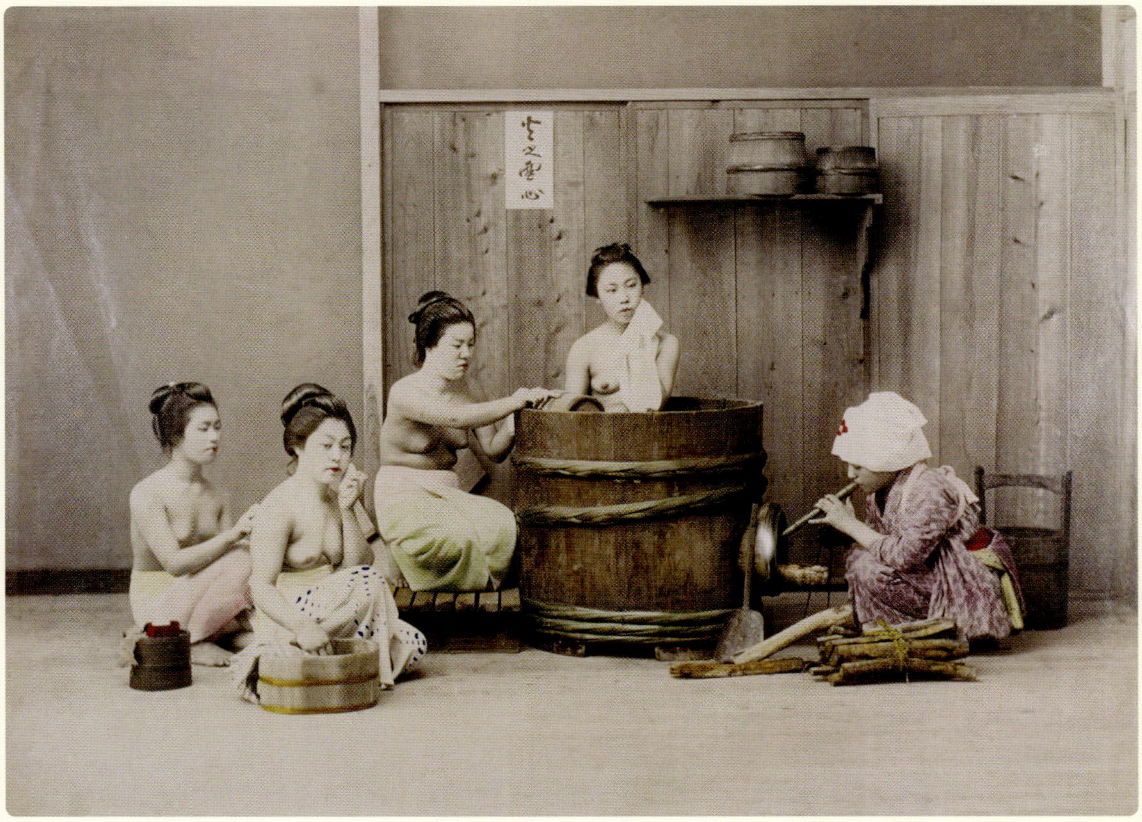

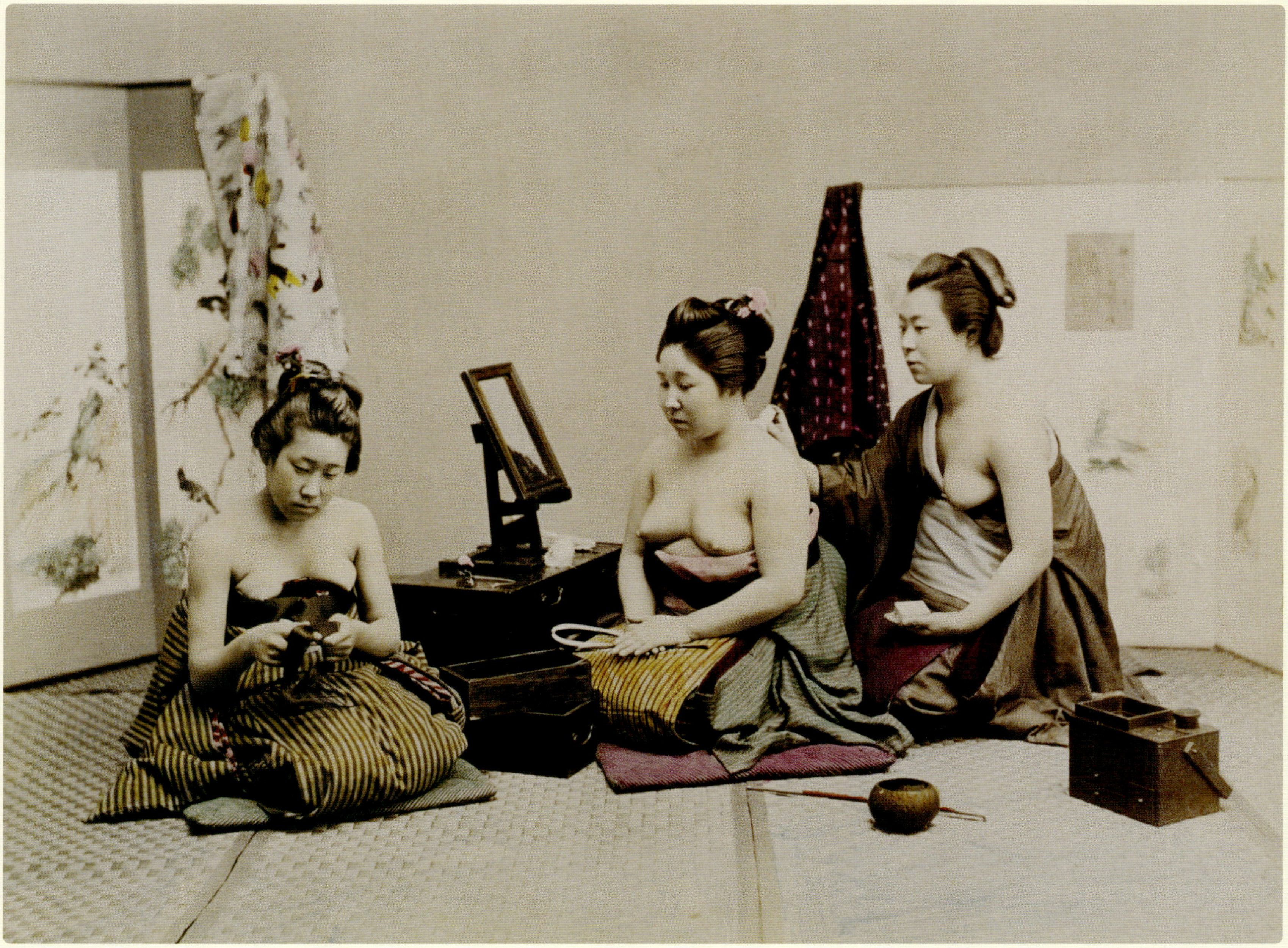

Dressing Girls, (Q47) (Baron Raimund von Stillfried, c. 1880)

This view of three topless women, according to the caption, catches them in the act of dressing. This soft-core pornographic image represents a genre forbidden in proper Victorian society. Pornographic woodcuts, *shunga*, had a respectable life in the Japanese art world. Sex and pleasure were an accepted part of Japanese life in the licensed quarters, where men were expected to relax and live out their fantasies. Pornographic photography flourished in the Meiji era and several recent books document the phenomena. The woman on the left of this photograph is holding a large lock of hair. The woman on the right appears to be applying some sort of device, possibly a medicinal cup, to the back of the woman seated in the middle.

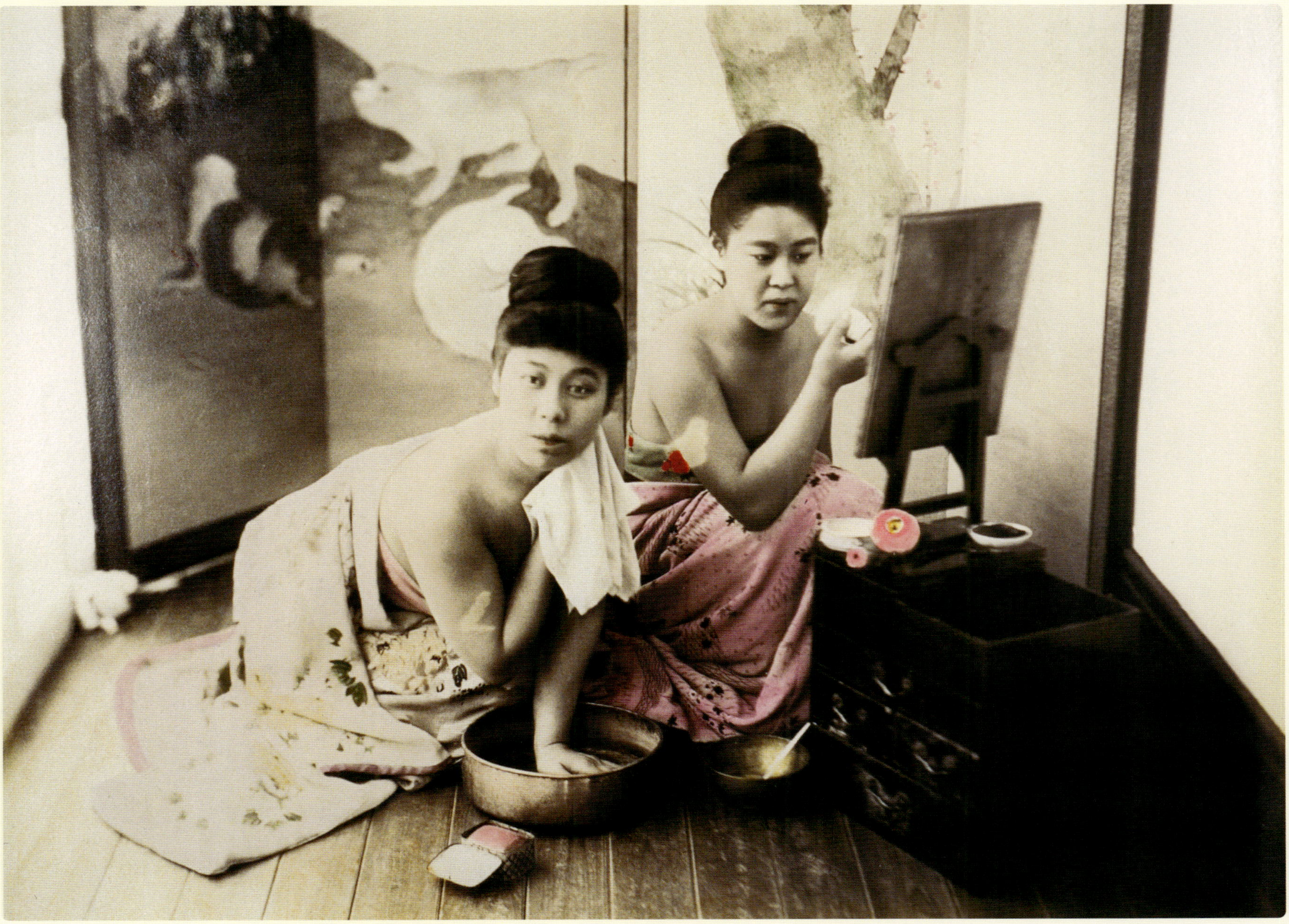

Dressing (F71) (attributed Kusakabe Kimbei, c. 1885)

The posed bathing scenes give a glimpse of a routine activity, however they all seem staged. This image appears to offer a visual surprise, as the camera has seemingly caught two women in the private act of their toilette, washing and grooming themselves.

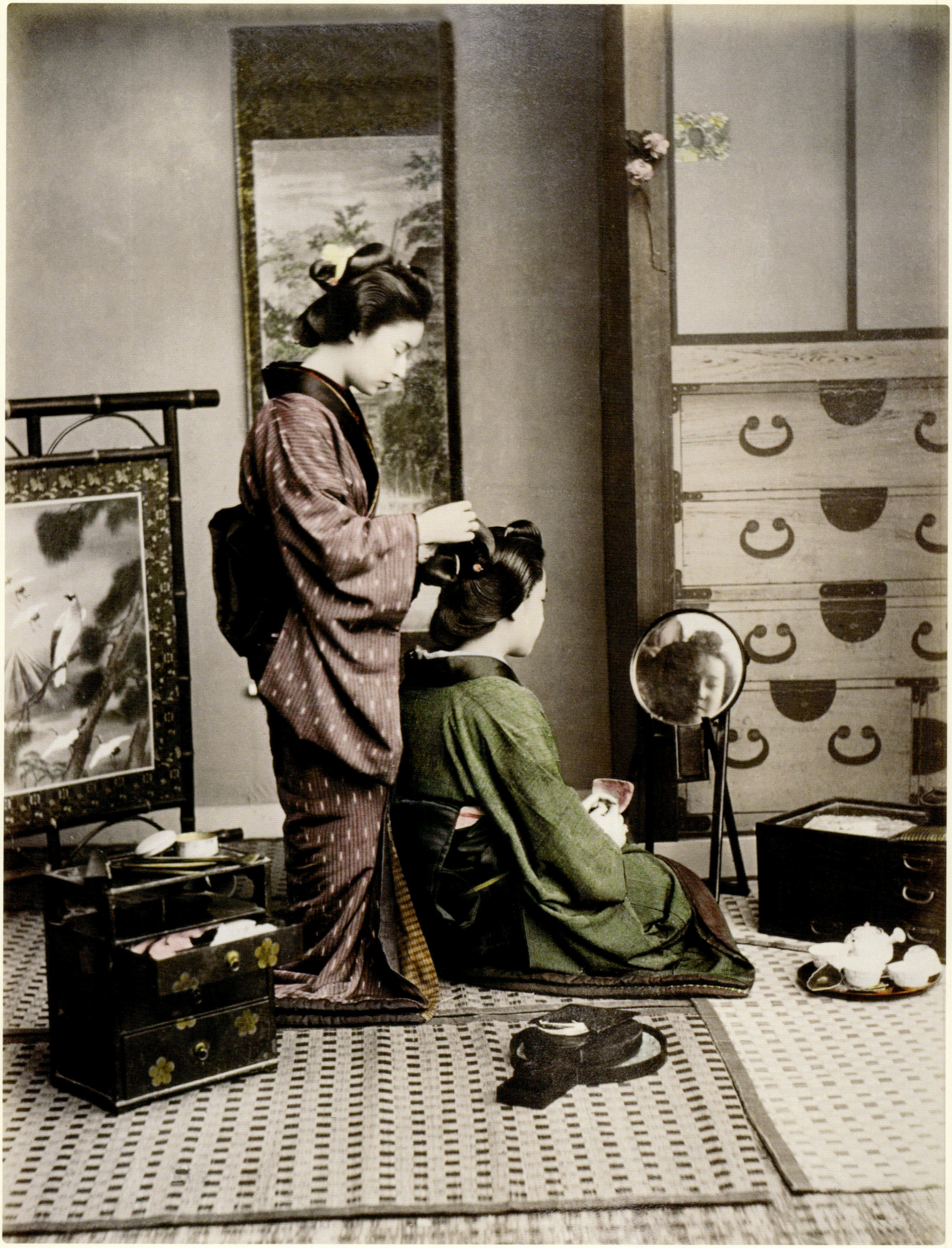

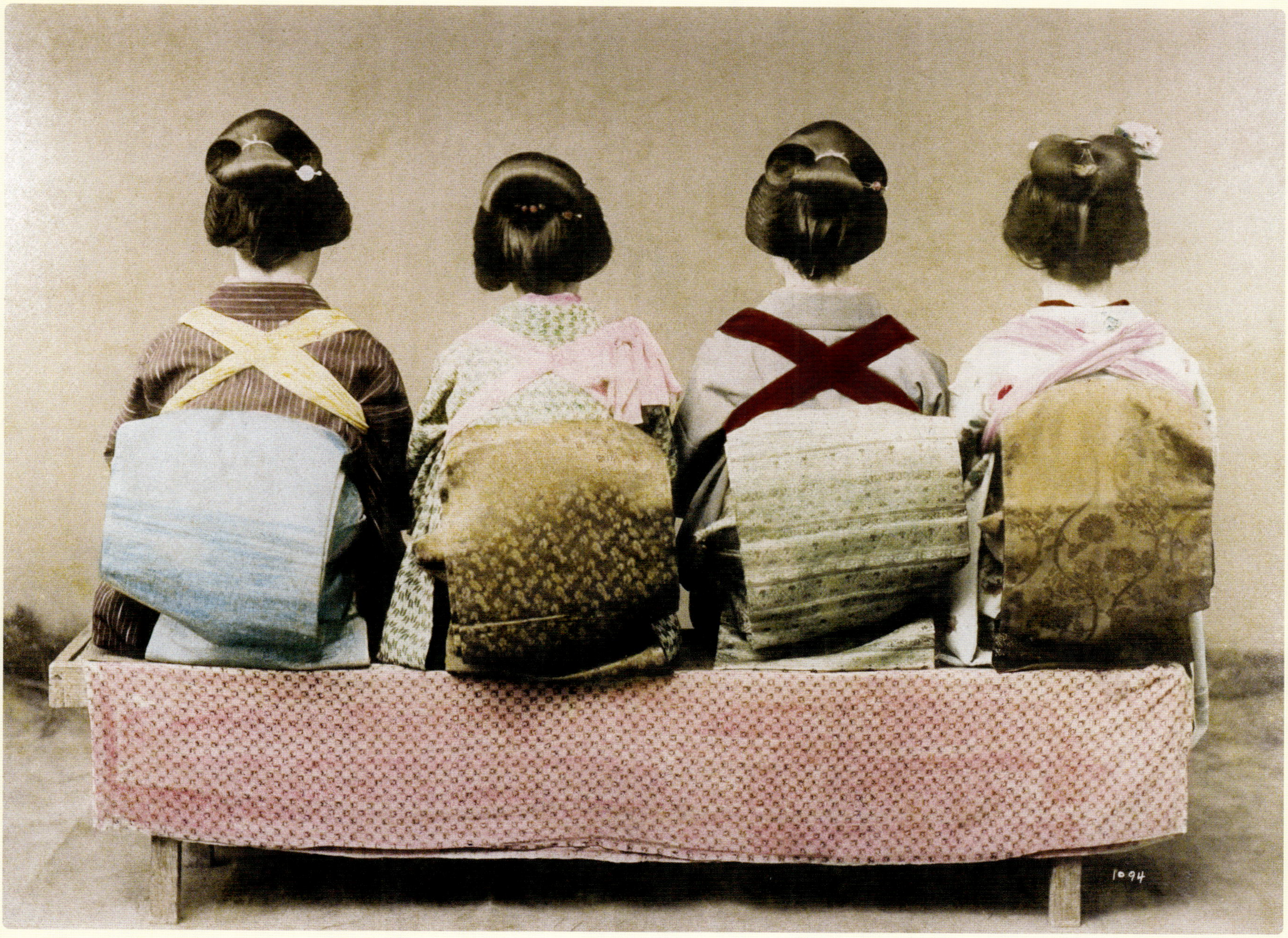

Showing Back Style (B1094) (unattributed, c. 1880)

In this era, a woman's dress, adornments, and hairstyle advertised her identity. Her outfit stated what part of the country she came from, what she did for a living, and especially her social class. In the geisha world, each city, and each *hamanachi* in that city, had particular hairstyles. A geisha's hairstyle, as well as kimono, indicated her rank and progression in the willow world. *Shimada*, one of the most common hairstyles, became popular in the nineteenth century. There are several varieties, such as *taka shimada*, worn by young women, and *tsubushi shimada,* worn by older women. The first hairstyle of a Kyoto *maiko* was *ware-shinobu*. It consists of a bagel-shaped roll of hair worn on the top of the head. The second style, after a *maiko* loses her virginity, is called *ofuko*, and the topknot is placed lower down. The last style before a *maiko* became a geisha was very ornate, and called *sakko*. Numerous other styles existed, as well as many for special occasions. In this era, most geisha, after years of having their hair pulled to create such ornate styles, had a bald spot in the center of their head. This photograph shows four different hairstyles. Ornaments were worn for special occasions. The type, and especially an excess, of ornaments identified a courtesan.

Hair Dressing (172) (Kusakabe Kimbei, c. 1885)

A geisha's hair, like the rest of her, had to be a work of art. Preparing it was a time-consuming and costly endeavor. In this image a geisha is having her hair prepared by her attendant. The implements for hairdressing and a tea tray are around her. In the twentieth century, with the relaxation of conventions, wigs became an accepted accessory. The advantage of a wig is that it can be designed and set in a particular style, and a geisha no longer had to spend hours getting her hair done. She was also able to interact outside of the geisha world, as her hair was not always set. Wigs were very expensive and it was imperative for geisha to own more than one, for different occasions and events. The costs added up, as the wigs had to be reset regularly and, after several years use, replaced. Historians are continually identifying makers of Japanese photographs by finding identified period albums. This photograph is published and attributed to Kusakabe Kimbei in the Nagasaki Albumen Photograph Database, having been removed from an album containing only his work. Kimbei has artfully placed the mirror and focused it on the woman's face. The room is beautifully decorated with tatami mats, scrolls, and decorative screens. These exact items, when found in other photographs, help to ascertain authorship of the photograph.

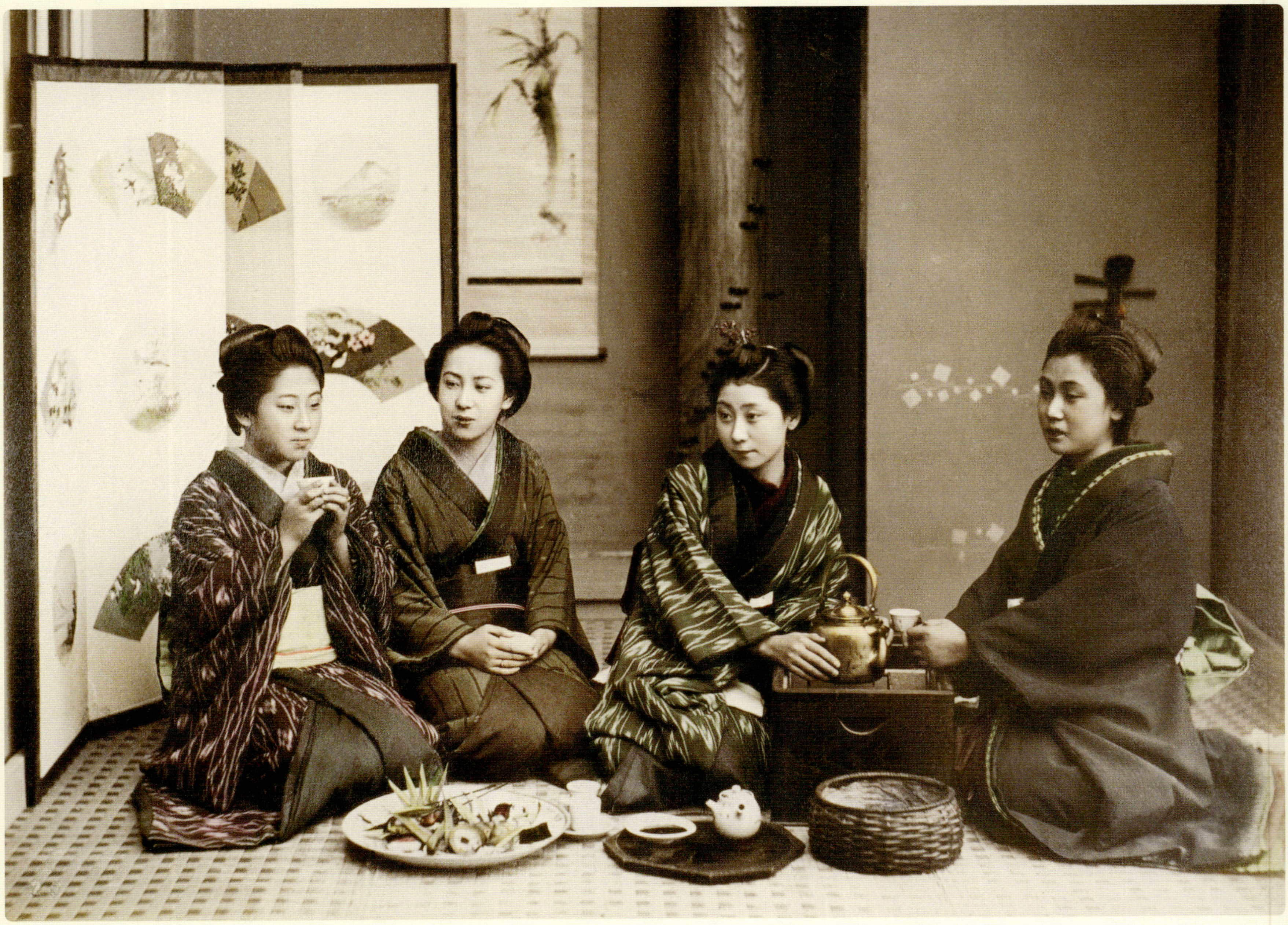

Afternoon Lunch (26) (Kusakabe Kimbei, c. 1890)

Geisha do not eat with their clients. When they attend a party or dinner they serve drinks and are expected to drink but not consume any food. Geisha and *maiko* typically ate twice a day at noon, after morning classes (for the *maiko*), and at 4:00 PM before getting ready for the evening. This exquisitely painted photograph is from an album by Kusakabe.

Singing Girls (P-26) (unattributed, c. 1885)

Geisha spent an inordinate amount of time in front of a mirror, all of it necessary, as makeup, hairstyle, and all other aspects of their appearance had to be perfect. The slow, contemplative application of makeup was a meditative process in which she evolved into her geisha persona. She was a living form of art and there was no compromise in presentation. A geisha's painted face is her occupation's mask to the world, each one similar yet different. This geisha, checking her final appearance, appears satisfied. The written designation on the bottom, "P- #," leads one to believe that the P series was produced by the same photographer. He also labeled them "Singing Girls" no matter what the scene showed (see other P-numbered photographs). While its tempting to say that they are all by one studio, the reality is that unless the backgrounds and persons match, all that they may be said is that they were labeled by the same studio. Other photographers could have supplied the negatives. The problem of attribution is a stumbling block for art and photographic historians, but not for those interested in the subject and what the image shows.

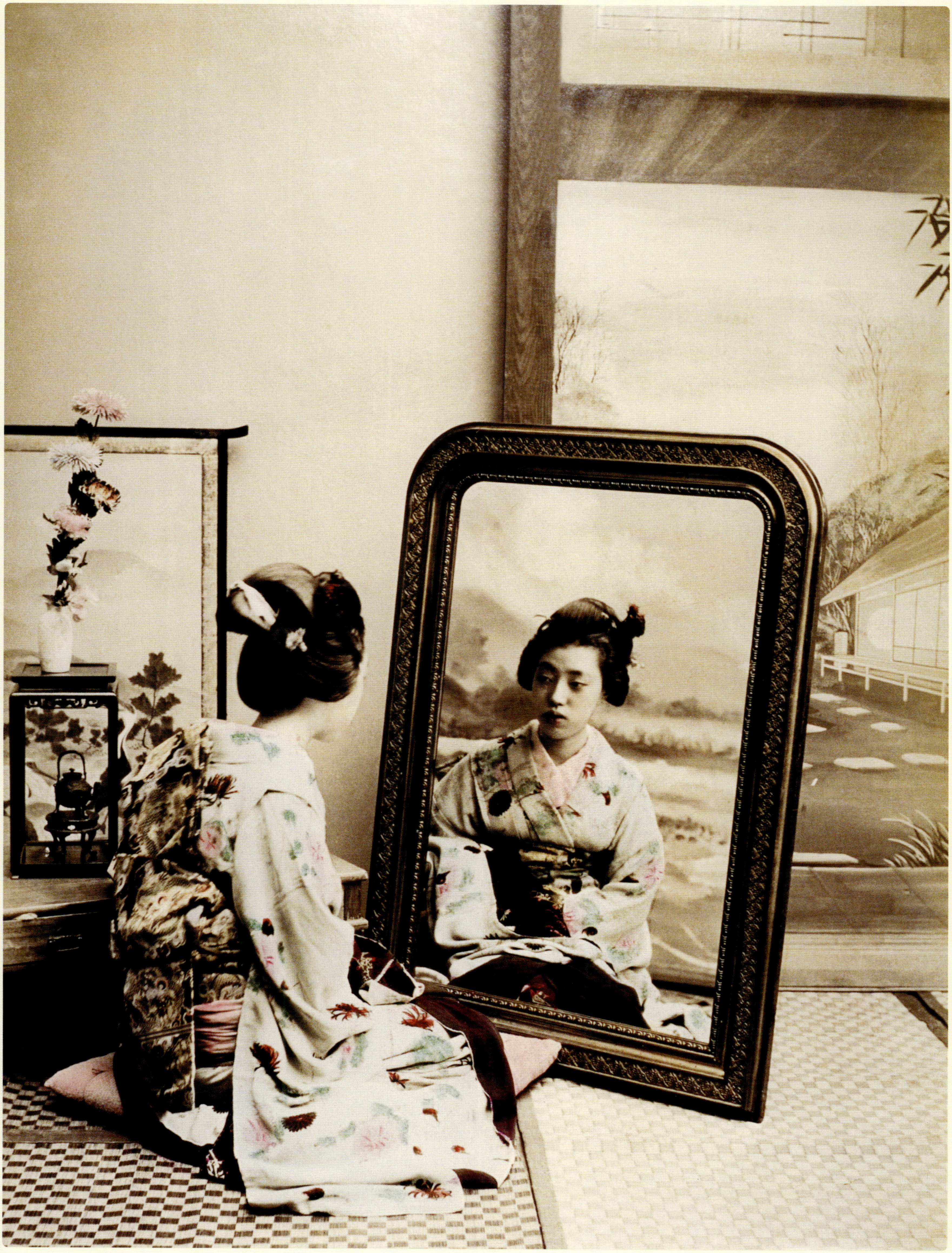

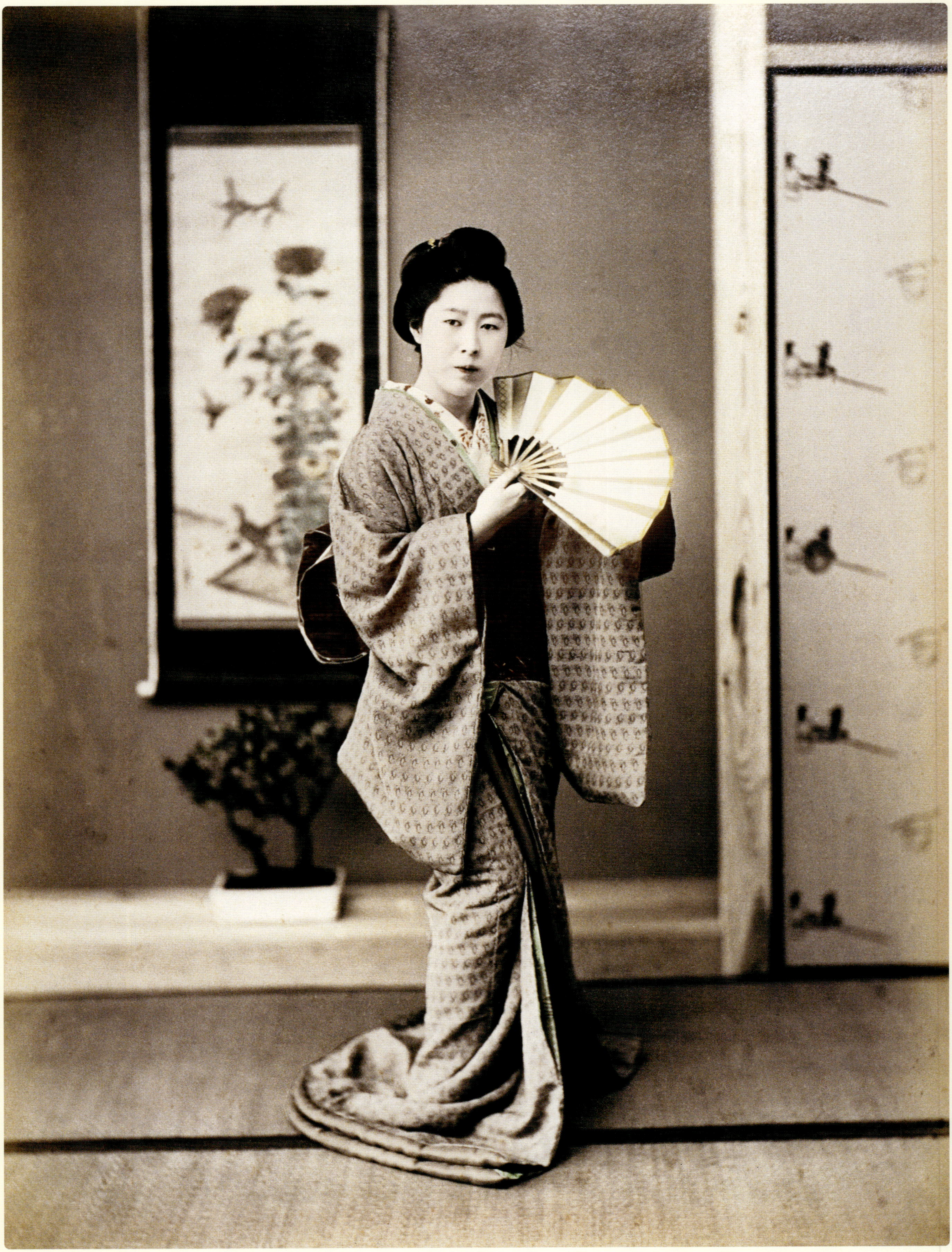

Dancing Girl with Fan (B1183)
(Baron Raimund von Stillfried, c. 1880)

The final formal presentation of a geisha (in a photograph) is not complete without her accouterments. For a musician it would be her instrument, a singer her music, and for a dancer—as seen here—it is her fan. The folding fan is the essential instrument of a geisha's dance routine. It can seductively shield a face or body part, as she sings and tantalizes her audience. The typical dance fan had ten ribs and was weighted so it could be quickly snapped shut or open. When the fans were thrown, the weights also enabled the fan to fall properly and be caught easily. The long, flowing kimono and its sleeves were often incorporated into the dance. The length of the sleeves were significant, as they indicated the level of the geisha or *maiko*. The *maiko*'s sleeves were so long they almost reached the ground.

Geisha Public Life

Geisha & Dog (attributed to Kusakabe Kimbei, c. 1885)

This unposed, snapshot-like image of a geisha taken outdoors is certainly one of the rarest of the genre. She walks in a garden, carrying her kimono in the classic style so as to show her undergarments in an erotic fashion, and is surprised by a dog who jumps up to greet her. No other such image from this early era has been found. This was discovered in an 1880s album by Kusakabe Kimbei.

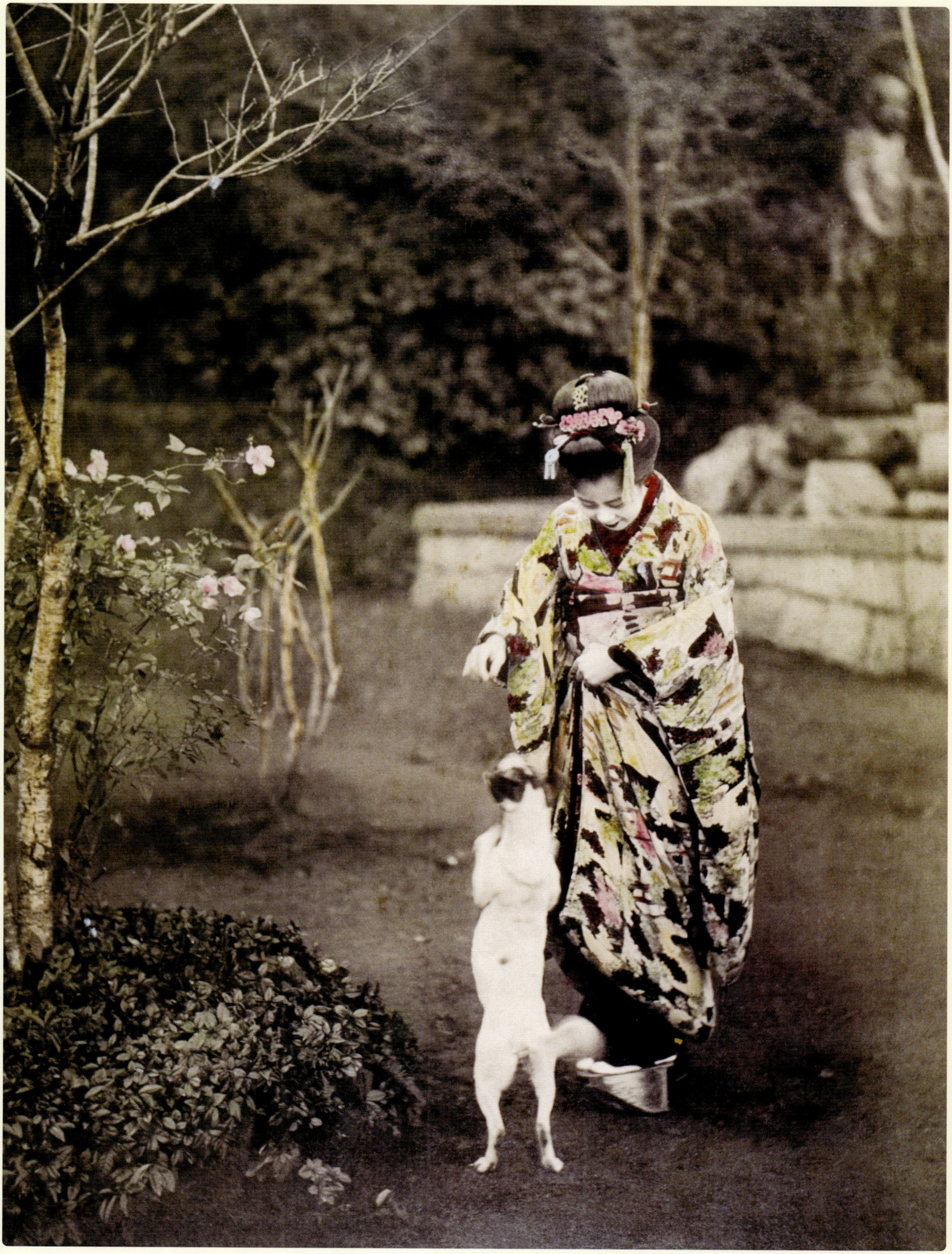

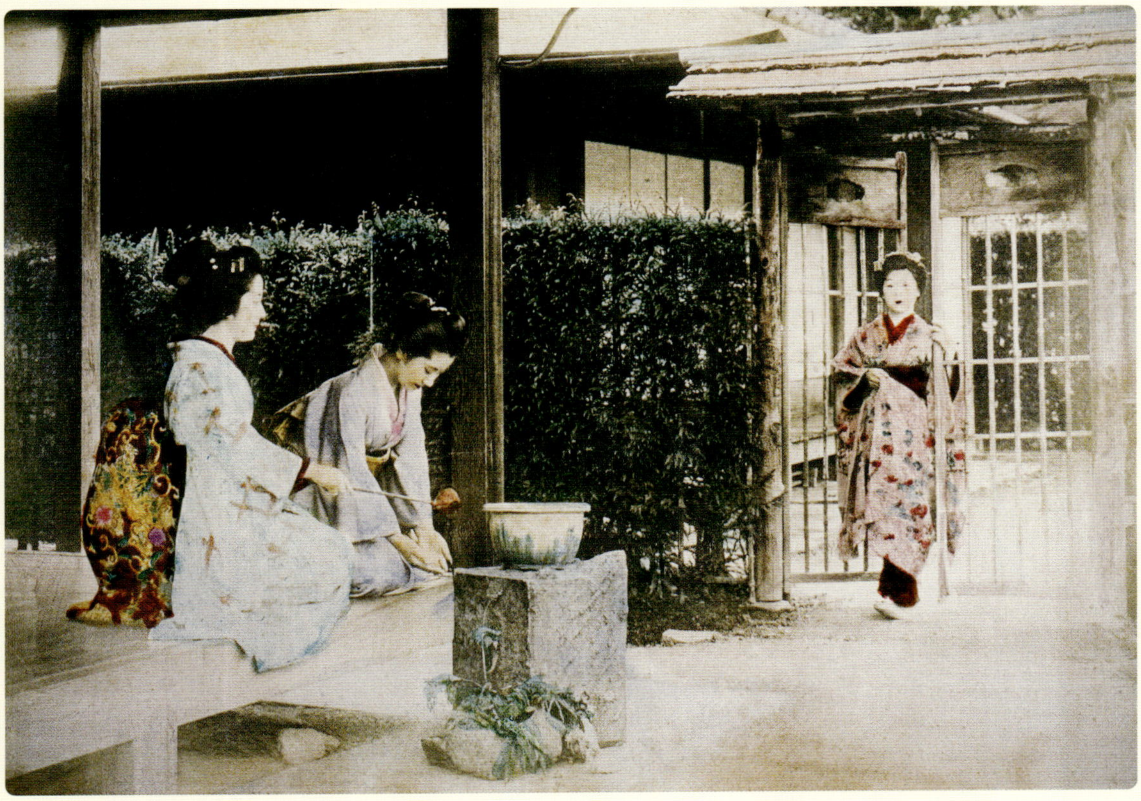

Washing Her Hand (1523) (unattributed, c. 1885)

A *maiko* enters the gate as two geisha wash their hands. The Japanese believed in frequent washing, unlike many Western countries. This lack of cleanliness aided the distrust the Japanese felt towards outsiders. Casually touching another person was not part of Japanese culture, which aided in avoiding disease. Attention to cleanliness and sanitation led to landmark medical accomplishments during the Russo-Japanese War (1904–5). They reversed the predicted death statistics. For every person who succumbed to disease, ten died in battle. Just several years before, during the Spanish-American War, for every ten who died from disease, one died in battle.

Bowing at Gate (unattributed, c. 1880)

The traditional greeting in Japan is not shaking hands or any other bodily contact, but bowing. How low one bows is proportionate to the respect and deference one has for that person. Kissing is not a Japanese custom for a greeting, or even for public display of affection. Kissing, called *seppun*, was considered private and part of special lovemaking by *yujo*, prostitutes, as part of their erotic repertoire in the eighteenth century.

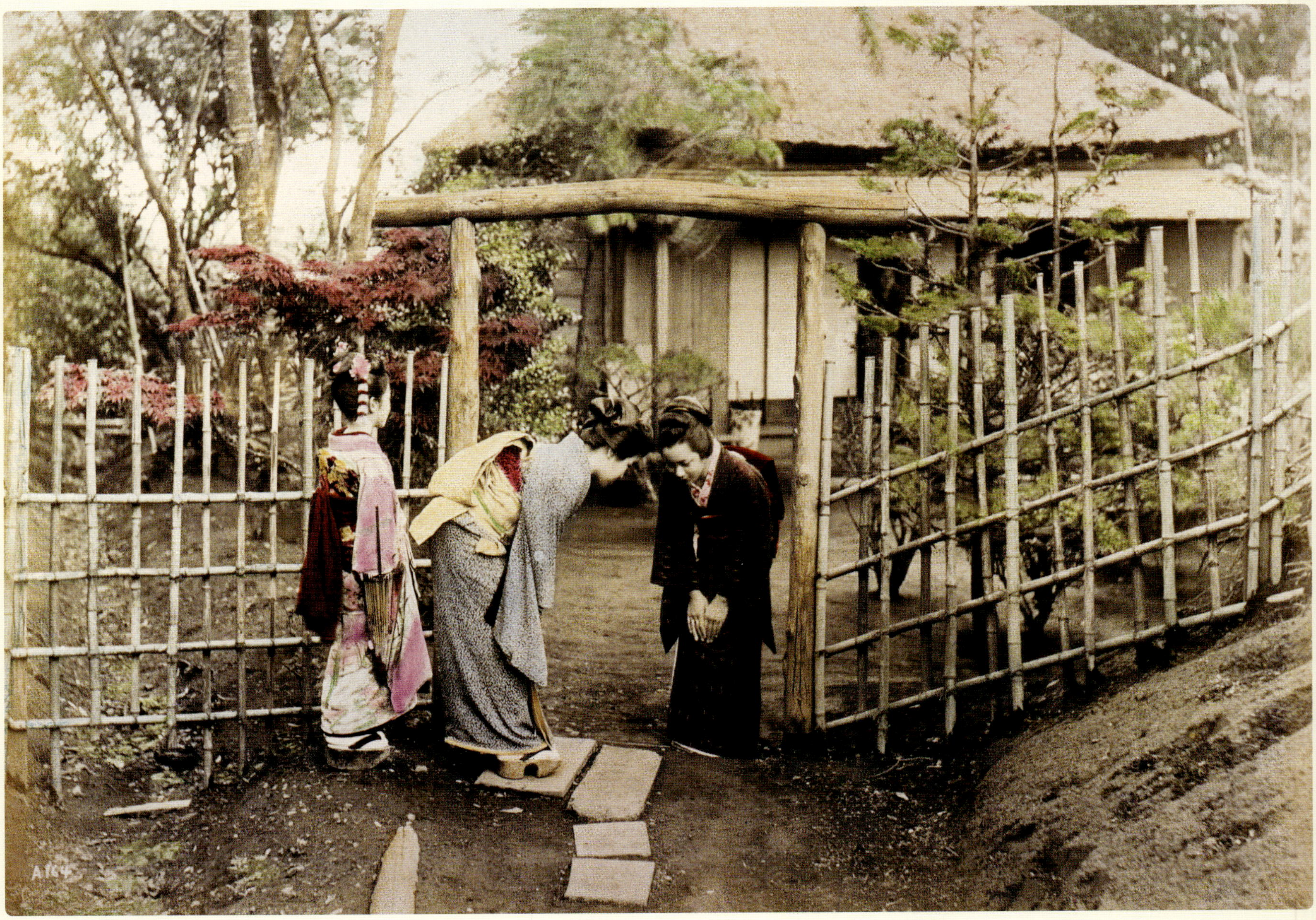

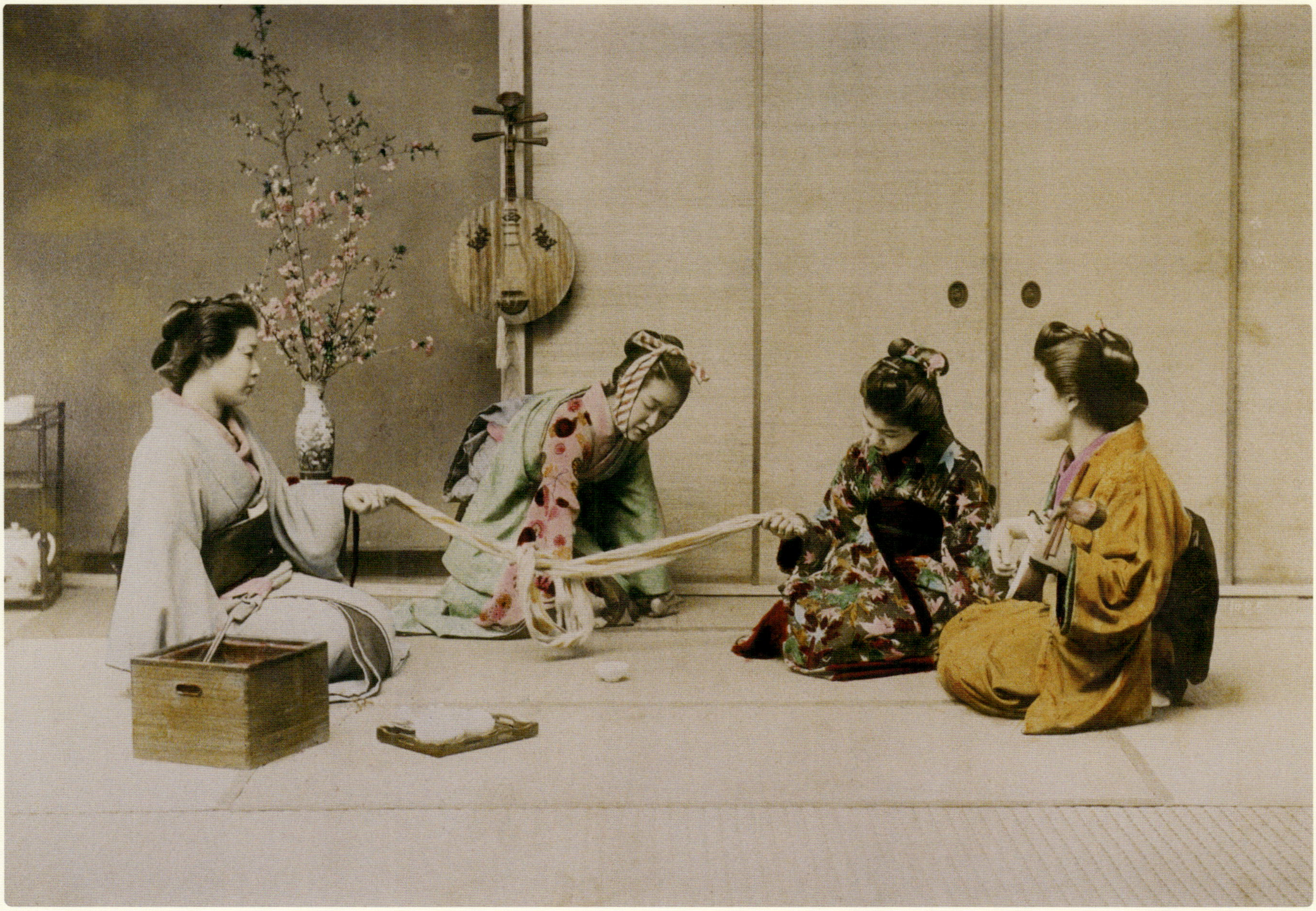

Girls Playing on Konkonchiki Game (B1085)
(unattributed, c. 1890)

Games were part the repertoire of entertainments geisha provide. Clients liked to play gambling and drinking games, many with sexual connotations. Geisha, when playing games with men, artfully let them win, except in drinking games. The game depicted here is *konkonchiki*, a fun test of speed and alertness, which obviously decrease if played while drinking. The woman in the center has to reach through the hole in the knot, grab the object on the floor, and safely draw it back through the knot before it can be tightened by the two geisha holding the ends. When played at parties for clients, the game is set to music and it is the men who have to grab the object. They must grab it at a certain time, indicated by the lyrics of an appropriate song. When they fail they have to drain their cup of sake. The geisha on the right is playing a *gekkin*.

Two Dancing Girls Holding Umbrella (B1164)
(attributed Kusakabe Kimbei, c. 1890)

Outdoor views of geisha became more common in the 1890s. These geisha stand under the cherry blossoms with a tea service and a plate of fruit on the bench beside them.

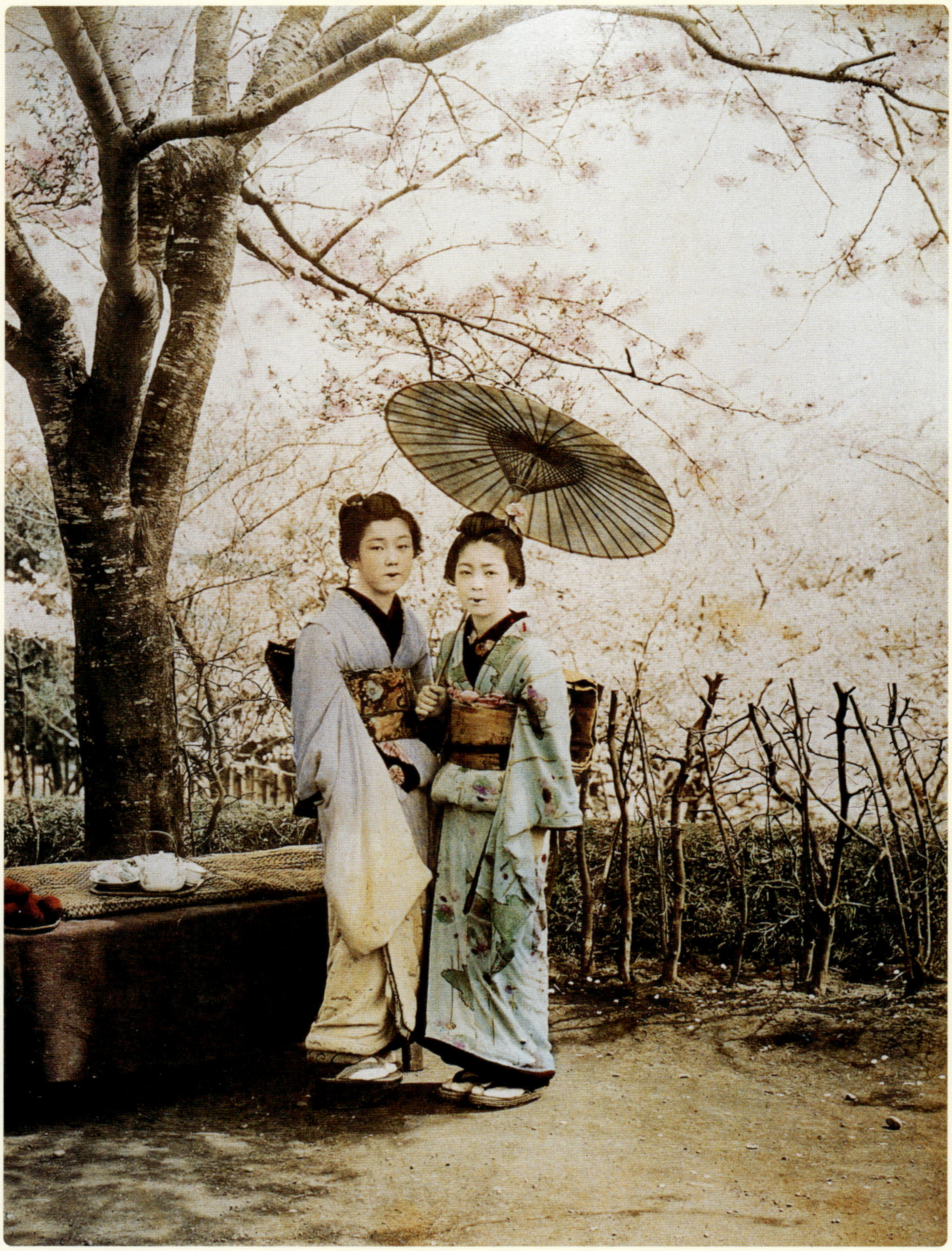

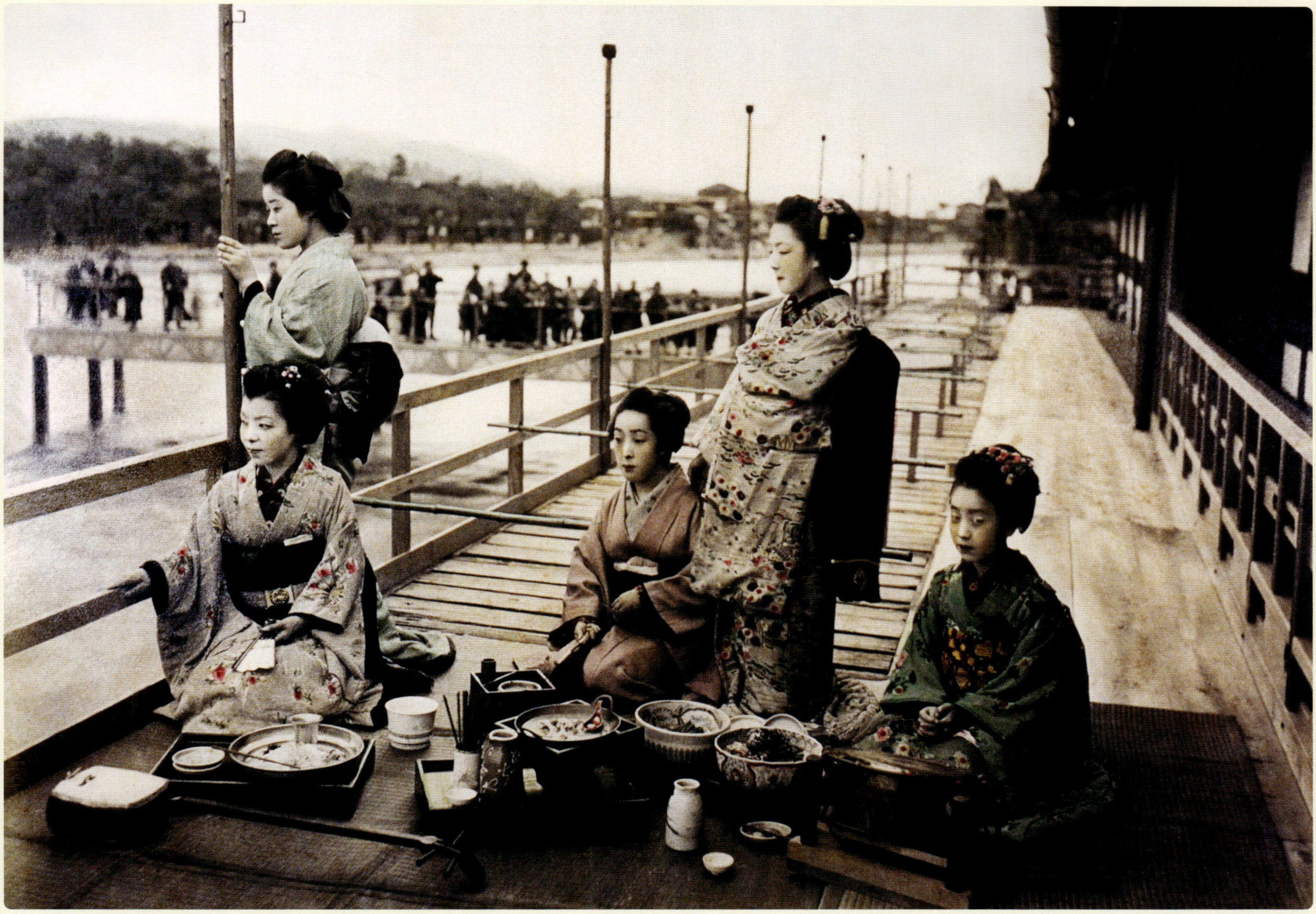

Coolness, Yojio, Kioto (M1) (unattributed, c. 1885)

This photograph was taken at a noted *ochaya*, teahouse, in Kyoto's Pontocho District on the Kamogowa River. It shows geisha having their afternoon meal. The image is one of many taken on the balconies of the noted teahouses along the water. The Pontocho essentially consists of two narrow, stone-paved streets. One, known as Pontocho, after which the district is named, is so narrow that it is more or less a pedestrian lane. It runs closest and parallel to the Kamogawa River. The entrances to the riverside teahouses are on this street. Pontocho was (and still is) the district in which Kyoto's noted *maiko* can be seen.

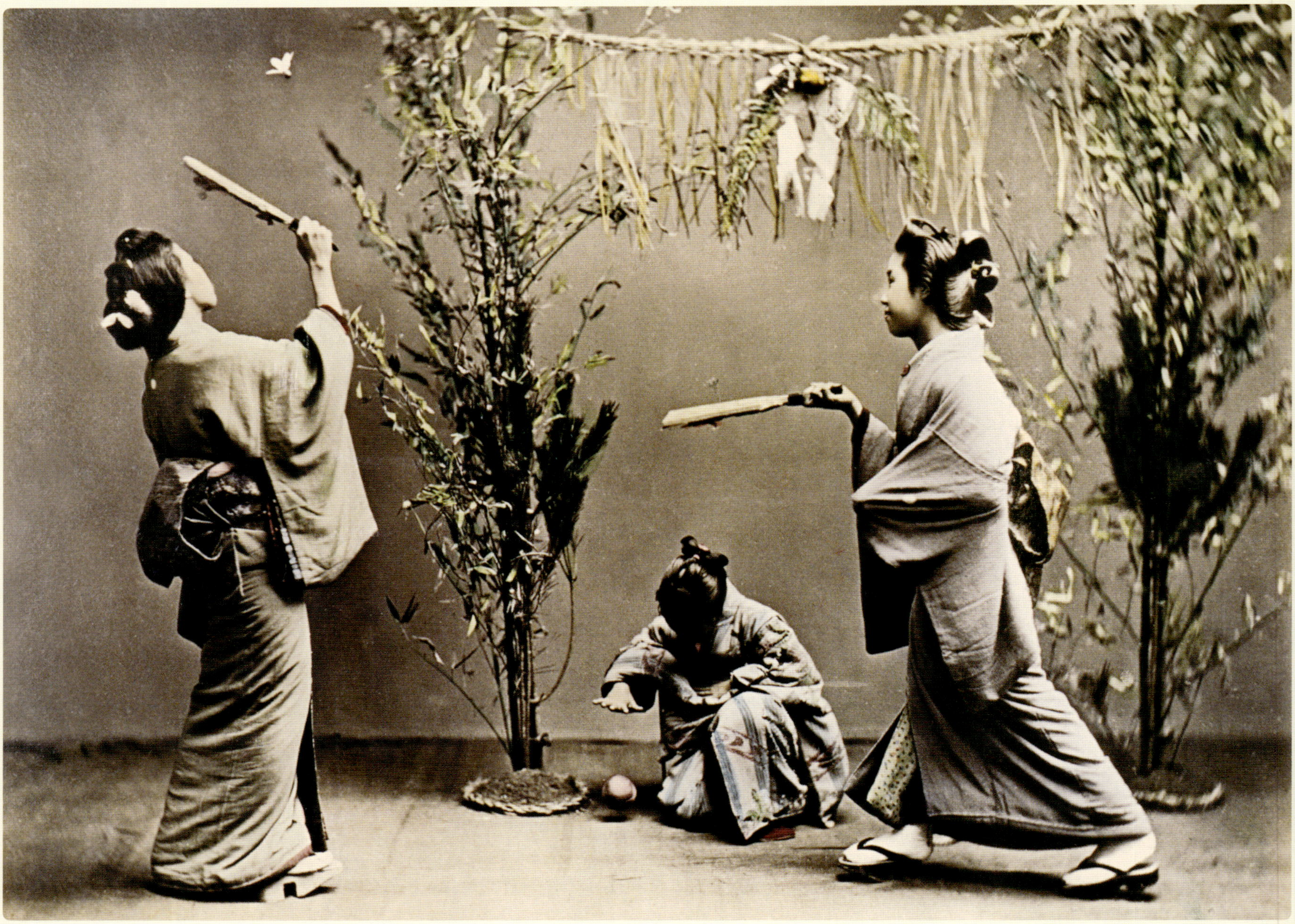

Girls New Years Games (152)
(attributed Kusakabe Kimbei, c. 1885)

New Year's celebrations are a time for games. In this photograph we see geisha playing *hanetsuki*, a game similar to badminton, with paddles and a shuttlecock but without a net. In the background a *maiko* engages in *temari asobi*, bouncing a thread ball. A *temari* is an embroidered ball that a geisha may own for entertainment.

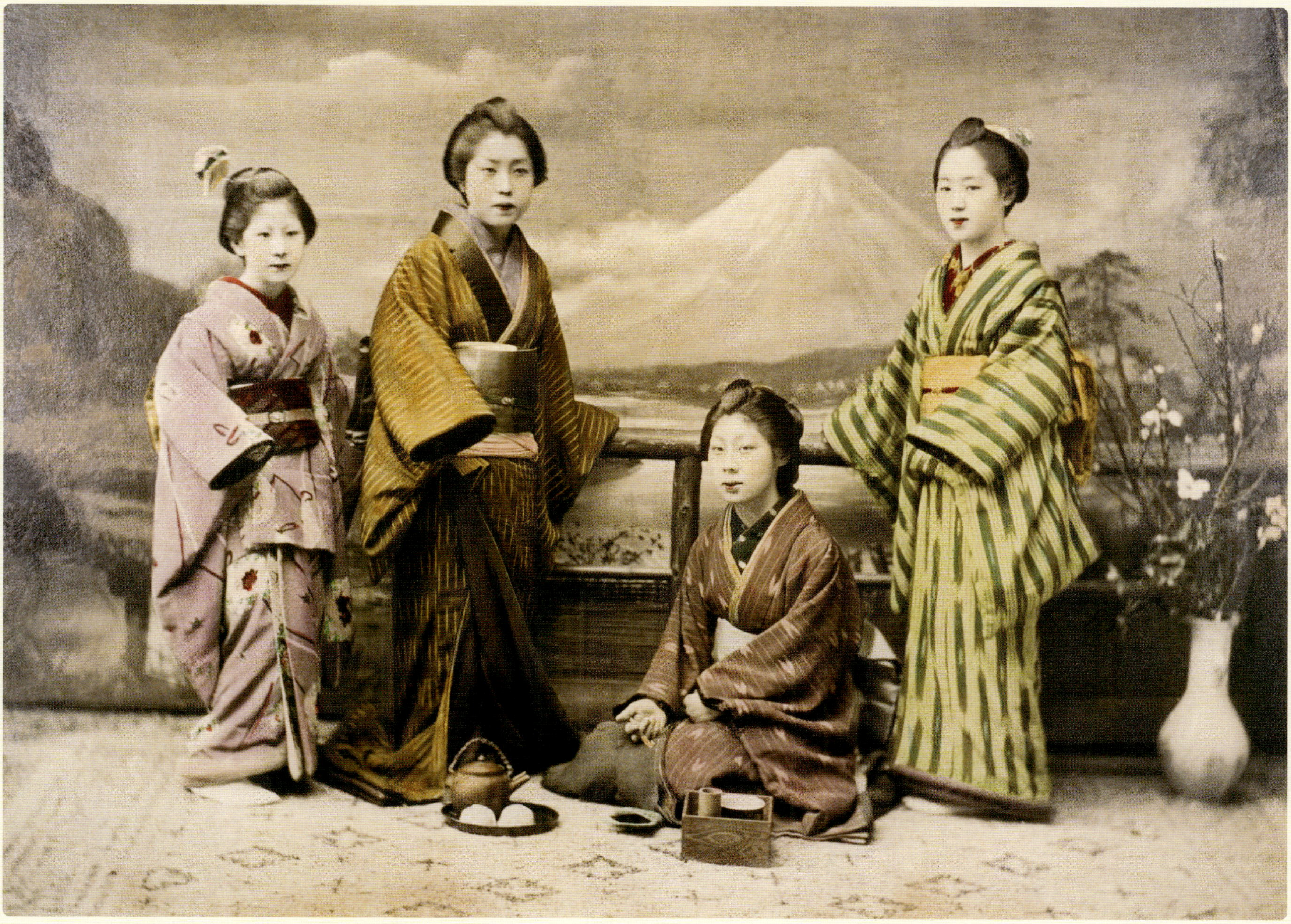

Posing "Before" Mt. Fuji (unattributed, c. 1890)

Three geisha and a *maiko* pose before a backdrop of Mount Fujiyama, a symbol of Japan. The trainee is easily identified by her red collar. Mount Fuji is the highest mountain in Japan, straddling the boundary between the prefectures of Shizuoka and Yamanashi just west of Tokyo. It can be seen from the city on a clear day. Mount Fuji is located near the Pacific coast of central Honshu and visiting or climbing it was a ritual for Japanese who could afford to travel. The most popular time for people to hike up Mount Fuji is from July 1 to the end of August. Today, an estimated 200,000 people climb Mount Fuji every year, 30 percent of which are foreigners.

Silk Store (56) (unattributed, c. 1890)

A geisha's kimonos were the possession she was most proud of and her greatest expense. At a silk store, a geisha would pick out fabric for her wardrobe, as her ensembles had to be distinctive. Her kimonos and obis represented her individuality and unique style. Often, if a geisha took over the teahouse clientele of her *onesan,* older sister, some of the older sister's kimonos were passed on so that the public recognized the outfit and its reputation. The type of silk used, along with its design and pattern, was dictated by the status of the geisha and the nature of her work. If her clients were among the very rich, her outfit would accordingly have to be of the best material. For a time, the geisha's outfits were by law understated and subdued so that they would not visually compete with the courtesans who were expected to wear the finest of silks and brightest of colors. As a result of the Meiji restoration in the 1870s, geisha became the heroines of the era for their role in protecting the samurai and politicians who were ultimately successful in overthrowing the shogunate. Geisha once again wore beautiful and elaborately designed kimonos. The kimonos' sleeves and body were fashioned from straight panels of material, which was free from darts, buttons, or other folds. The swathes of silk seen draped in the store gave the purchaser a good idea of how the garment would present. Each kimono was individual and a unique work of art that the purchaser has created. Today, geisha are the only Japanese women to routinely wear kimono. A modern fine silk kimono can cost over $15,000. Antique Kimonos from the seventeenth century can cost over $300,000.

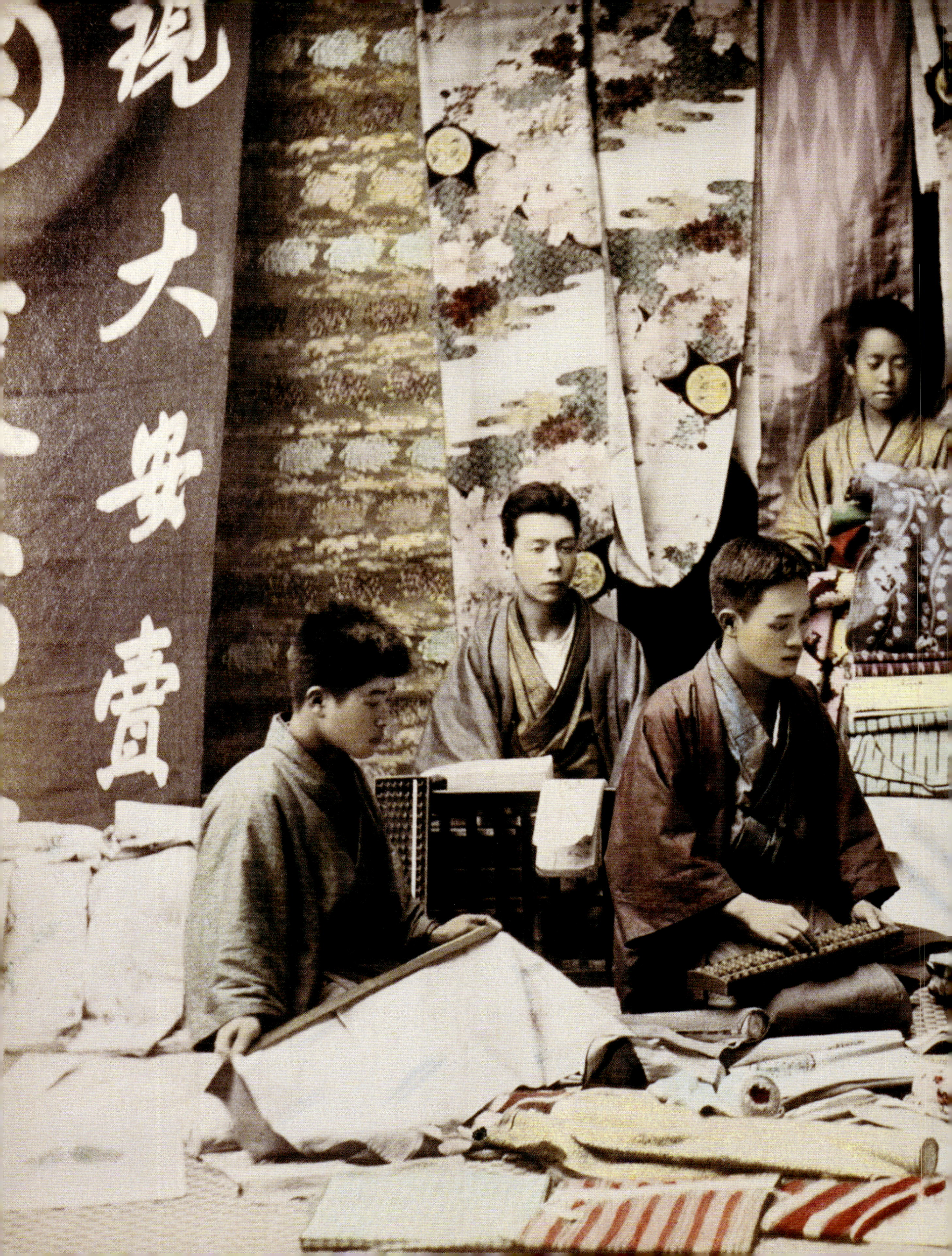
現大安賣

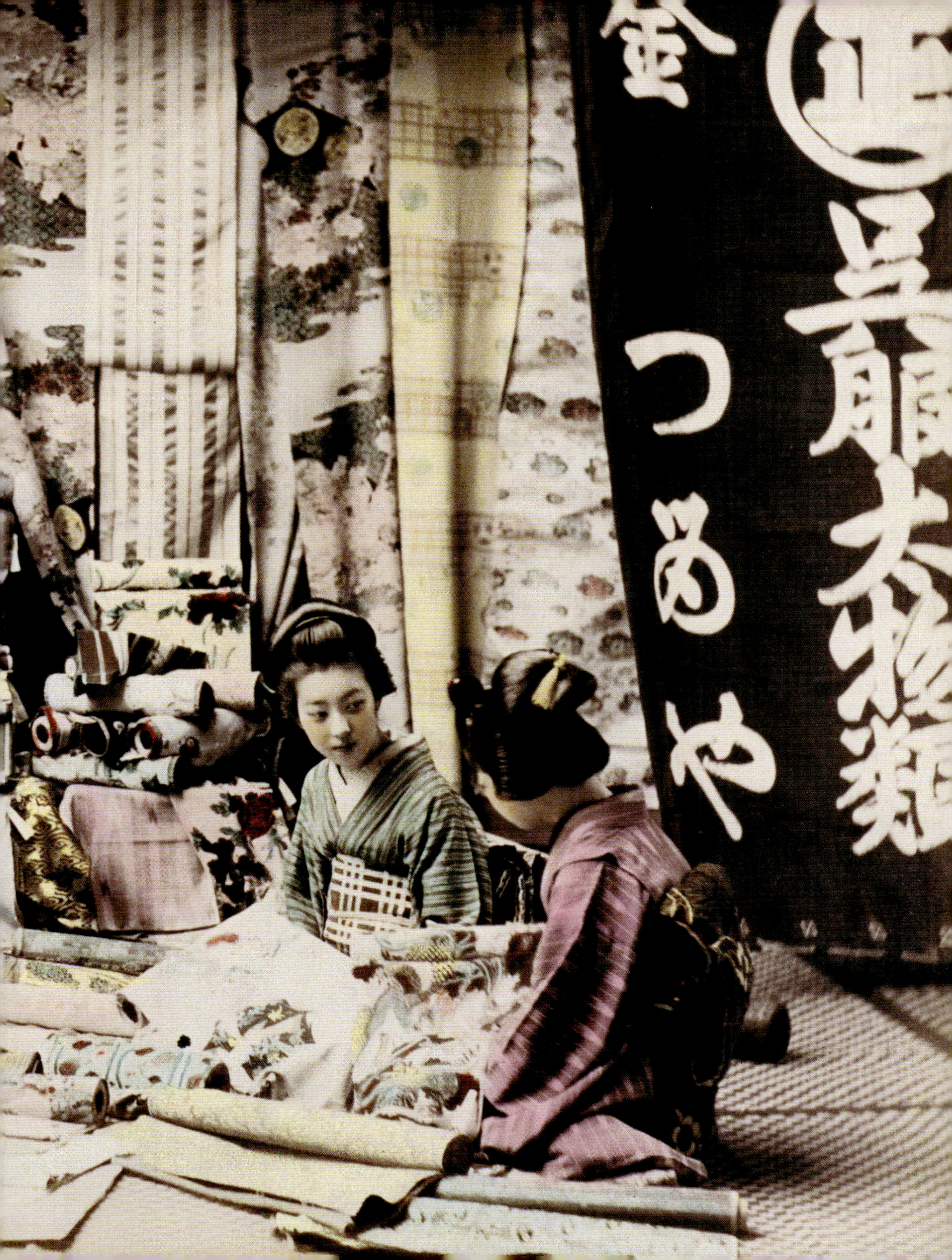

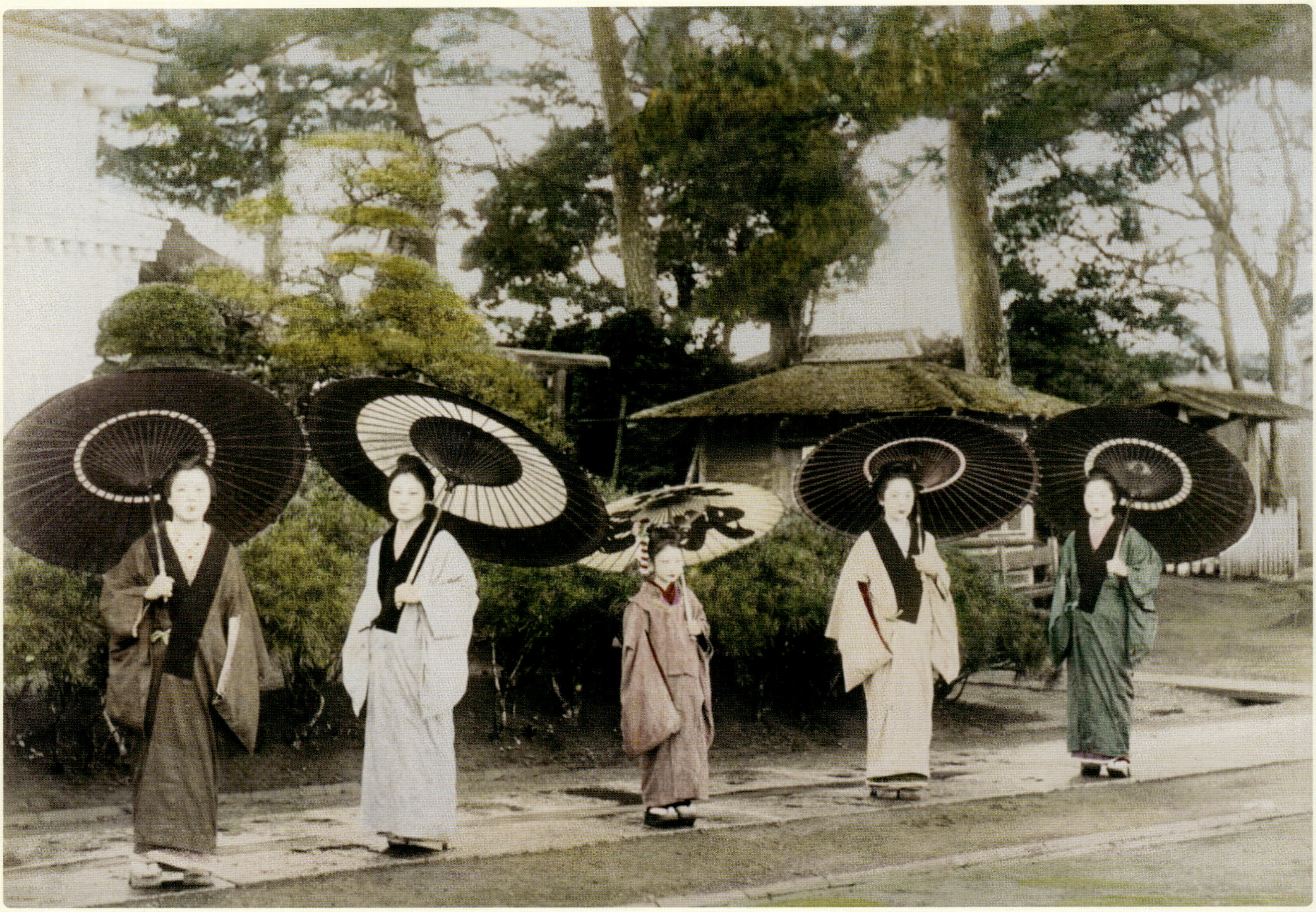

Geisha Outside with Umbrellas
(attributed Adolfo Farsari, c. 1890)

Nineteenth-century photographs of geisha outdoors are usually in parks or gardens, rarely in the street. Photographs could only be taken on sunny days, so geisha are often posed with umbrellas, which were necessary to protect their delicate skin. Geisha and *maiko* could not get sunburned, since they painted their faces stark white as part of their appearance. *Oshiroi*, the white facial masking substance of the era, contained lead, and some geisha suffered from lead poisoning.

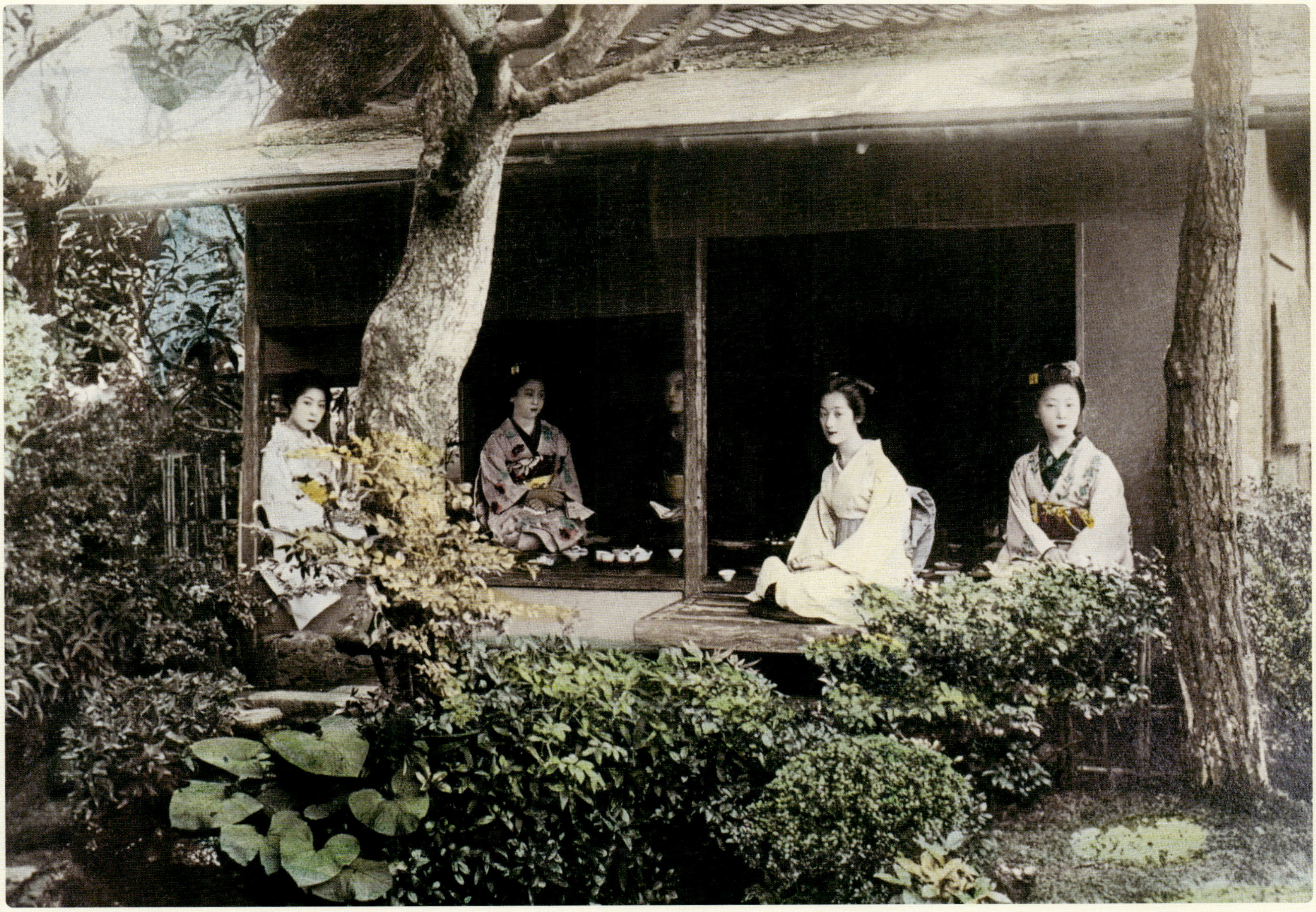

Teahouse Restaurant in Kyoto
(Tamamura Kazaburo, c. 1895)

This is one of the photographs Tamamura sent to the United States to be incorporated in *Japan: Described and Illustrated by the Japanese*, Francis Brinkley's 1897 ten-volume text on Japanese life. The images in the books are accompanied by full captions and are among the only nineteenth-century tourist photographs that are identified with such detailed descriptions of the period. The Japanese government approved the text and photographs for export as representative of their nation. Captain Brinkley presents this photograph in volume three and writes, "The ordinary teahouse furnishes only slight refreshment to the wayfarer, but a variety of special lines of business are occasionally associated with the teahouse. Thus every little railway station has its teahouse which undertakes to purchase the traveler's ticket and check his baggage. Teahouses serve as ticket agencies for the Tokyo theatres, practically preventing patrons from dealing directly with the box office. The larger teahouses provide for the entertainment of their patrons in many ways, arranging for banquets, singing, dancing, etc., etc." This photograph of a roadside teahouse with geisha in full regalia is representative of the fine small establishments available to travelers.

Singing Girls (P31) (Adolfo Farsari, c. 1890)

This geisha pens a letter, or perhaps a poem, while an apprentice observes. The geisha apprentice has a red collar, which is indicative of trainees in towns other than Kyoto. In Edo (Tokyo), geisha trainees are called *akaeri*, literally "red collar." In Kyoto, the trainees are called *maiko*. Photographs of geisha reading or writing were a popular convention. Poetry and literature are essential to educated Japanese life. A Heian court noble woman, Murasaki Shikibu, wrote the world's first full-length novel, *The Tale of the Genji*, around the year 1000. It contains 54 chapters and about 1000 pages, firmly establishing women in literature. Courtesans in the eighteenth century and geisha by the nineteenth century were trained to know the literary masters, recognize noted works, and be able to recite famous poems. Only about 15 percent of Japanese women could read by the time of the Meiji restoration (1868). Geisha were not only well read, but also took lessons in calligraphy, composition, poetry, and correspondence. Writing "love letters" and poems to clients was a necessary part of developing a lengthy, profitable relationship. A broad understanding of literature and poetry both ancient and modern made the geisha a clever conversationalist, and much of a geisha's entertainment had to do with verbal innuendos and enticements in which she often recited erotic works. To be a gifted wordsmith was honored in Japan, and for men to be able to talk intelligently with a beautiful, educated woman was a delight and quite seductive. The intelligentsia and literati were drawn to geisha for their knowledge, witty responses, and understanding of the world. Until the twentieth century, few Japanese women were as well versed in arts and letters.

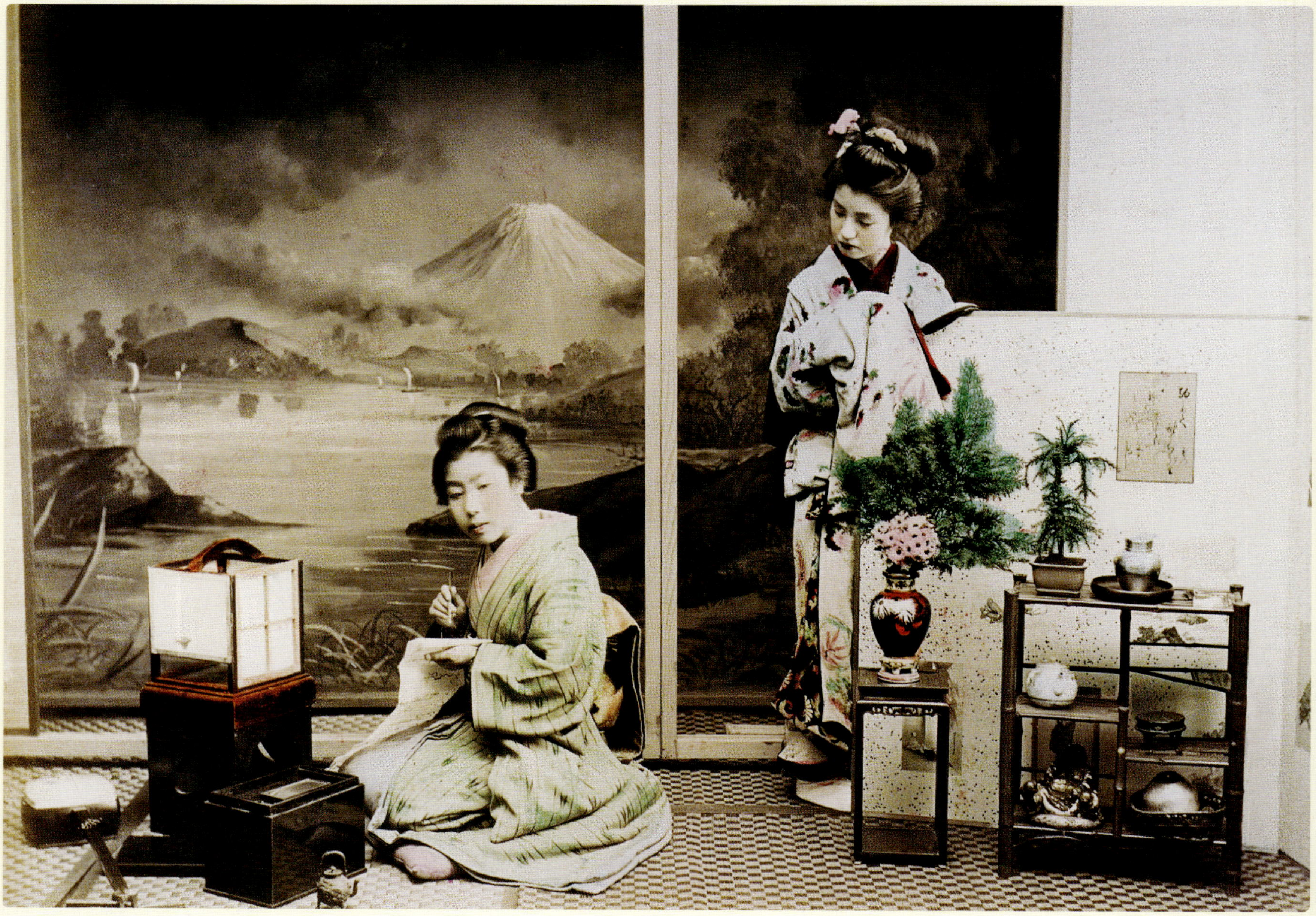

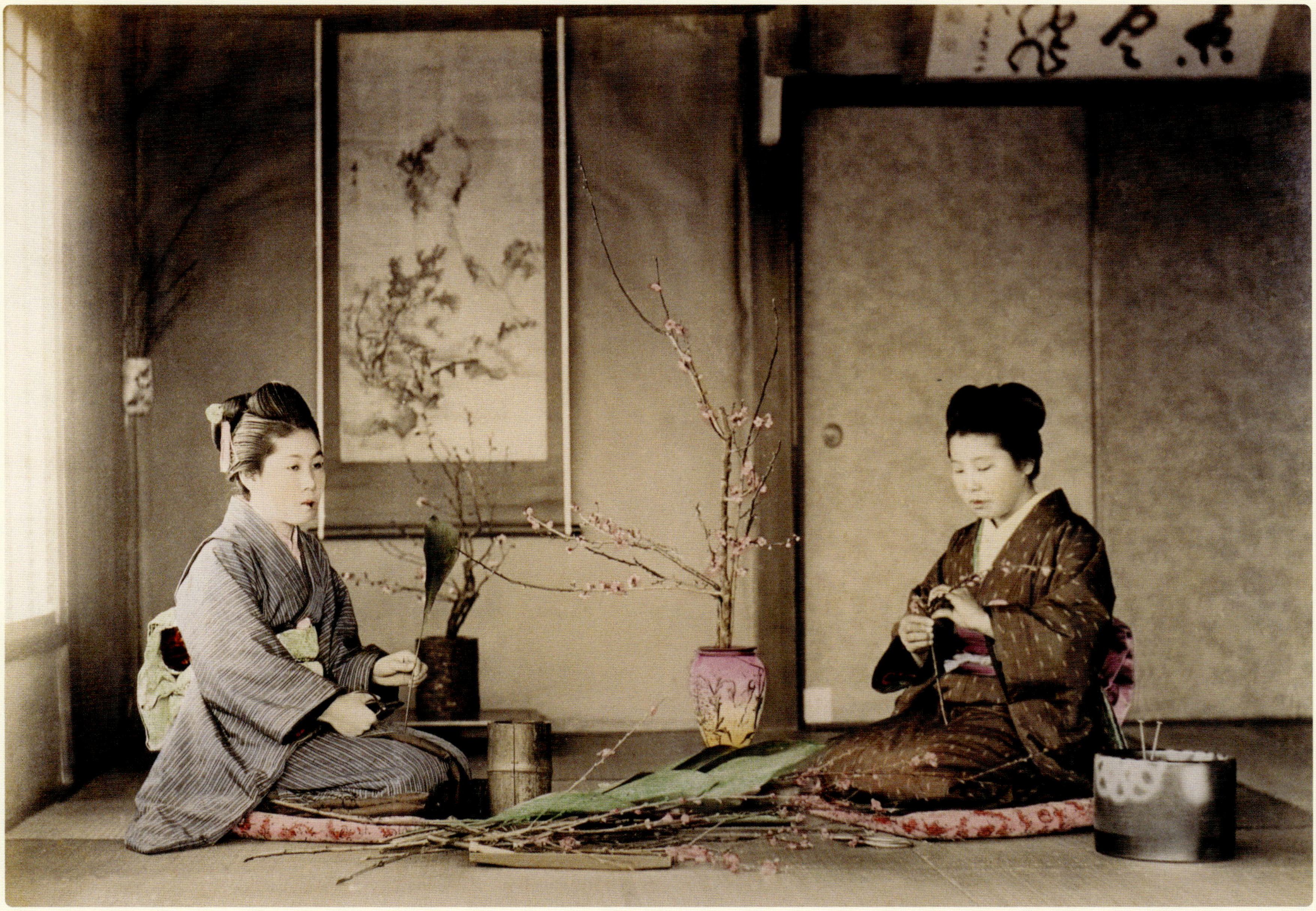

Ikebana: Flower Arranging (attributed Adolfo Farsari, c. 1890)

The traditional art of flower arranging was part of a geisha's training. Rooms in Japan were sparsely decorated, furniture was minimal, and floor covering was limited to tatami mats. Wall scrolls, lanterns, painted screens, mirrors, bonsai trees, small chests, and vases with flower arrangements were among the items used for decoration. It is not only the flower, but also the vase or pot, that is chosen for the arrangement and completes the artistic expression. Arrangements vary with the season and these geisha have chosen a ceramic vase decorated with cherry blossoms, an appropriate complement to the cherry blossoms they are preparing. There is a minimalist esthetic to flower presentation, which places emphasis on natural shapes. Ikebana originated from the practice of offering flowers at shrines and became associated with the tea ceremony during the feudal era.

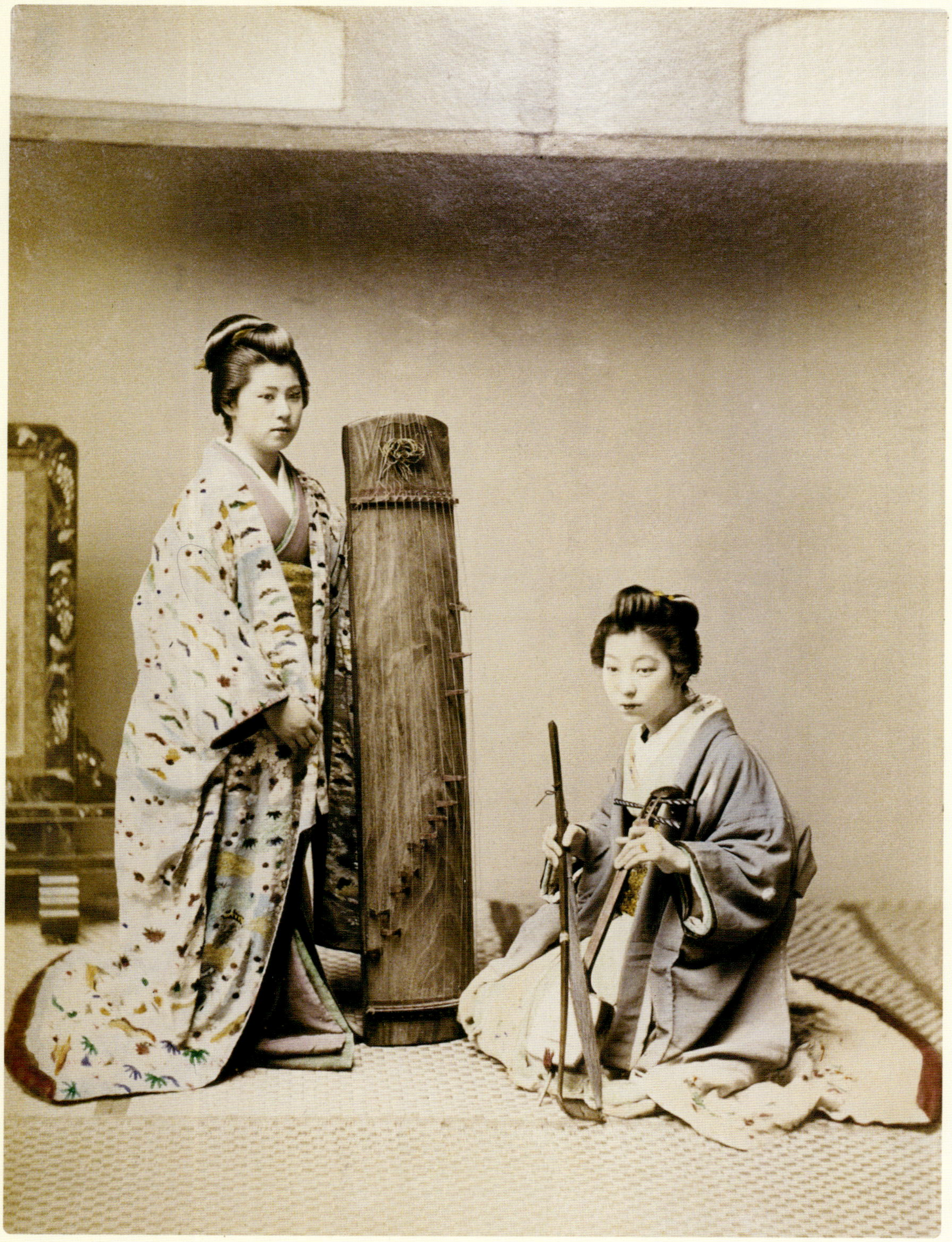

Playing Koto & Kokyu (215) (unattributed, c. 1885)

Geisha had to become proficient in at least one instrument, so as to accompany other geisha in their performances. In addition a geisha had to be an expert in some aspect of entertaining, either in singing, dancing, playing, or even conversation. These geisha pose with their instruments. The koto is a large, broad, thirteen-stringed harp-like instrument. The *kokyu* is a string instrument akin to the violin.

Singing Girl (Tsudzumi, Taiko) (P28) (unattributed, c. 1895)

This geisha plays a *tsudzumi*, a shoulder-supported drum. It is one of the few musical instruments invented by the Japanese. The geisha holds one hand on the internal strings, which altering the sound by increasing or releasing tension. The *tsudzumi* is banged with the other hand on the drum face. It was developed during the Heian era from a hand drum. The drum on her lap is an *otsuzumi*, on the floor a *taiko*.

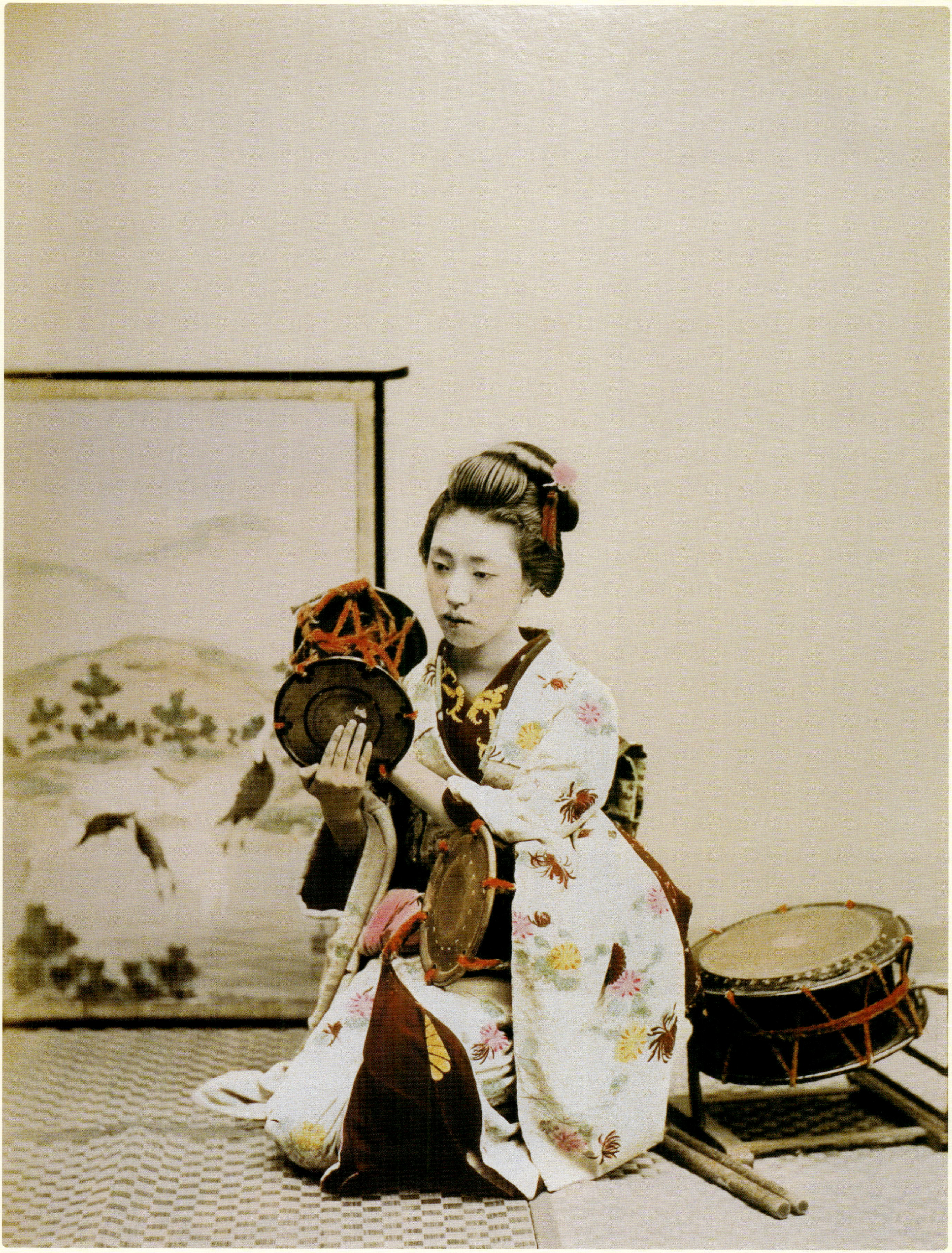

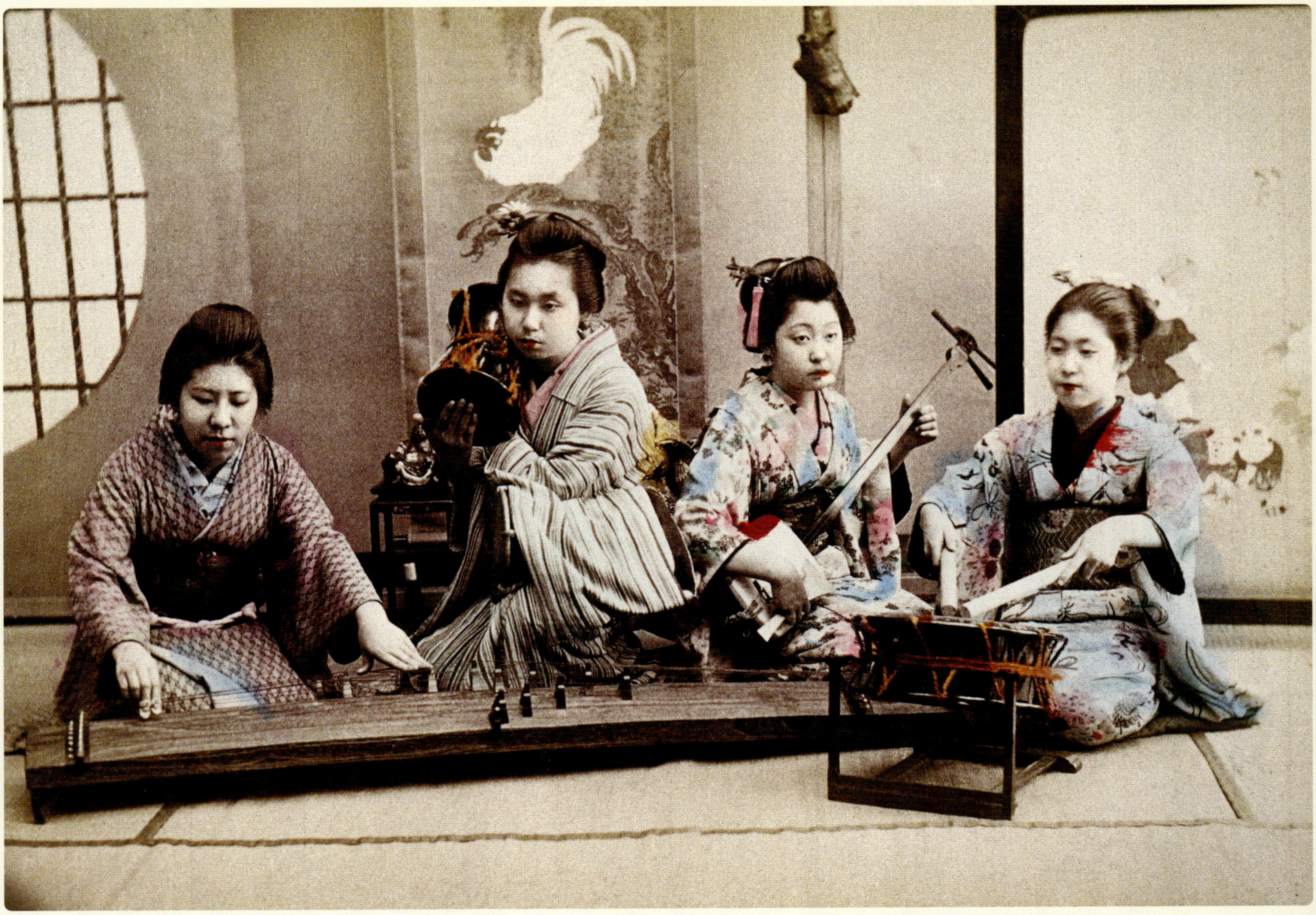

Geisha Band (attributed Adolfo Farsari, c. 1890)

A full geisha band includes the sharp-sounding shamisen, the mellower, harp-like koto, and at least two different styles of drums. At times, a fife or anther string instrument was added. Drums, *taiko*, are an essential part of Japanese music, and large drums were especially important in shrine and temple ceremonies. The *taiko* on the right is played with two sticks, *daiko*. The over-the-shoulder drum, *kotsuzumi*, is an original Japanese invention, unlike the shamisen and the koto.

Geisha with Gekkin (unattributed, c. 1895)

All geisha learned to play the shamisen, and some also studied other instruments, such as *taiko*, *kokyu*, and koto. Others trained in flute and fife: these added a melodic sound to a band and allowed for solo performances. In order to be unique and a desired performer, some geisha learned other, more exotic instruments. *Gekkin*, the string instrument in this photograph, was developed from a Chinese mandolin.

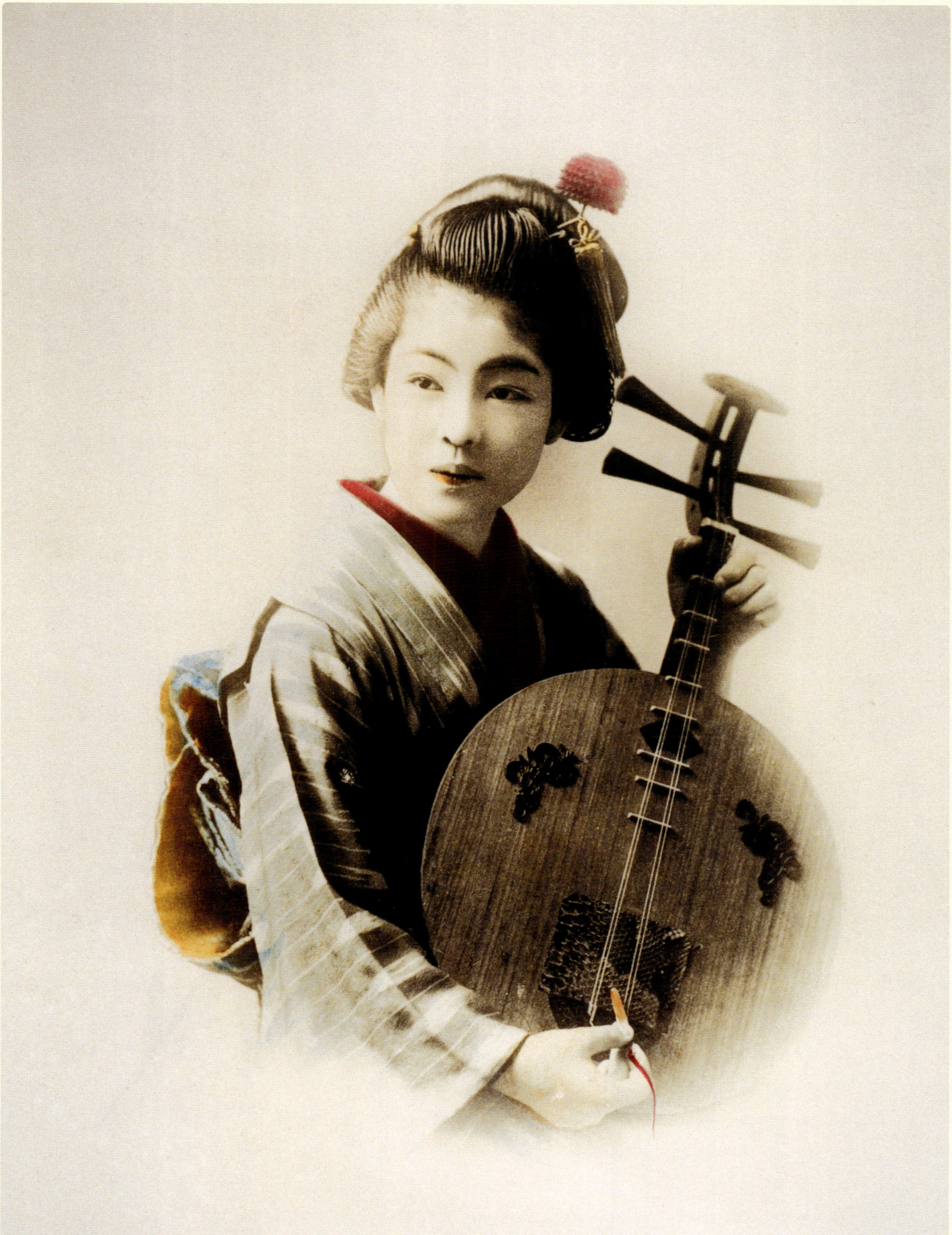

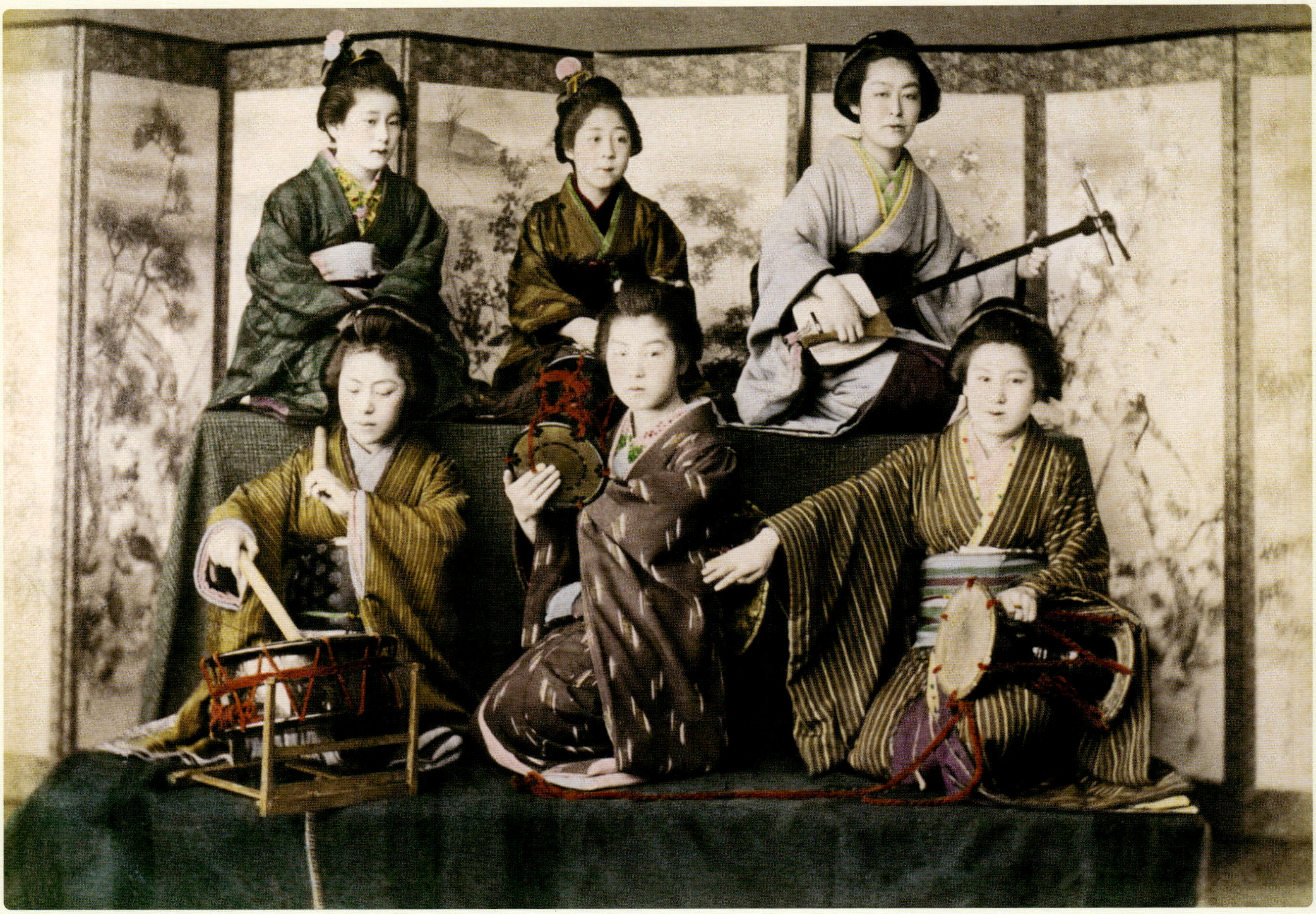

Geisha's Dancing (63) (unattributed, c. 1895)

This geisha band has the standard shamisen and three drums, the shoulder-held *kotsuzumi*, the lap-held *otsuzumi*, and the *taiko* on the floor being played with sticks. Two dancers sit next to the shamisen player. The following photograph has the next number in the photographer's series, and hopefully the two images together will ultimately provide clues to the photographer.

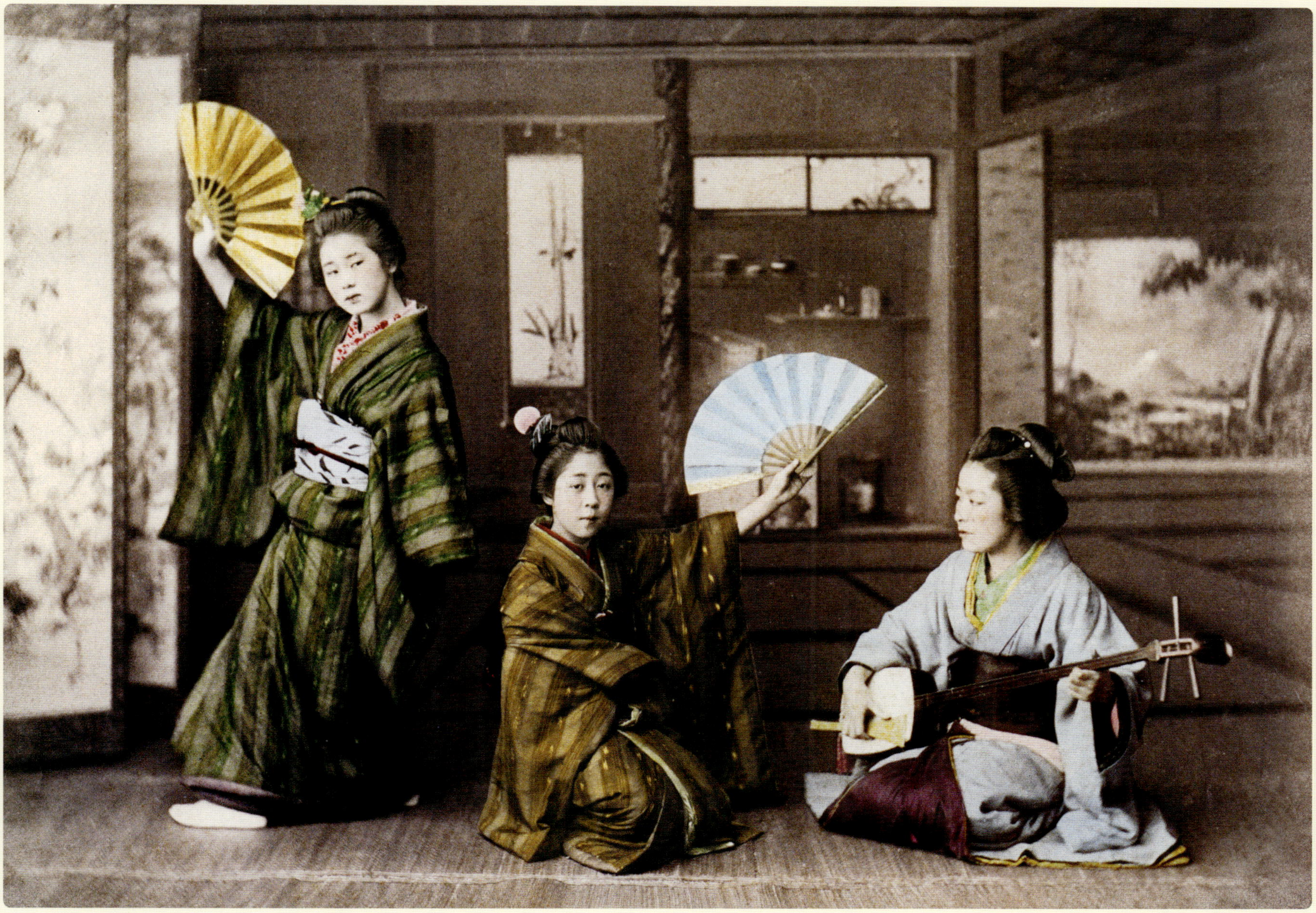

Geisha's Dancing (64) (unattributed, c. 1895)

The same shamisen player is depicted in the preceding image, as are the dancers. The dance fans, *maiogi*, are larger than regular fans. The fans are weighted for quick folding and falling in a special way. Some dances require throwing or tossing the fans for effects. Dancers had several fans: some adorned with decorations of birds, flowers, or other objects to be used in a particular dance. The dance fan represents femininity and underlines the eroticism of the geisha.

Celebrity Geisha

Geisha Holding Cherry Blossom (unattributed, c. 1885)

This geisha with a cherry blossom epitomizes Japanese femininity. She is beautifully dressed, with traditionally-styled hair and impeccable makeup. Her downward glance transmits the air of subservience and submissiveness. This attitude was the popular western concept of Japanese women. Perhaps this was true of housewives, but certainly not geisha. Geisha were not submissive. They were revered artists, they demanded respect, and they knew that they deserved to be treated well in all of their dealings with men. The traditional Japanese male's idea of masculinity and authority required that women wait on them. However the client was not in charge, the geisha was. Geisha are trained to appear subservient, to pamper men, and make them feel singular. They accomplished this with unparalleled style and grace.

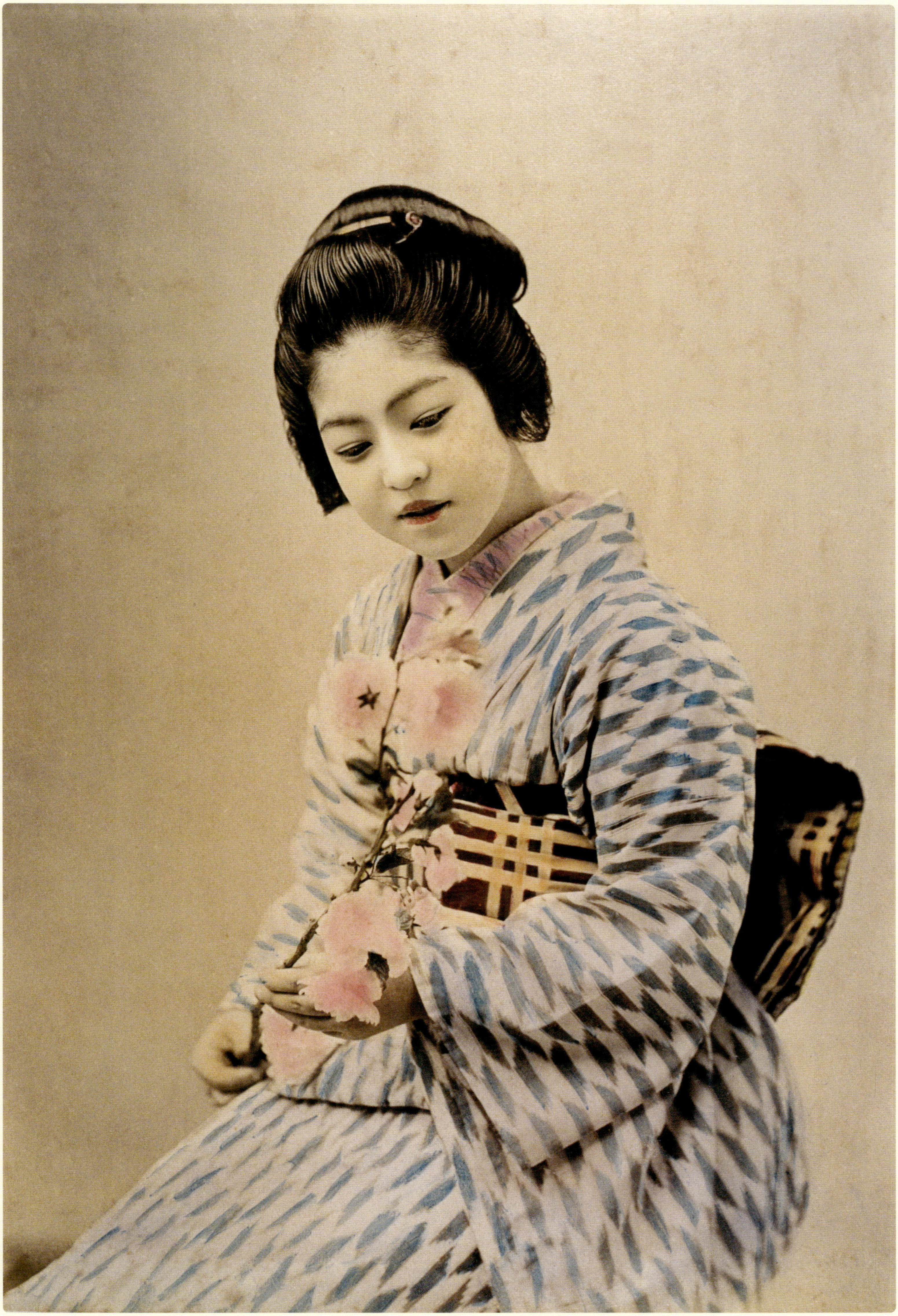

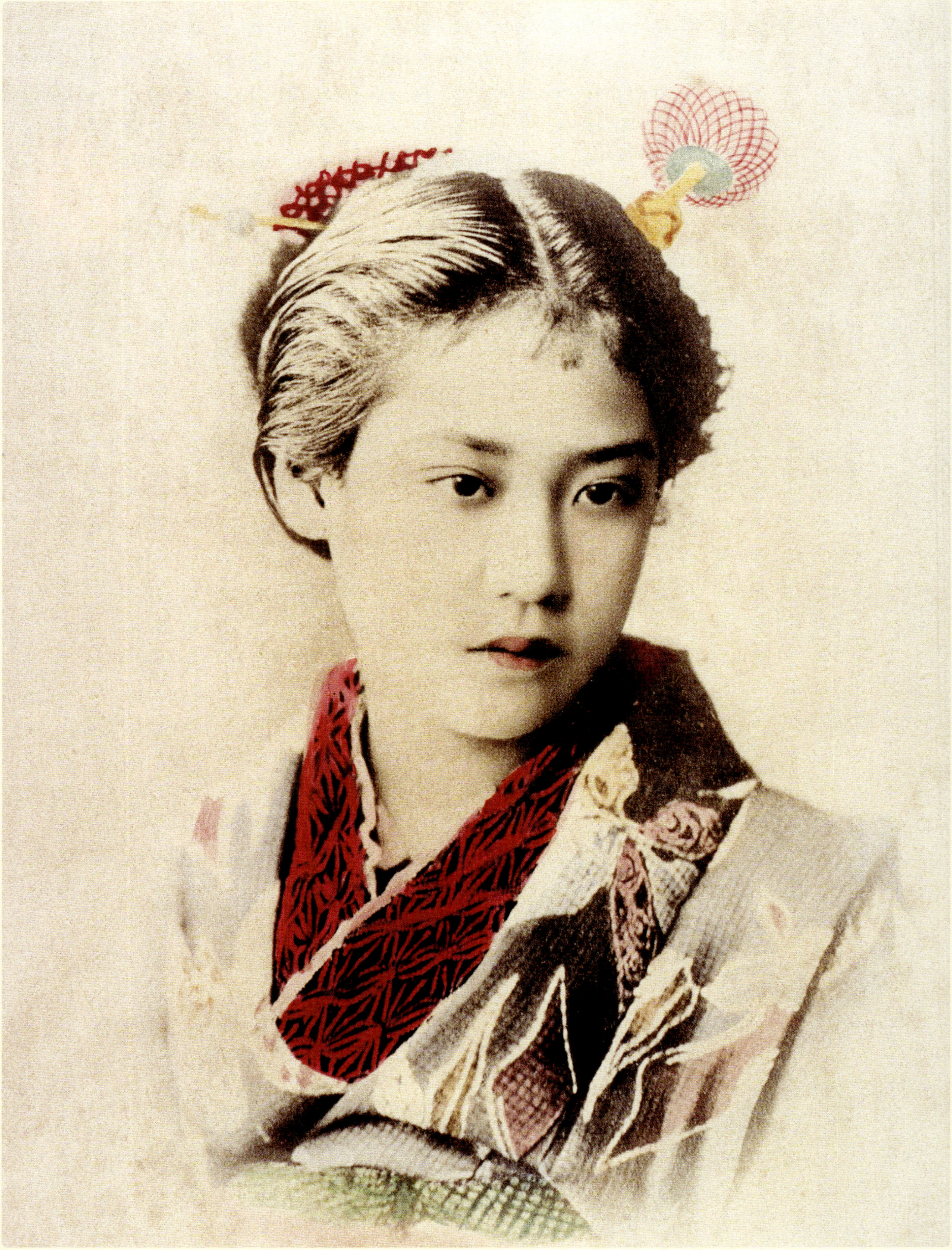

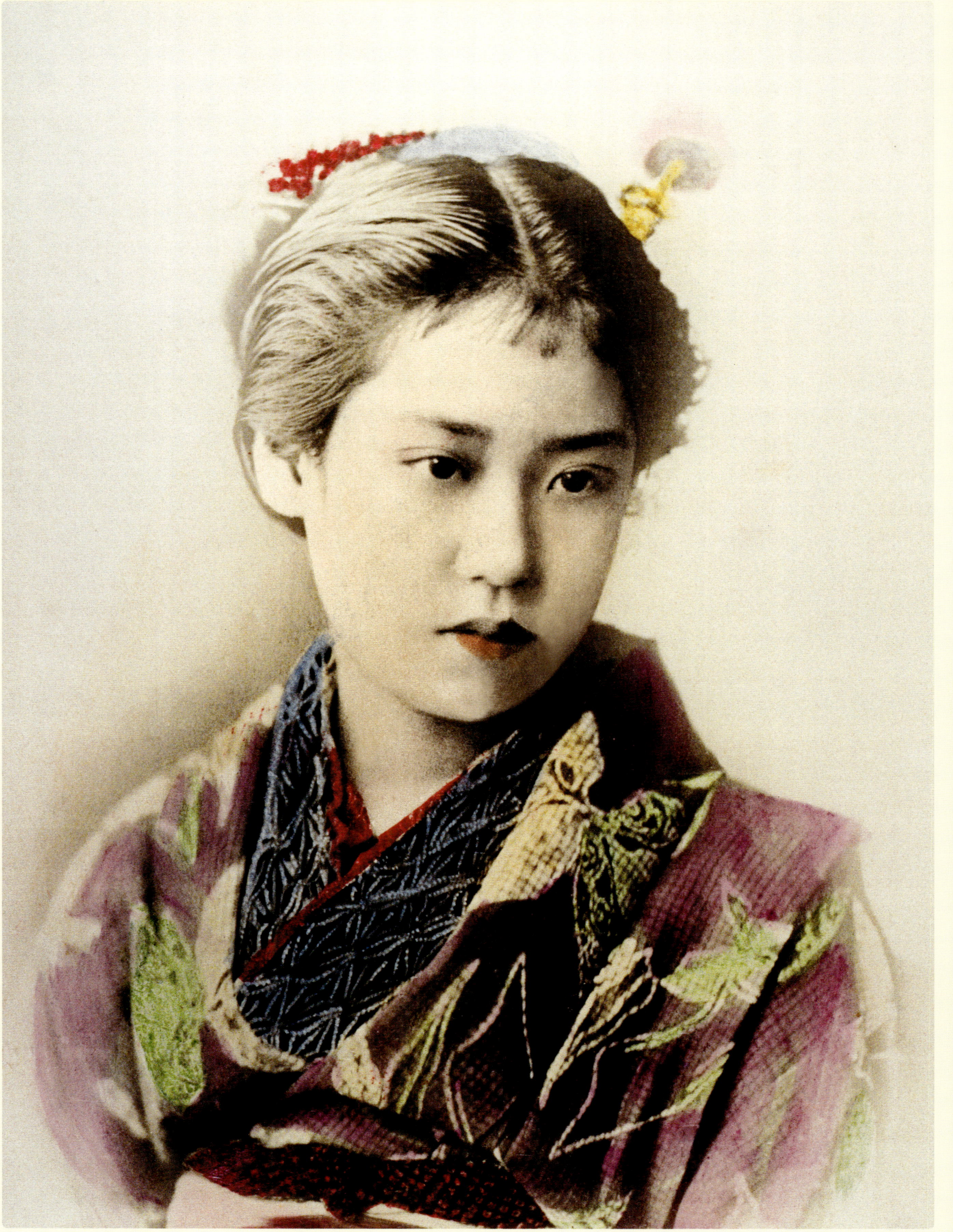

Geisha with a Flower in her Hair (unattributed, c. 1885)

The close-up portrait was the conventional style for photographing important people. In the late 1880s, close-up images of noted geisha became popular as a result of their rising celebrity. They were idolized by the general population and foreigners. By the early 1890s geisha images had become a collectable item for the Japanese, like photographs of well known actors and movie stars of the twentieth century. When the photographic postcard was authorized in 1900, the inexpensive cards were available to the Japanese working classes. A negative of this image passed though various photographers' hands and each adjusted the portrait. Painting the kimono, collar, obi, or flower different colors easily changed this print. Adding a bow, extra flowers, or even replacing it with a bird ornament are other examples of altering this photograph. The two presented may be from the same studio, as the hair decorations are similar. The image has become well known, having been published in several historic texts. Some authorities attribute this image to Adolfo Farsari.

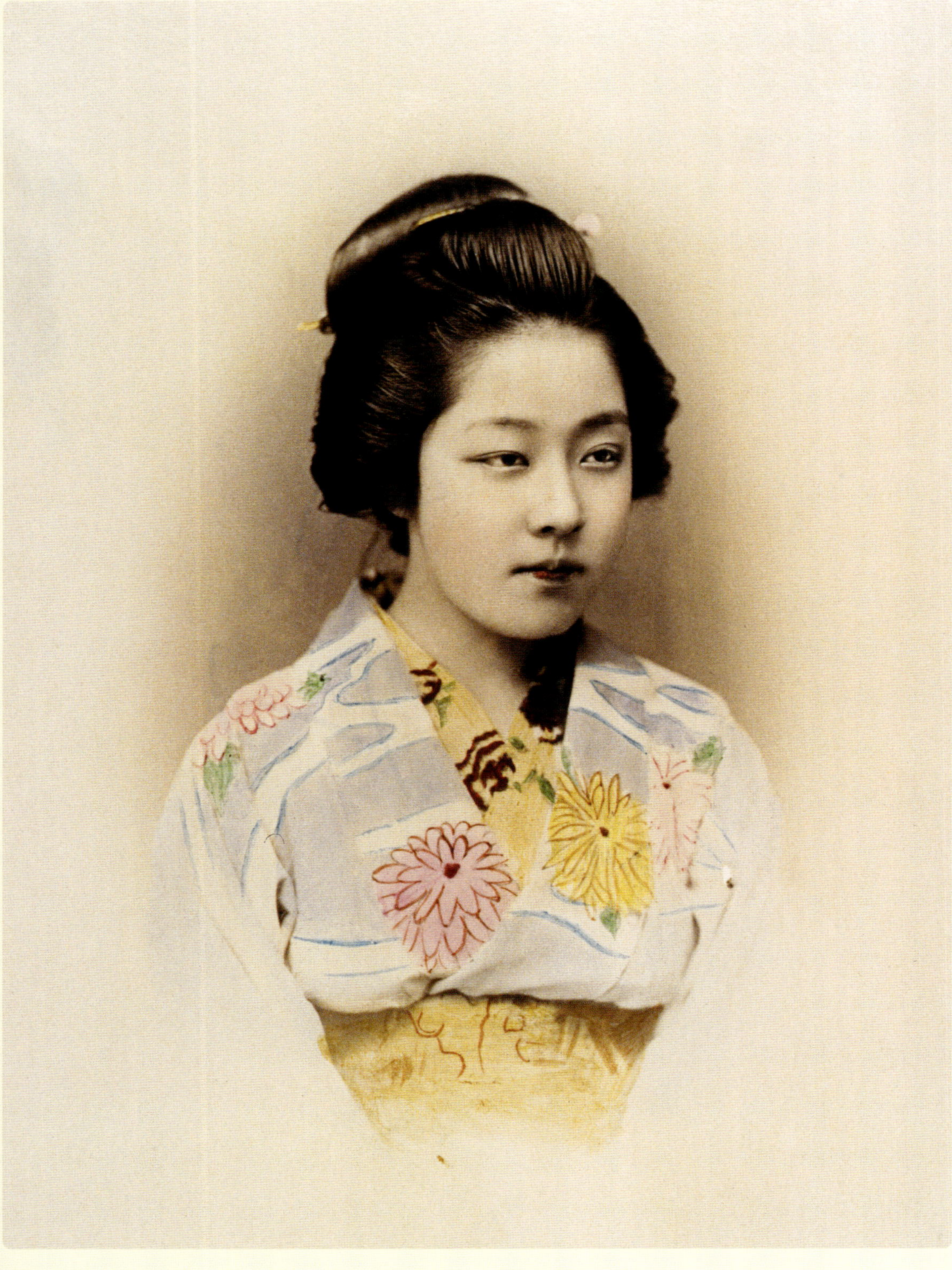

Geisha in a Yellow Obi (unattributed c. 1880)

This is a classic 1880s close-up portrait of a geisha. It highlights her lovely flowered kimono, under kimono, and obi. Her serious expression is typical of geisha portraits.

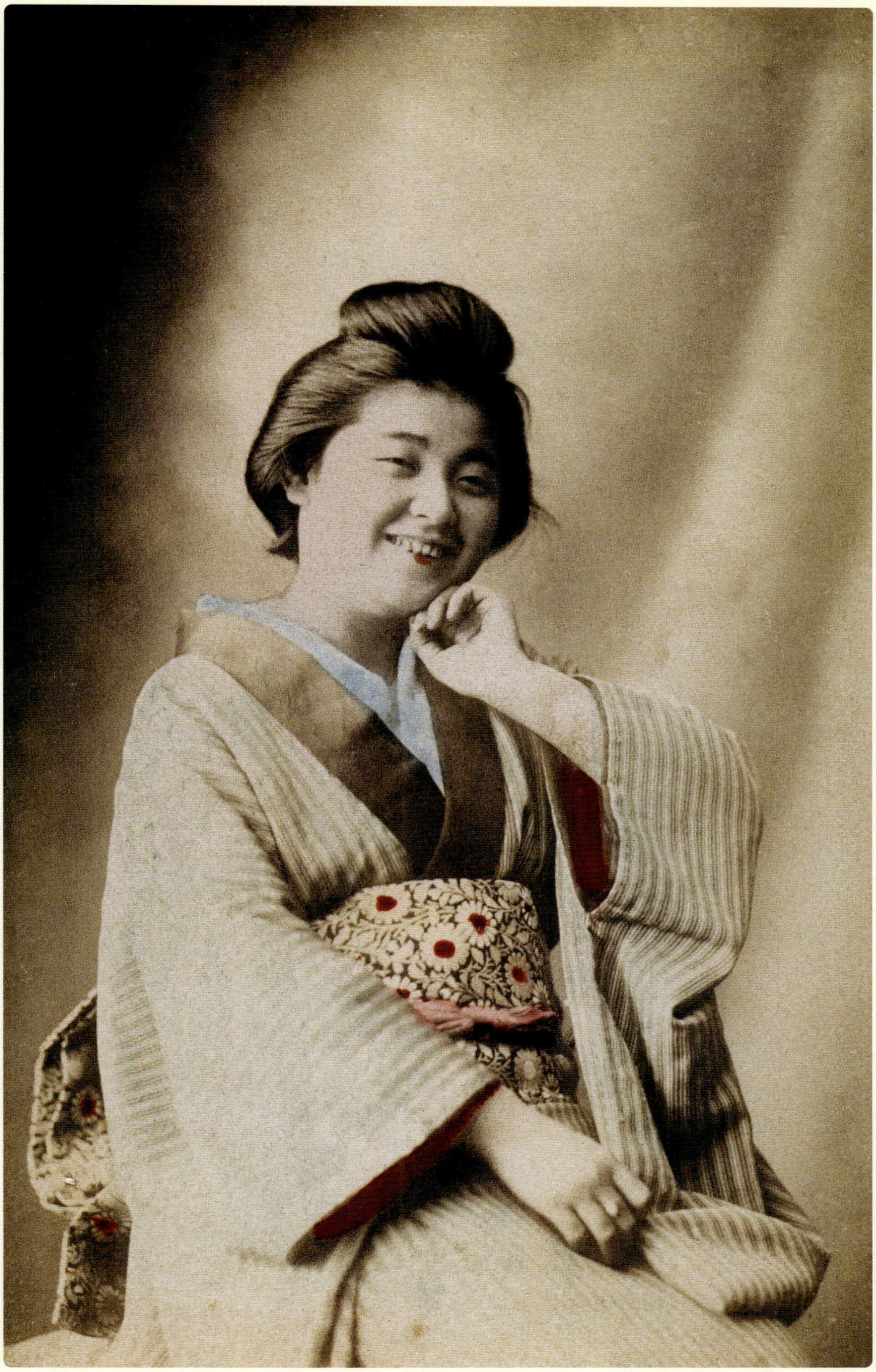

Laughing Geisha (unattributed, c. 1895)

There are no portrait photographs of other geisha laughing in this era. Photographs of this geisha appear in many of the later albums (1890–1910), as well as on postcards. She is depicted in various positions, numerous outfits, suggestively undraped, and with assorted props, including an umbrella. Images from the laughing geisha series are perhaps the most frequently reproduced geisha photographs. They were most likely taken to satisfy foreign tastes. Her smiling image contrasts with the conventional contemplative and serene portraits of geisha.

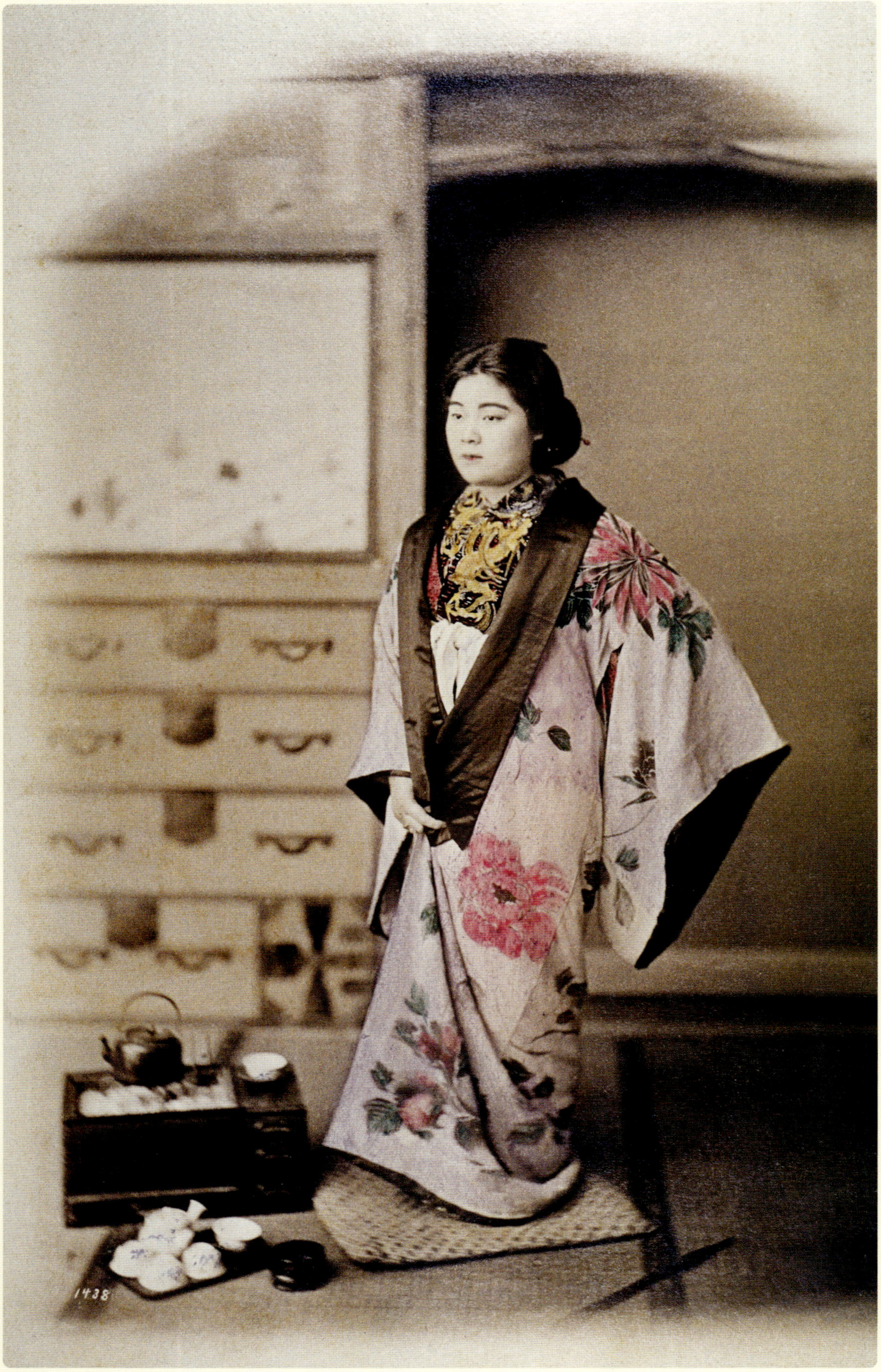

Geisha in Flowered Robe (1438)
(attributed Felice Beato/Baron Raimund von Stillfried, c. 1870)

This image is typical of the early photographs of geisha by Beato or von Stillfried. Von Stillfried began his photographic career around 1872, and took over Beato's studio in 1877. Ten years after Beato had himself given up commercial photography. Beato took his photographs of personalities during the Edo period, concentrating primarily on the individuals of the feudal era. After the Meiji restoration, in 1868, Beato continued to work, but he took images of landscapes and official photographs for various governments. Both he and von Stillfried produced books on customs and costumes, and this painted photograph clearly emphasizes the kimono. Von Stillfried's images seem artificially posed and stiff compared to Beato's, and the vignetting is typical of Beato, not von Stillfried. The number on the image indicates it is from von Stillfried's studio. However as he took over Beato's studio it could easily be by Beato and numbered by von Stillfried.

Wind Costume (155E)
(attributed Baron Raimund von Stillfried, c. 1880)

Outdoors photographs of people in motion were not possible with early photographic processes. In order to create action, various props were used in the studio, as well the technique devised by Baron von Stillfried of using fine wires to hold up parts of clothing and make it appear as if caught in the wind. One of the most popular setups was the geisha in a rain or snowstorm. Another popular image was the upset rickshaw, in which a person has fallen and their clothes are still in motion.

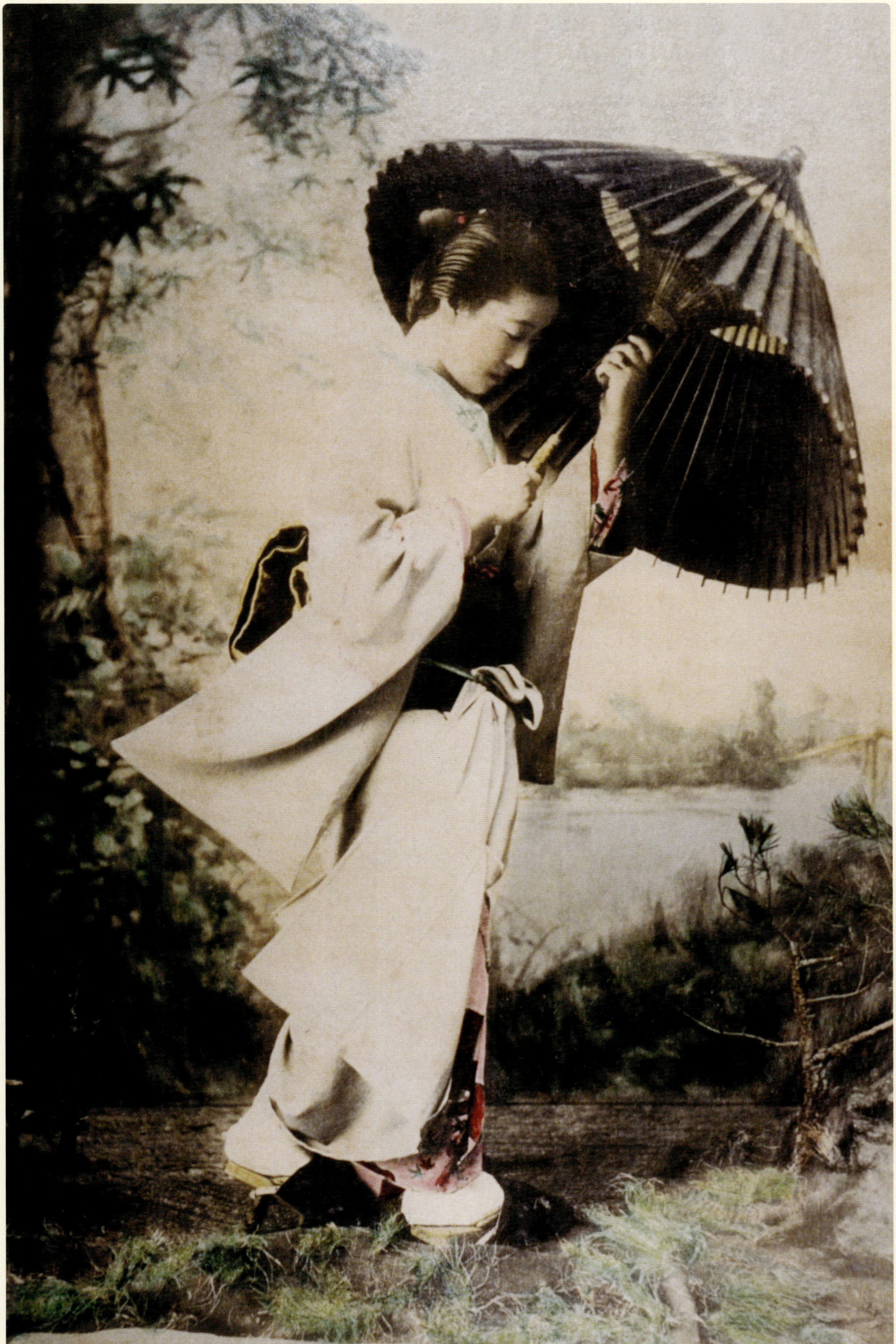

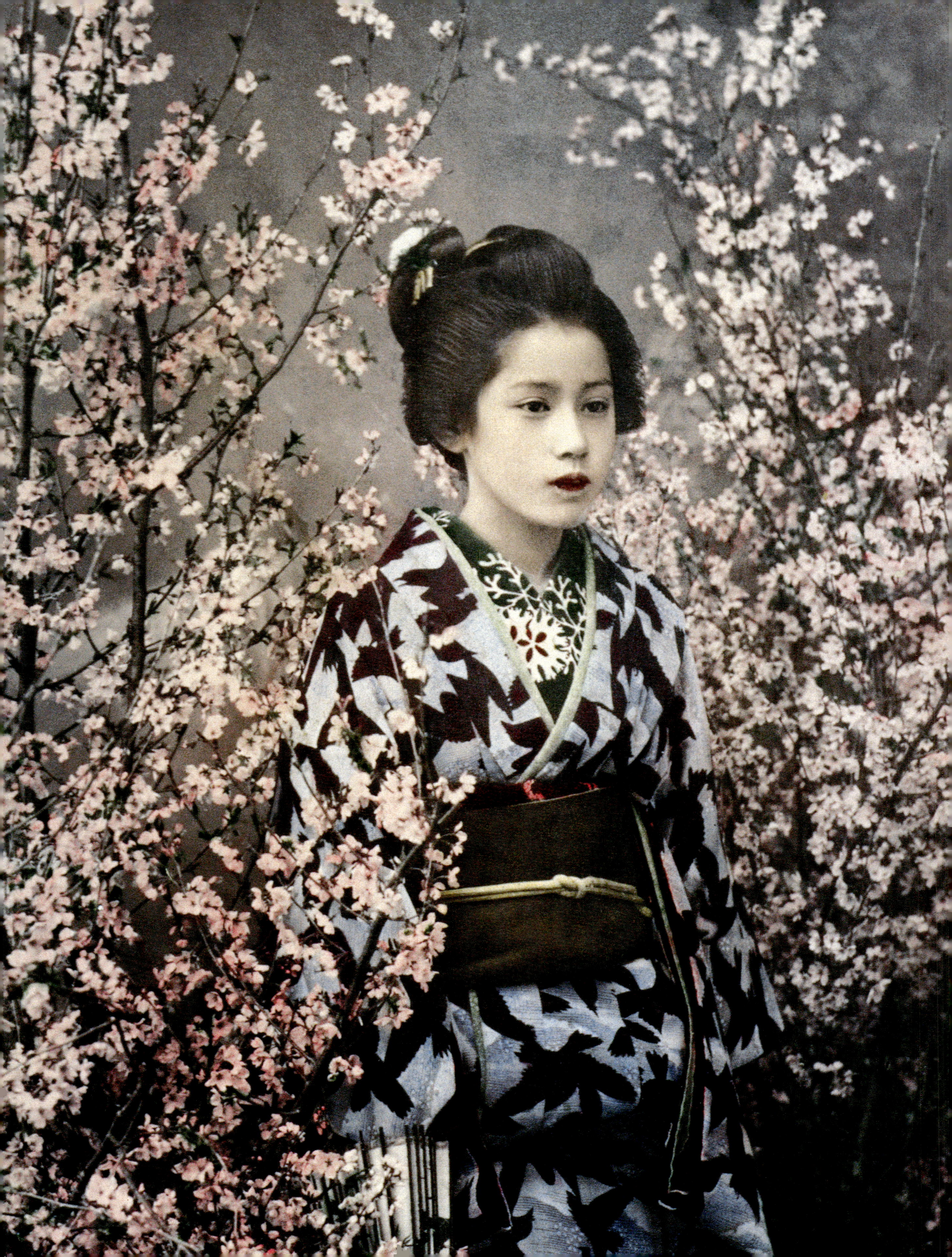

Geisha Among Cherry Blossoms (Ogawa Kazumasa, c. 1891)

This photograph captures two classic symbols of Japan, the geisha and the cherry blossom. This photograph was one of the most widely distributed geisha images, as it appeared in Francis Brinkley's *Japan: Described and Illustrated by the Japanese.* Tamamura Kozaburo sent about a half million photographs to be tipped by hand into the various editions of the ten-volume series. From the selection of images in the books, it's obvious Tamamura used photographs from all the commercial photographers from 1862 onwards. By 1891, all the Western commercial photographers had left Japan. In light of renewed Japanese patriotic pride at having taken over the industry, it was probably easy to develop the American series with cooperation from all the studios. This was the era in which Japan was emerging as a world power. By 1897, Japan was an industrialized country, although not yet recognized as such by the Western world. When the British fleet attacked in 1864, Japan had no navy. By 1899, it had the largest battleship in the world and an impressive modern navy that would soon defeat Russia. During this era of industrialization, however, it was photographs of "feudal" Japan that were exported for publication.

Postcards

These postcards depict three distinct formats of photographic reproduction. The top image, dated April 1912, is a hand-painted silver-gelatin photograph of *maiko* at the Kyoto Cherry Dances. The middle postcard, circa 1906, is a hand-painted albumen print of the Gion dancers. The bottom photograph, circa 1908, is a silver-gelatin print. It shows geisha riding in an automobile. The image of geisha in a car is representative of the special place geisha had in society. They were expected to always travel first class and in this era a car was the privileged way of travel.

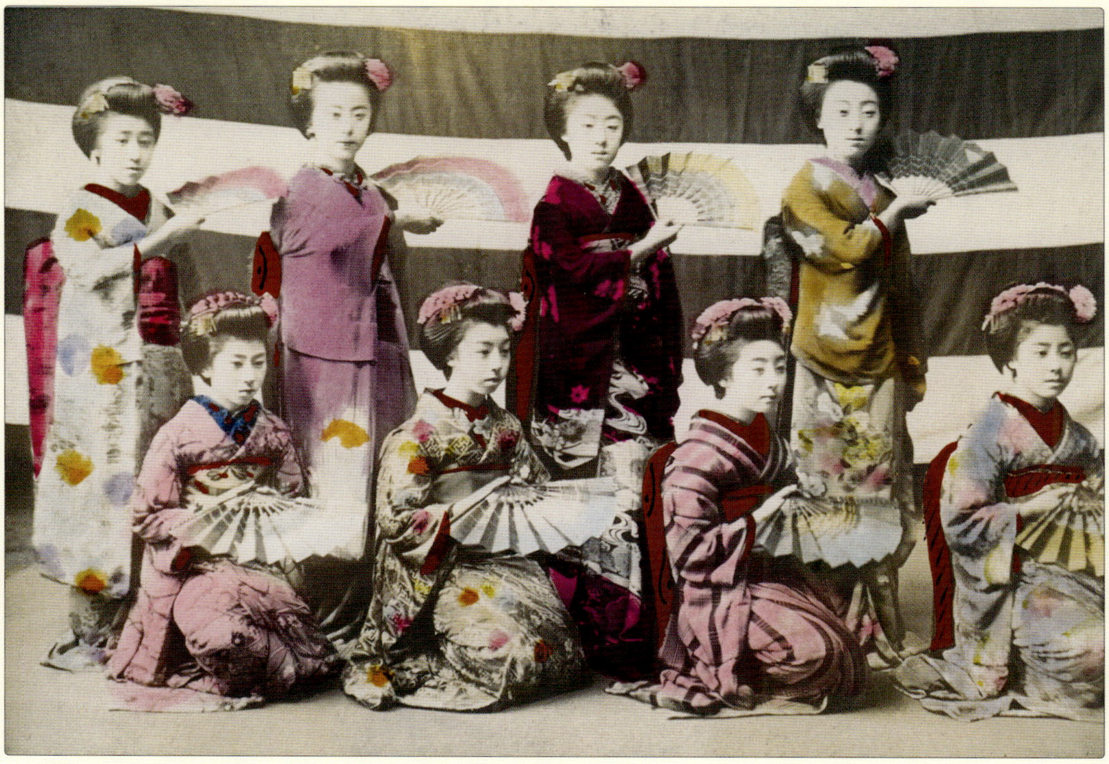

Maiko at Kyoto Cherry Dances

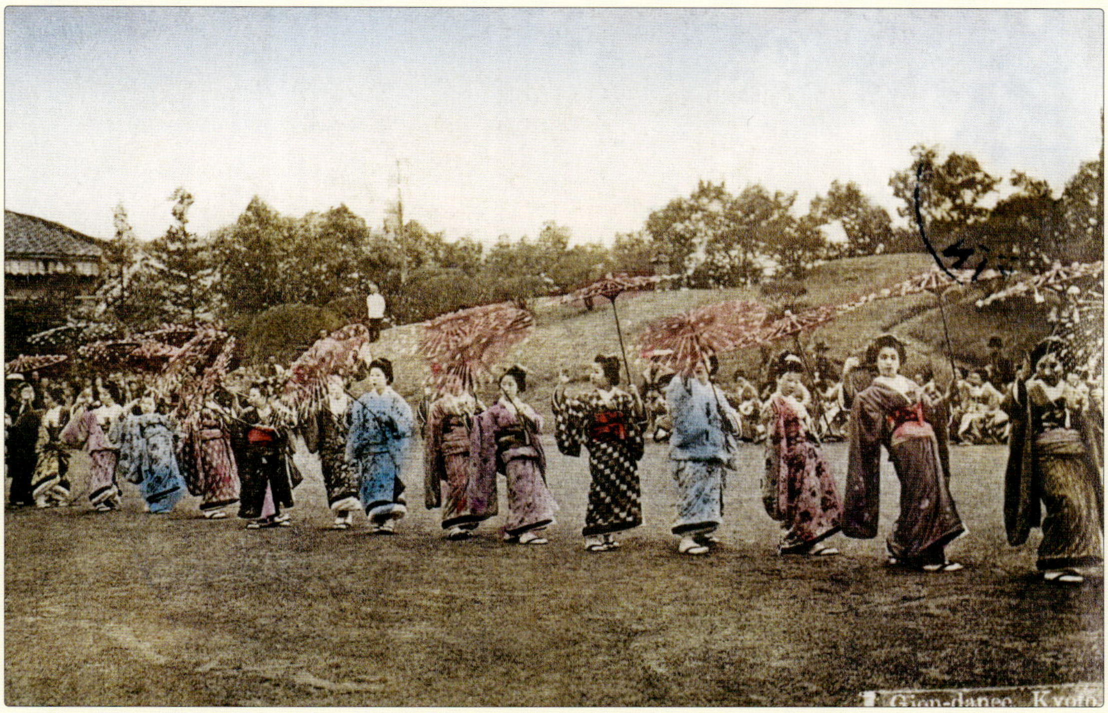

Gion-dance, Kyoto

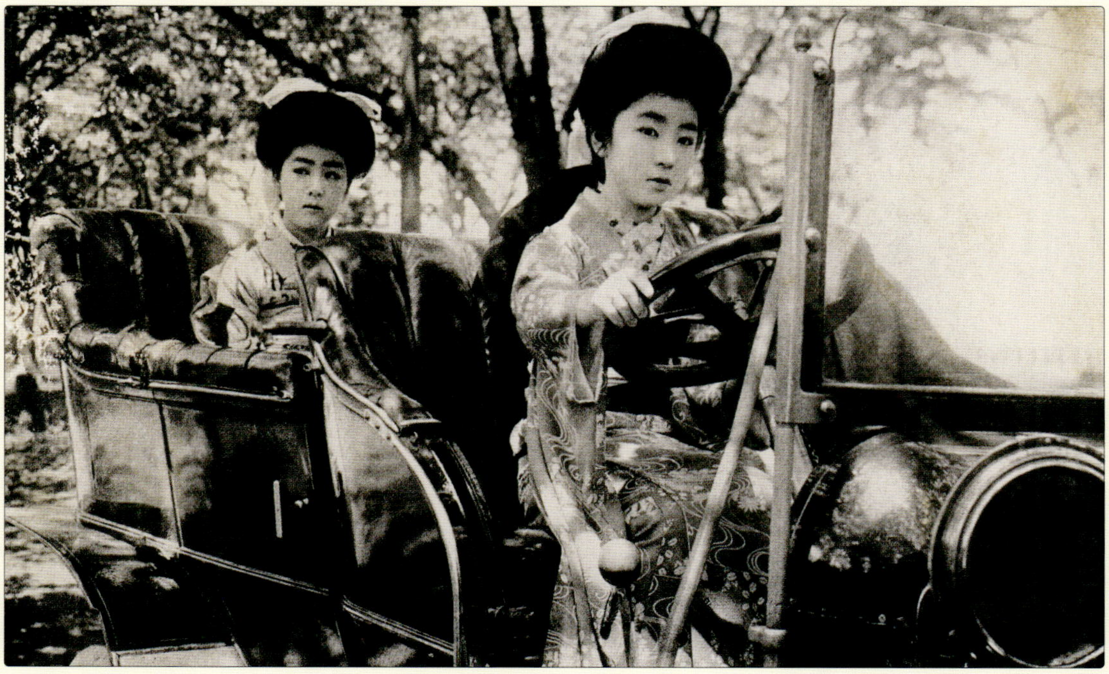

Geisha in Car

These postcards depict three distinct formats cf photographic reproduction. The top image, circa 1910, is a hand-painted silver-gelatin photograph of *maiko* at the Cherry Dances. The middle postcard, circa 1906, is a hand-painted albumen print of the Gion dancers. The bottom photograph, circa 1908, is a silver-gelatin print. It shows geisha riding in an automobile. The image of geisha in a car is representative of the special place geisha had in society.

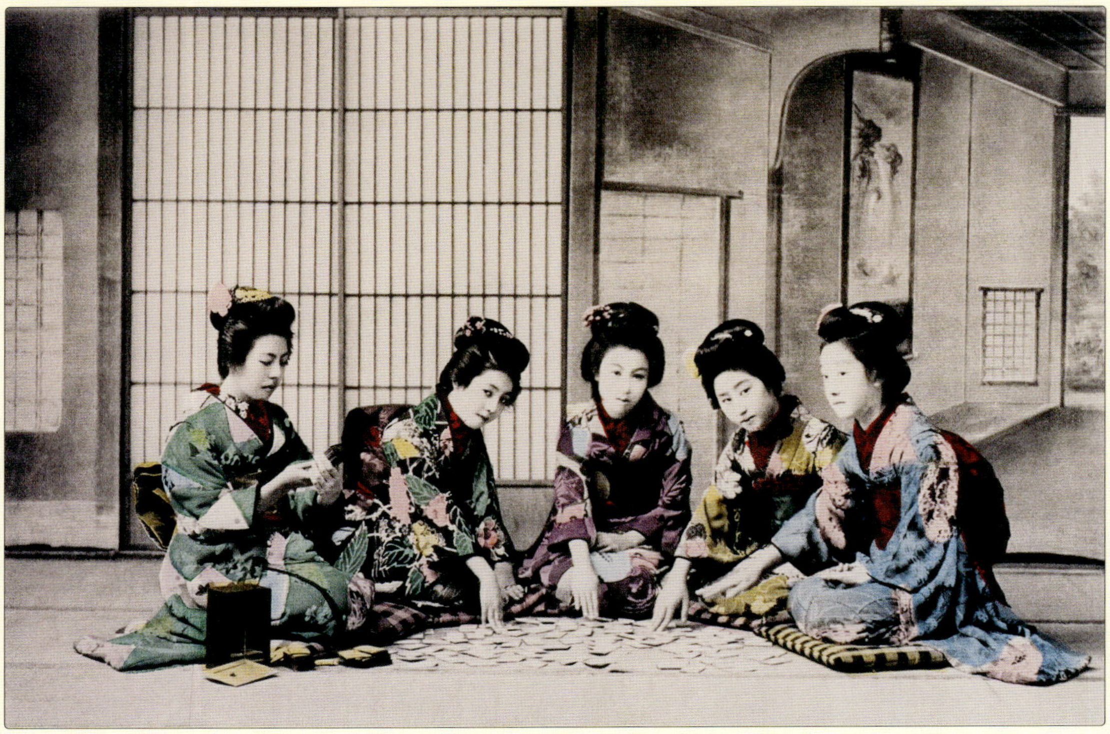

Playing Uta-Garuta

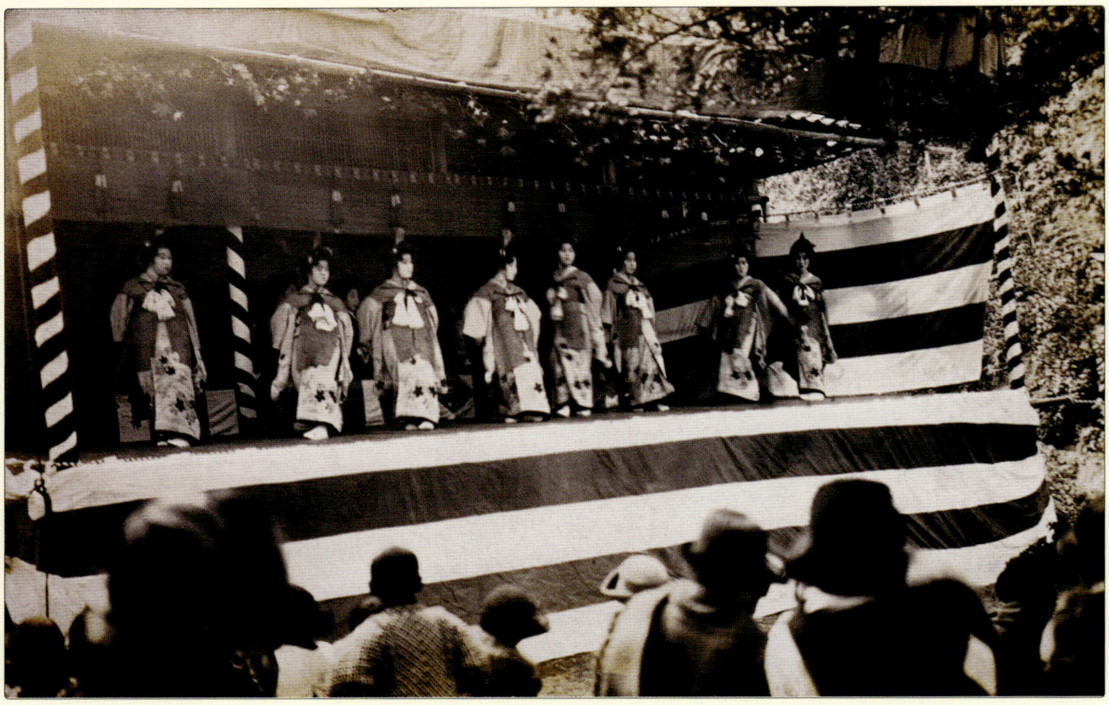

Amateur Photo at Festival

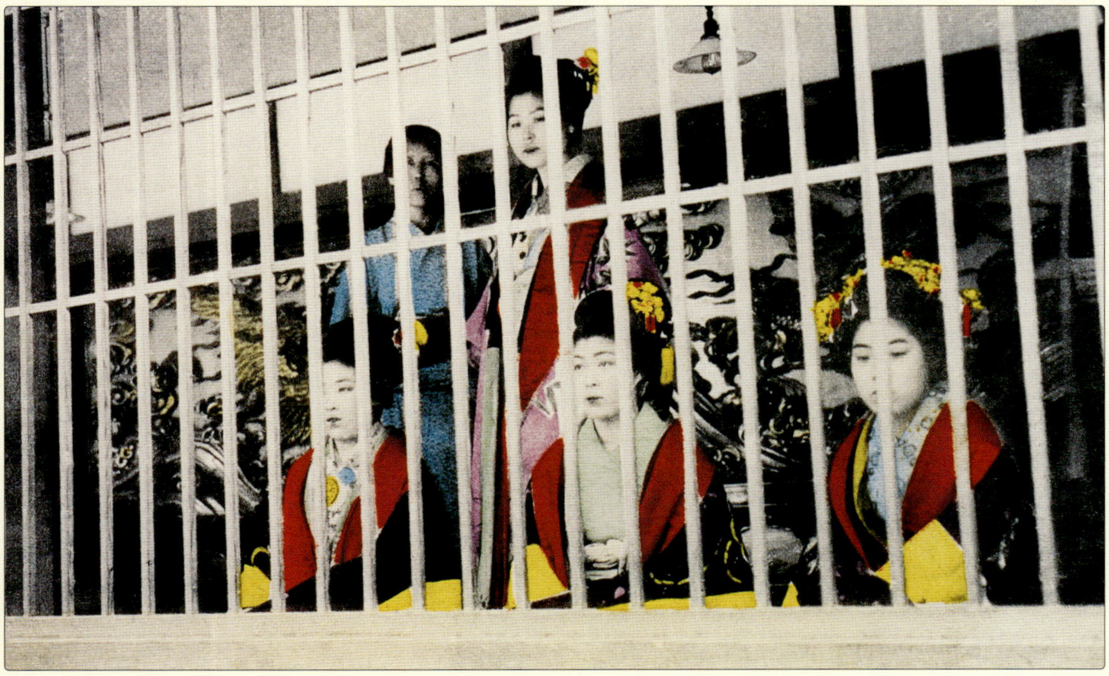

Yoshiwara Prostitutes

The top two postcards, painted collotypes, are from the popular *akaeri* trainee series. The upper one depicts a group of *akaeri* most likely at a spring dance festival. The second depicts *akaeri* in a studio preparing a meal. The bottom view is an amateur's silver-gelatin photographic postcard of a street in Kobe, taken circa 1910. Tamemasa's postcard and photograph shop provides a rare view of a noted Japanese vendor's establishment. Tamemasa, a photographic dealer based in Nagasaki, had stores throughout the nation selling albums and cards. A Japanese gentlemen looks in the window. Magnification of the postcard shows that the images on the right half of the window he is looking in are pornographic, and the images on the left are of geisha.

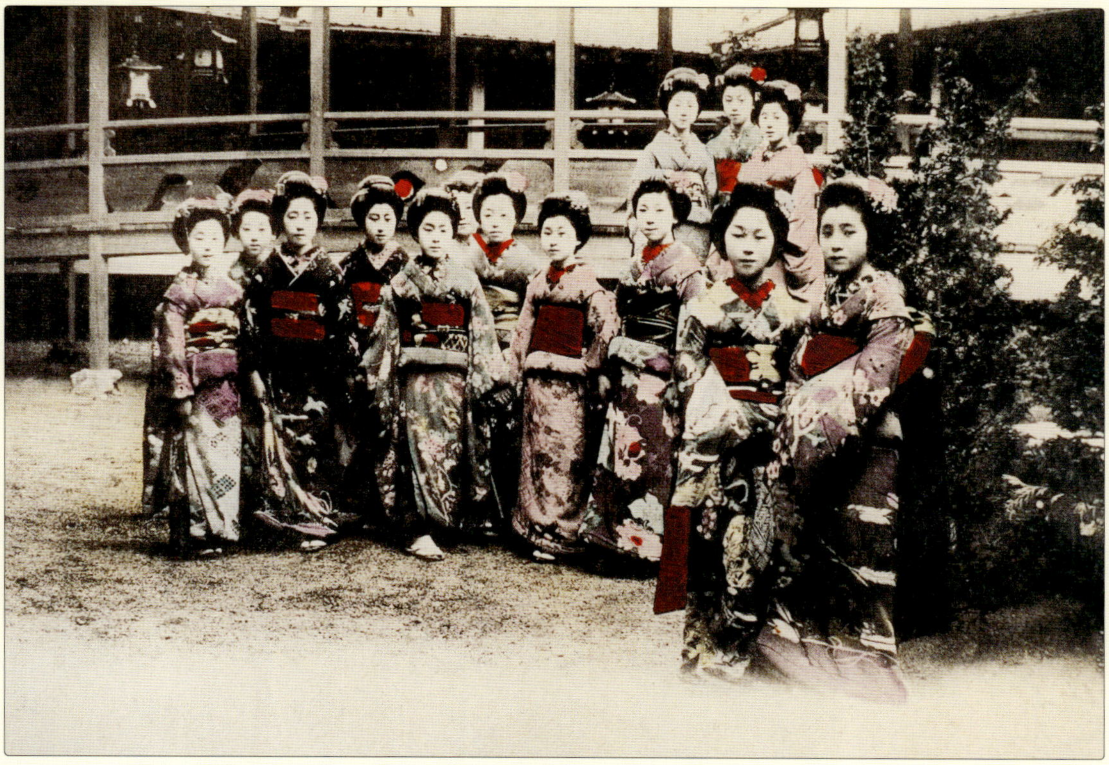

Akaeri in Tokyo

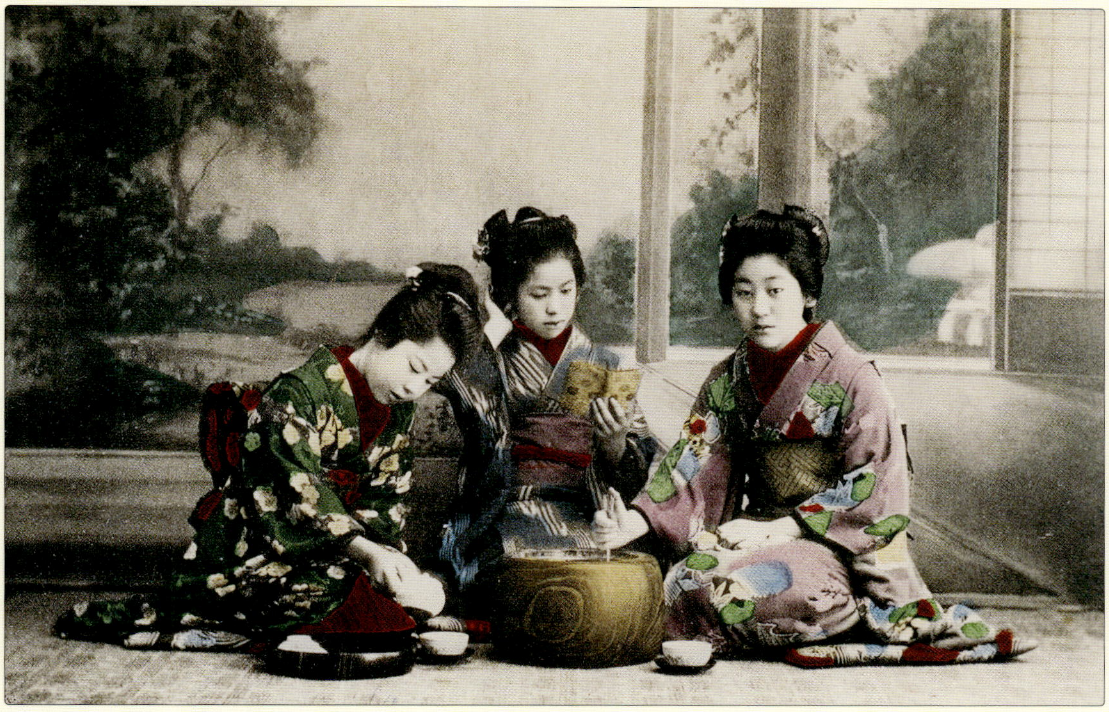

Akaeri Preparing a Meal

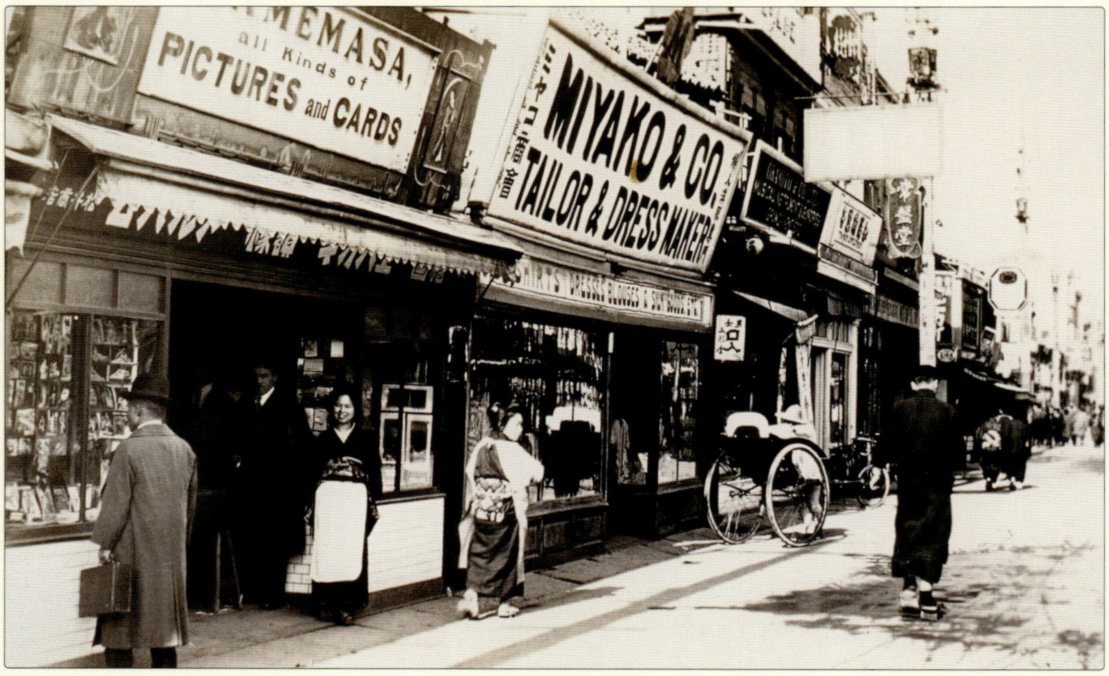

Tamemasa's Postcard & Photograph Shop

Pin-up Postcards

Celebrity Geisha

During the first decade of the twentieth century, the celebrity geisha postcard became a collectible item for the Japanese. The style of the postcards changed in each decade. These silver-gelatin photographic cards were popular around 1910. The photograph on the lower left is signed, across the image, by the renowned geisha.

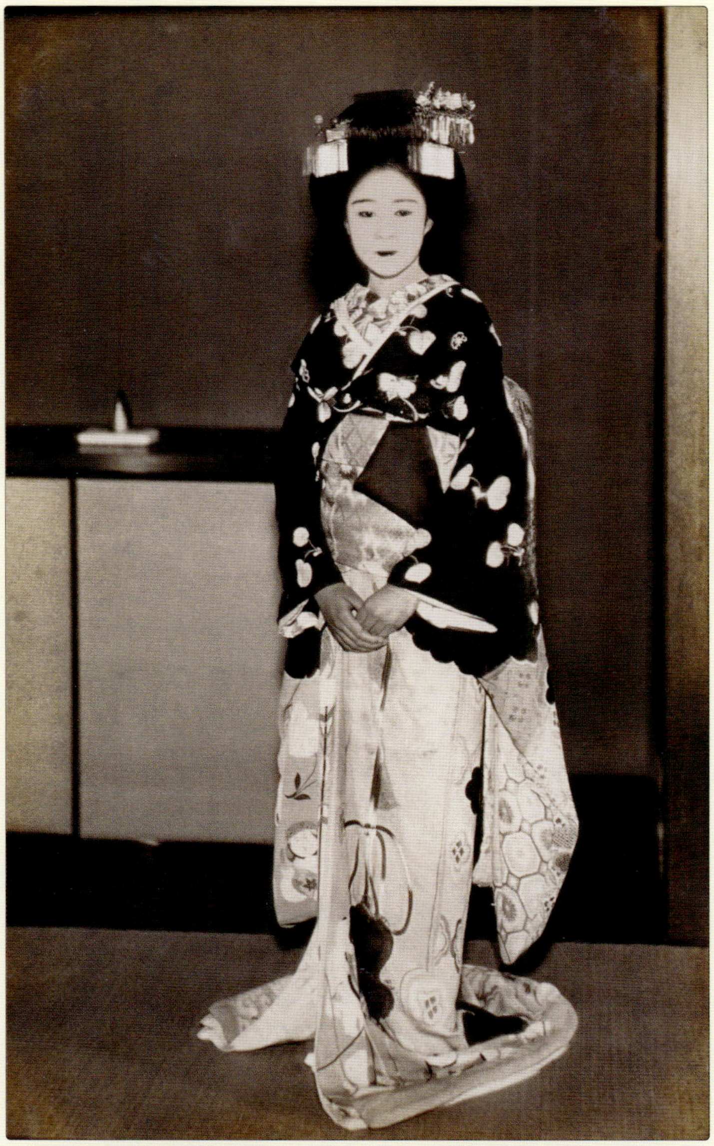
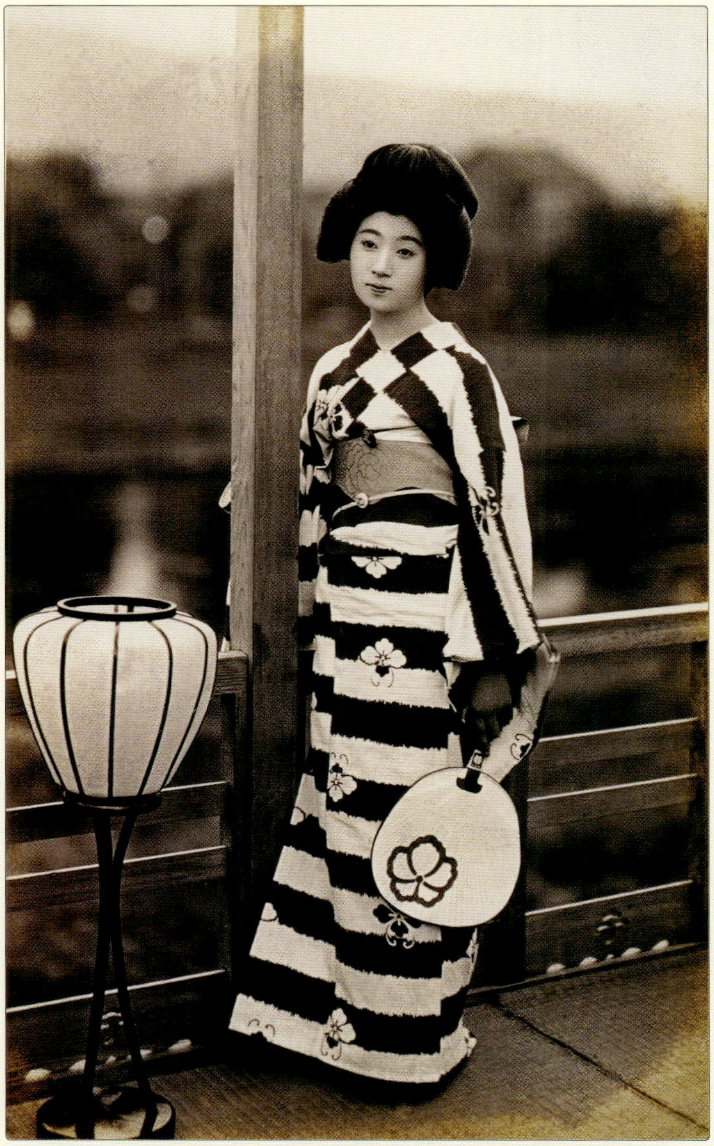
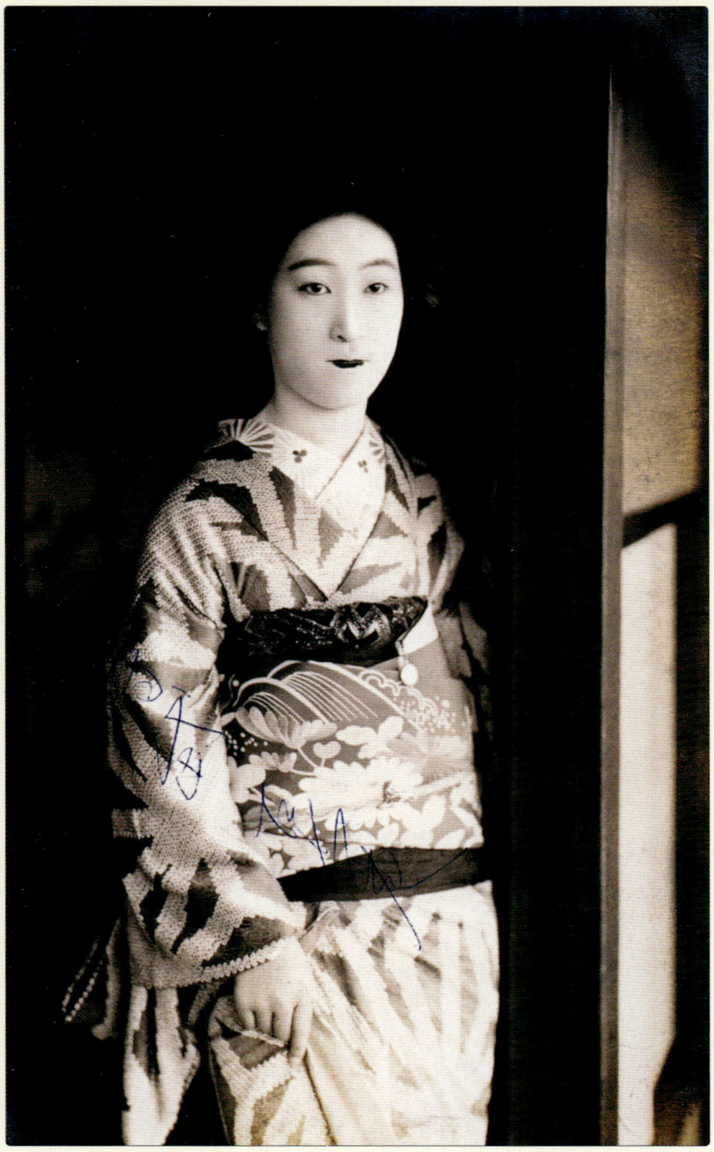
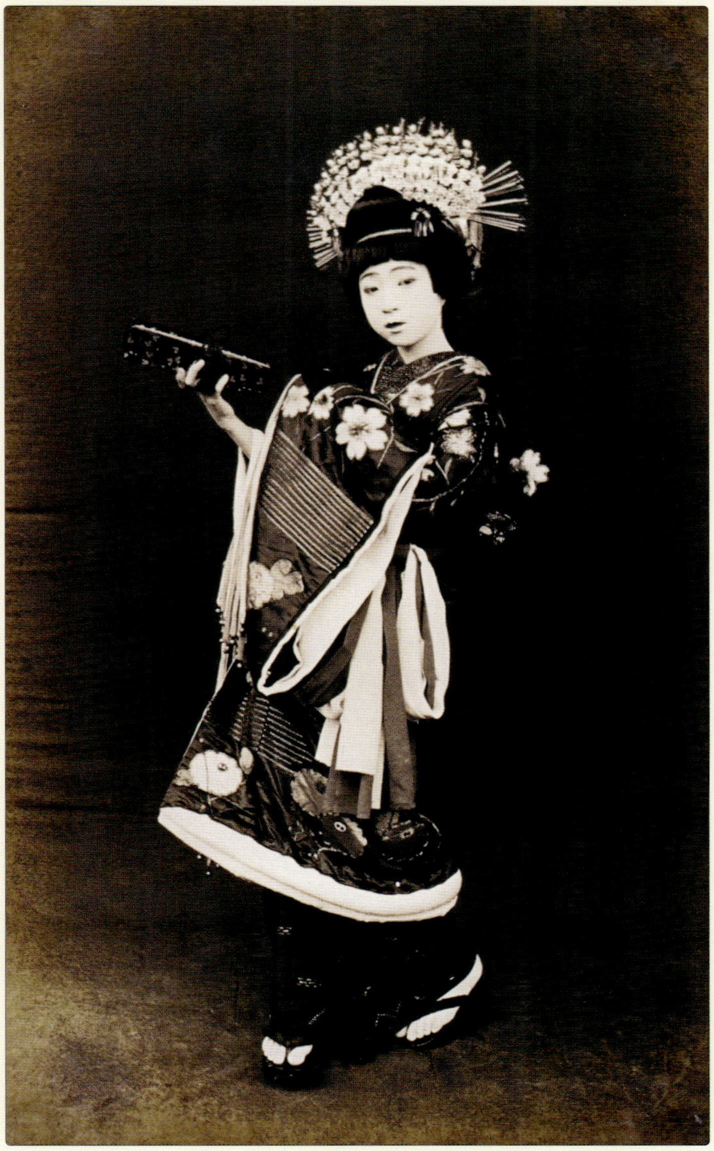

akaeri — the term used for a geisha trainee in Edo (Tokyo) and other towns derived from the red-colored collar they wore, literally "red collar."

beni — rouge that geisha and *maiko* use to highlight the lips and eyes.

chanoyu — tea ceremony.

chaya-musume — teahouse serving girl.

daidaiko — large ceremonial drums.

danna — the patron of a geisha, literally "master."

denoisho — the formal dress of a geisha, literally "going-out outfit."

en musubi — a special bond, used by analogy, to mean marriage of a young apprentice to an "older sister," literally "the tying together of destinies."

furisode — long-sleeve kimono typically worn by *maiko*, literally, "swinging-sleeve."

geiko — Kyoto dialect for geisha.

hakoya — the male attendant who carried a geisha's boxed shamisen or other necessities to parties outside her *ochaya*.

hana kanzashi — flower hair ornaments.

hanamachi — the geisha quarters of a city or town, literally "flower town."

hanadai — a geisha's wages, literally "flower money."

han-gyoku — term for an apprentice geisha in Tokyo (also called *akaeri*).

hiiki — a patron of the arts who supports one or more geisha: a geisha may have several.

hiki iwai — the ceremony or official procedure for a *maiko* or geisha leaving her profession.

hakujin — a type of amateur prostitute in Kyoto, literally "white ones."

ikebana — traditional flower arranging.

iroke — Japanese concept and traditional notion of feminine allure.

iromuji — kimono of solid color.

jikata — seated shamisen players, literally "ones on the ground."

kaburenjo — geisha district headquarters.

kamuro — courtesan's child attendant.

kanzashi — hair ornament.

karyukai — term for geisha community, literally "the flower and willow world."

kenban — the registry office in a geisha district.

kiseru — bamboo pipe with a long stem.

ko-uta — short song usually performed by geisha playing shamisen.

machiai — older Tokyo term for geisha entertainment venue.

maiko — apprentice geisha in Kyoto, literally "dancing girl."

misedashi — debut of a *maiko*.

mizuage — deflowering of a *maiko*, after which she becomes a full-fledged geisha.

mizu shobai — the sex industry, literally "water trade."

obijime — the cord that is tied around the obi.

ochaya — teahouse.

odoriko — dancing girls.

oiran — high-level classification of courtesan in Edo (Tokyo).

okiya — house where many geisha live.

oniisan — respectful name used for guests at a party, literally "big brother."

onnagata — male Kabuki actor who portrays female characters.

oshiroi — white face makeup.

otoko geisha — eighteenth-century term for male geisha.

otosan — respectful name used for older guests, literally "father."

ozashiki — private party room, or term used by geisha for a party.

ryokan — traditional inn.

ryotei — modern term in Tokyo for restaurants in which geisha entertain.

san-san-kudo — the sisterhood binding ceremony of exchanging cups of sake, literally, "three times three, nine times."

sarashi — long strip of linen used to wrap the chest.

seppun — kissing.

shikomi — first-level geisha trainee.

shinzo — apprentice *oiran* (*furisode shinzo*, young virginal apprentice; *banto shinzo*, older apprentice).

shirabyoshi — popular dancers and courtesans from the tenth through sixteenth centuries (term derived from their song and dance).

shugi — tip given to a geisha.

tabi — the split-toed socks (usually white) worn with sandals.

taiko — drum.

tachikata — modern term for geisha who specialize in dance.

taikomochi — male geisha or jester, literally "drum bearer."

tayu — highest-ranking courtesans of Kyoto.

tsuzumi — hourglass-shaped drum.

uchi geisha — geisha employed by one teahouse.

uchiwa — geisha's flat, round fans, usually printed with their crests and names.

ukiyo — literally "floating world."

ukiyo-e — literally "pictures of the floating world."

yujo — sex professional.

yukata — simple cotton kimono for everyday use.

Stereoviews of Geisha from Platt Book, Herbert Ponting, 1904–5

These photographs of geisha are from the original platt book of stereoviews taken by Herbert Ponting. A platt book is a book of original photographs a photographer produces and presents to clients to order images. It is essentially a "contact sheet." Pontine's book was made not for the public but for photographic publishers to produce the images as a series of stereoviews or lantern slides. His stereoviews were reproduced by various clients, including the A.C. White Company and the Keystone View Company. Some of the images were not chosen for reproduction and the platt book contains the only surviving copies. Ponting, who preferred to be called a "camera artist," is best known as the pioneer of polar photography. He was the first professional photographer to be hired on an Antarctic expedition. He traveled on the ill-fated voyage of fellow Englishman Captain Robert Scott to the South Pole. (Scott reached the South Pole just one month after Norwegian Roald Amundsen and unfortunately did not survive the journey back.) Ponting, before heading south, made several trips to Japan and the Far East. During the Russo-Japanese War he worked for *Harper's Weekly*. This half-page from Ponting's platt book was taken during the war and depicts geisha at various activities. He was also commissioned by Underwood & Underwood to photograph Japan. He traveled there many times, as the country held a constant fascination for him. In 1910, Ponting published *In Lotus-land Japan* (London: Macmillan and Co.), reproducing many of his noted images of geisha.

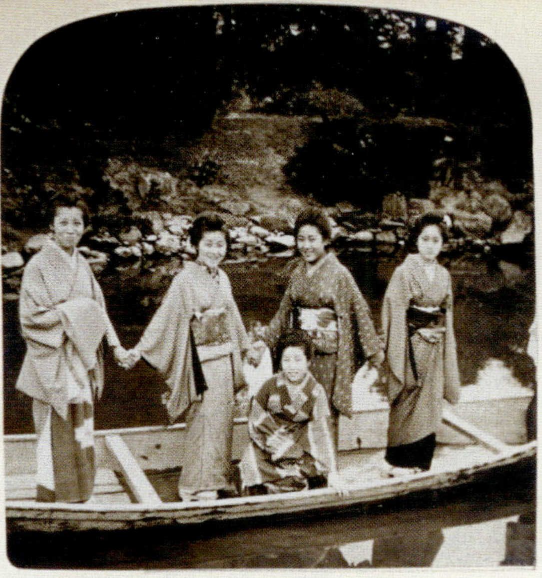
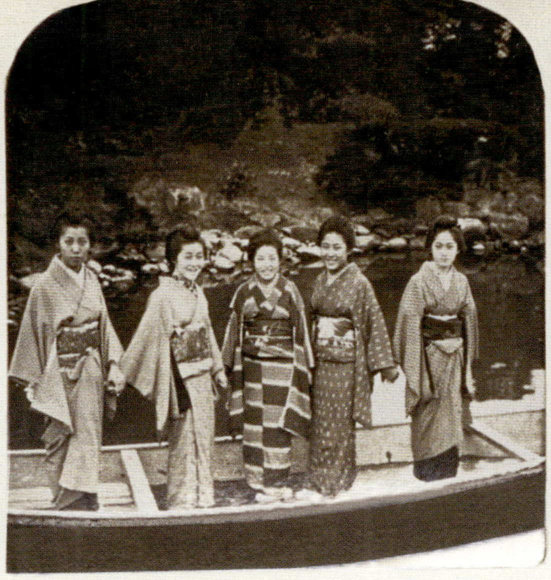
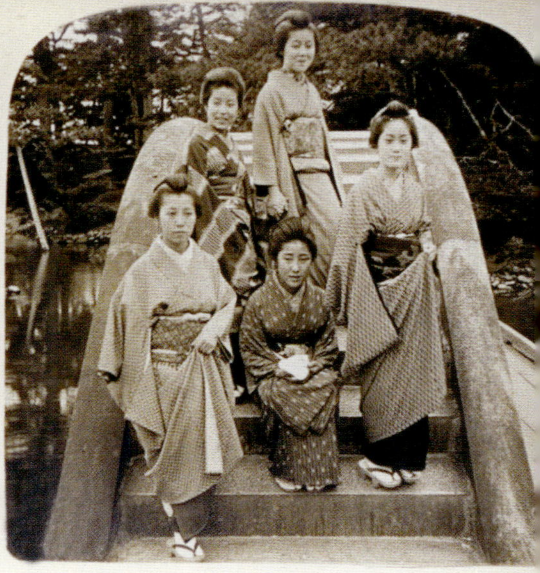
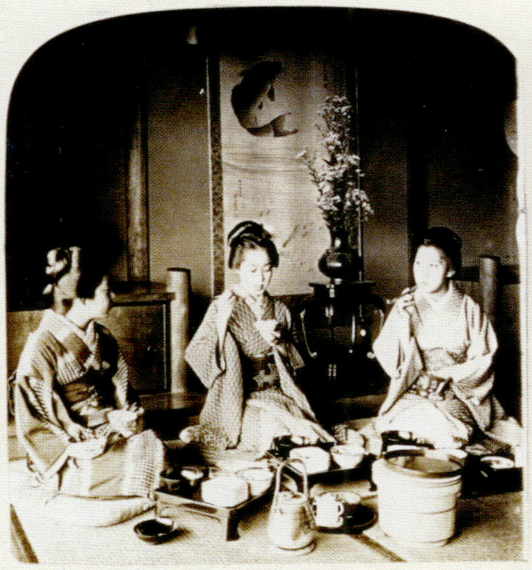
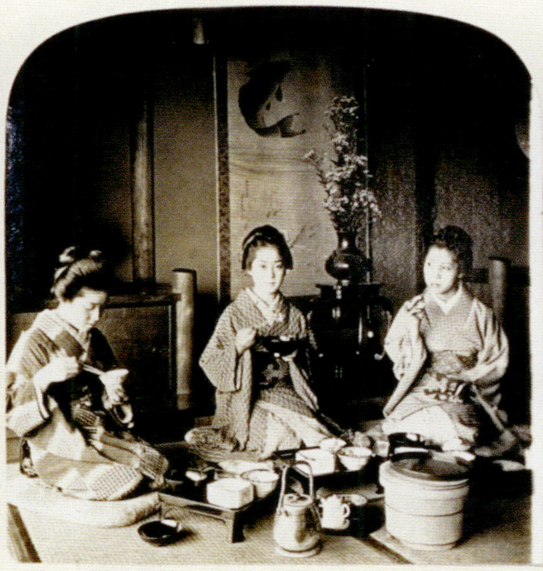
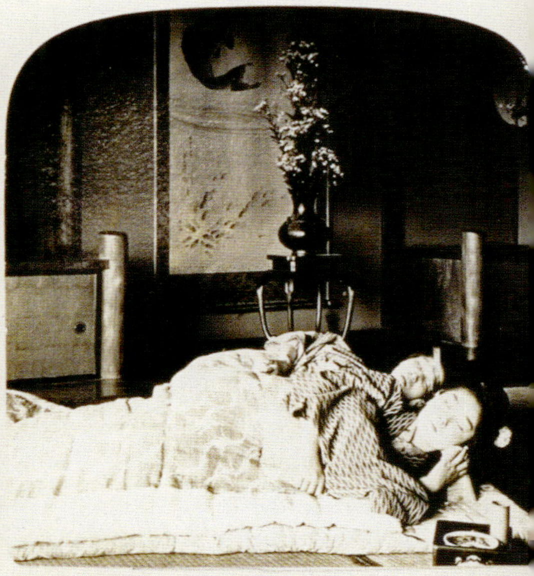
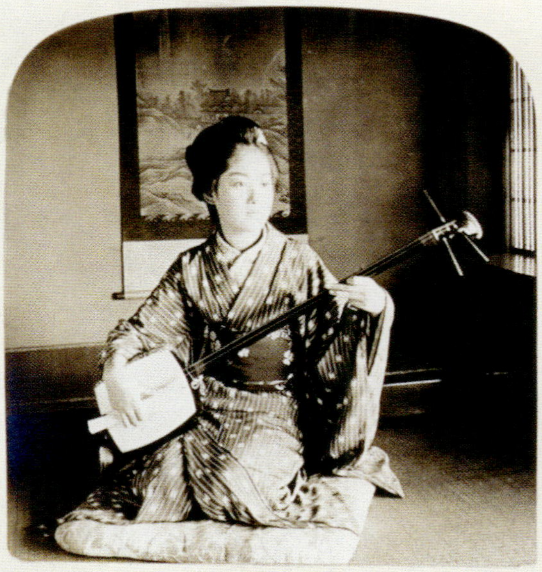
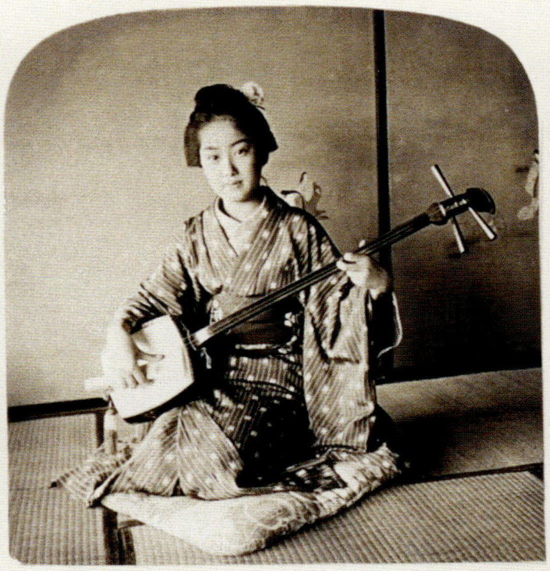
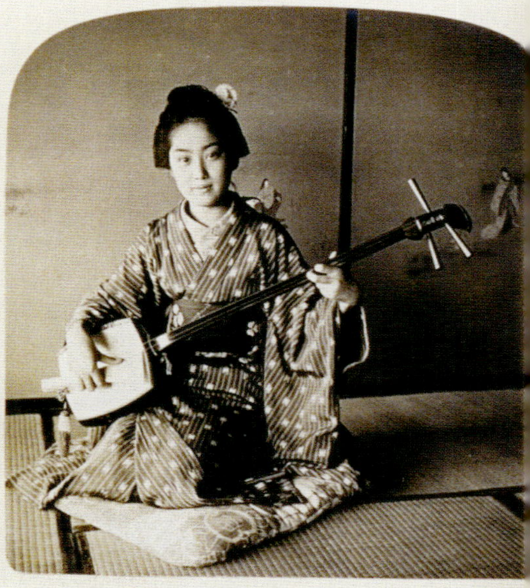
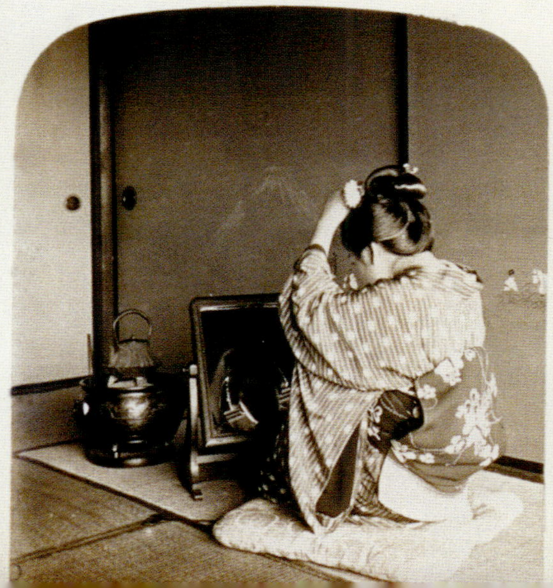
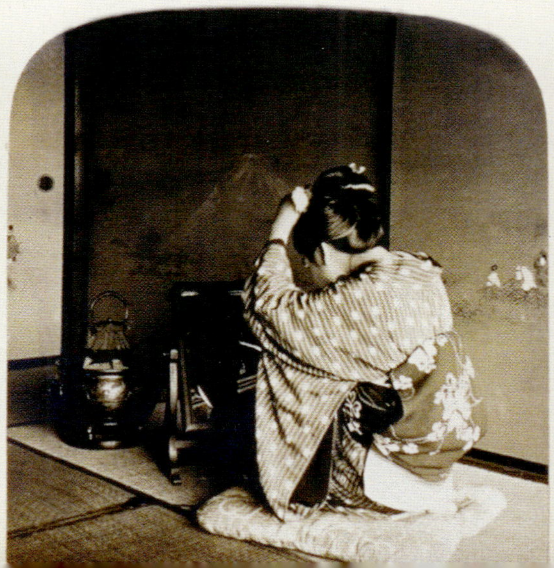
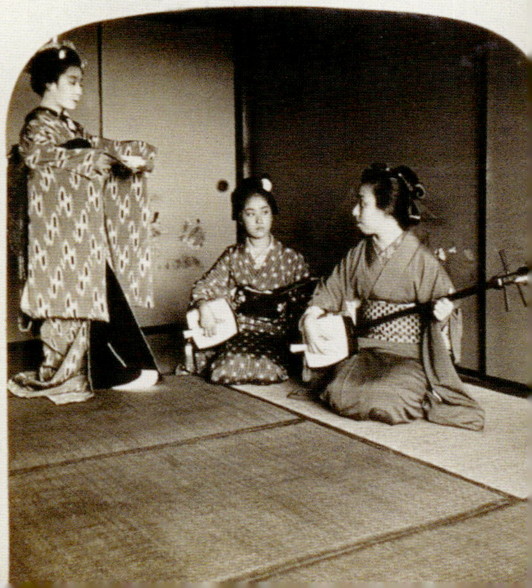

Bibliography

Beasley, W.G., *The Japanese Experience: A Short History of Japan*. Berkeley: University of California Press, 1999.

Benfey, Christopher, *The Great Wave: Gilded Age Misfits, Japanese Eccentrics, and the Opening of Japan*. New York: Random House, 2003.

Bennett, Terry, *Early Japanese Images*. Rutland, VT: Tuttle Publishing, 1996.

Blood, Katherine L., et al., *The Floating World of Ukiyo-e: Shadows, Dreams, and Substance*. New York: Harry N. Abrams, in Association with the Library of Congress, 2001.

Brinkley, Francis, *Japan and the Japanese, Volumes I through X*. Boston: J B Millet Company, 1897.

Clark, John, *Japanese Exchanges in Art 1850s to 1930s: with British, continental Europe, and the United States*. Sydney: Power Publications, 2001.

Cobb, Jodi, *Geisha: The Life, the Voices, the Art*. New York: Alfred A. Knopf, 1995.

Cortazzi, Hugh & Terry Bennett, *Japan: Caught in Time: Great Photographic Archives*. London: Garnet Publishing, 1995.

Crombie, Isobel, *Shashin: Nineteenth-Century Japanese Studio Photography*. Melbourne, Australia: Council of Trustees of the National Gallery of Victoria, 2004.

Dalby, Liza, *Geisha*. Berkeley: University of California Press, 1998.

Dalby, Liza, *Kimono: Fashioning Culture*. Seattle: University of Washington Press, 2001.

Dalby, Liza, *Little Songs of the Geisha: Traditional Japanese Ko-Uta*. Rutland, VT: Tuttle Publishing, 2000.

Dobson, Sebastian, et al., *Art & Artifice: Japanese Photographs of the Meiji Era*. Boston: MFA Publications, 2004.

Dower, John, *A Century of Japanese Photography: Japan Photographers Association*, New York: Pantheon Books, 1983.

Downer, Lesley, *Madame Sadayakko, The Geisha who Bewitched the West*. New York: Gotham Books, 2003.

Downer, Lesley, *Women of the Pleasure Quarters: The Secret History of the Geisha*. New York: Broadway Books, 2001.

Du Castel, Dider, et al., *Le crépuscule des geisha*. Paris: Editions Marvel, 2002.

Edel, Chantal, *Once Upon a Time: Visions of Old Japan. Photographs by Felice Beato and Baron Rainmund von Stillfried*. New York: Friendly Press, Inc., 1986.

Fabian, Rainer & Hans-Christian Adam, *Masters of Early Travel Photography*. New York: Vendome Press, 1983.

Gallagher, John, *Geisha: A Unique World of Tradition, Elegance, and Art*. New York: Sterling Publishing, 2003.

Ishiguro, Keisho, *Pornography In the Meiji Era: 1890-1910, A Color Pictorial Reference Book on Erotic Japanese Photos*. Tokyo: Photo Musee, 1996.

Iwasaki, Mineko, *Geisha, A Life*. New York: Atria Books, 2002.

Iwasaki, Mineko and Rande Brown, *Geisha of Gion: The Memoir of Mineko Iwasaki*. London: Simon & Shuster, 2002.

Kazuma, Ogawa, *Geisha of Tokyo: One Hundred Beauties of Tokyo*. Tokyo: Ogawa, 1902.

Louis, Lisa, *Butterflies of the Night: Mama-sans, Geisha, Strippers, and the Japanese Men they Serve*. New York: Tengu Books, 1992.

Marbot, Bernard, *Objectif Cipango: Photographies anciennes du Japon*. Paris : Paris Audiovisuel, 1990.

March, Philipp & Claudia Delank, *The Adventure of Japanese Photography 1860–1890*. Heidelberg: Kehrer Verlag, 2002.

Meech, Julia and Gabriel P. Weisberg, *Japonisme Comes to America: The Japanese Impact on the Graphic Arts, 1872–1925*. New York: Abrams, 1990.

Peabody Essex Museum, eds, *Geisha: Beyond the Painted Smile*. Salem, MA: George Brazillier, Inc. 2004.

Pedlar, Neil, *The Golden Age of Yokohama Postcards*. Self-published..

Prasso, Sheridan, *The Asian Mystique: Dragon Ladies, Geisha Girls, & Our Fantasies of the Exotic Orient*. New York: Public Affairs, 2005.

Rousmaniere, Nicole Coolidge, & Mikiko Hirayama, eds, *Reflecting Truth: Japanese Photography in the Nineteenth Century*. Amsterdam: Hotei Publishing, 2004.

Scott, A C, *The Flower and Willow World: The Story of the Geisha*. London: Heinemann, 1959.

Shimukowa, Kuhshi, *History of the Japanese Porn-Photos*. Tokyo: Koshi Pub., 2003.

Skinner, Tina & Mary L. Martin, *Geisha: Women of Japan's Flower & Willow World*. Atglen, PA: Schiffer Publishing Ltd., 2005.

Tucker, Ann Wilkes, et al., *The History of Japanese Photography*. New Haven: Yale University Press, 2003.

Underwood, Eleanor, *Life of a Geisha*. New York: Smithmark publishers, 1999.

Winkel, Margarita, *Souvenirs from Japan: Japanese Photography at the Turn of the Century*. London: Bamboo Publishing, Ltd., 1991.

Worswick, Clark, *Japan: Photographs 1854–1905*. New York: Pennwick/Alfred A. Knopf, 1979.

REFERENCES

1. Beasley, W.G., *The Japanese Experience: A Short History of Japan*, Berkeley, University of California Press, 1999, p. 148.
2. Ibid. p. 149
3. Benfey, Christopher, *The Great Wave: Gilded Misfits, Japanese Eccentrics and the Opening of Japan*, New York, Random House, 2003, p 31.
4. Ibid. p. 76
5. Peabody Essex Museum, Eds, *Geisha: Beyond the Painted Smile*, Salem MA., George Brazillier, Inc. 2004, p. 51
6. Rousmaniere, Nicole, & Mikiko Hirayama, Eds, *Reflecting Truth: Japanese Photography in the Nineteenth Century*, Amsterdam, Hotei Publishing, 2004, p.41
7. Wilkes-Tucker, Ann, et al. *The History of Japanese Photography*, New Haven, Yale University Press, 2003, p.30
8. Louis, Lisa, *Butterflies of the Night: Mama-sans, Geisha, Strippers, and the Japanese Men they Serve*, New York, Tengu Books, 1992 p.60

Acknowledgements

Several dealers and historians have supported our projects over the years. We particularly want to thank Adrien London Saks and William Clark Planta of The London Clark Gallery in Washington DC, dealers who offered images from their personal collection to help complete our compilation. They also lent us, for this publication, the ukiyo-e print and bathing scene. We would also like to express our appreciation to Japanese photographic historian Terry Bennett for his generosity in sharing his knowledge. He has written more books on the subject than any one else. He also shared his extensive geisha and Yokohama photograph collection so that we could get a better perspective on the early work. His third book on the history of Japanese photography will be published in the fall of 2006 and his perspective and understanding of the subject helped guide us in some of our final analyses of the photography of the geisha. We would also like to thank J-sun Burns for his editorial assistance; Mark Suroff for his support; Jennifer F. Dinsmore for help with research; Mine Suda for her design of the book; Nicholas Weist for his editing skills; and Craig Cohen and Daniel Power for the opportunity of working with powerHouse Books in publishing this work.

Stanley B. Burns, MD, a practicing New York City ophthalmic surgeon, is also an internationally distinguished photographic historian, author, lecturer, curator, and collector. For the last three decades he has concentrated on collecting photographs relating to unexplored areas of history and photography. The collection now contains over 800,000 images, including the most comprehensive compilation of early hand-colored photography. In 1995, he published *Forgotten Marriage: The Painted Tintype and the Decorative Frame*. In this exposé on the art of painting photographs, he explored the close relationship that hand-colored photographs have to paintings. He now explores the painted photographs of Japan, produced from 1872 to 1912, concentrating on the portrayal of geisha and their traditional arts. Photographs from his collection have been featured in numerous publications, films, and museum exhibitions. The Burns Archive, his stock photography and publishing entity, is a valuable photographic resource for both researchers and the media. Dr. Burns is also a consultant for Hollywood feature filmmakers, as well as independent producers. Some of his film credits include Adrian Lyne's *Jacob's Ladder*, Robert Altman's *Dorothy Parker and her Vicious Circle*, Tom Cruise's *The Others*, and Al Pacino's *Looking For Richard*. He is a contributing editor for seven medical specialty journals. Utilizing his unique collection, Dr. Burns has written seventeen critically acclaimed photographic history books, hundreds of articles, and curated dozens of exhibitions. His award winning books on memorial and post-mortem photography, *Sleeping Beauty* (1990 and 2002), became the focus of films and exhibits, including one at the Musée d'Orsay in Paris. France's Channel Plus created a documentary on his work as part of their series *Great Collectors of the World*. Currently, he is working on producing a documentary series, *Hidden Histories*, based on his collection of photographs of forgotten, but significant historic events.

Elizabeth A. Burns is the Creative Director of The Burns Archive and Press. She has curated and organized numerous exhibitions and books, including *Sleeping Beauty II* and *The Burns Archive Medical Specialty Series*. In 2002, under a grant by the United States and Israeli governments, she produced *A Dream Deferred, The African-American Experience 1848–1928*, the inaugural exhibition at the Center for the Study of the United States in Haifa, Israel. Other exhibits she has prepared feature works on early flight, spirit photography, criminology, Lewis Hine and the playground, African American history, and a special exhibition on respiratory disease entitled *BreathTaking Photographs*. Currently she is working on developing an exhibition of nineteenth-century hand-painted geisha photographs.

Books

2007 *Seeing Insanity: Photography & The Depiction of Mental Illness*

2006 *Patients & Promise: A Photographic History of Mental & Mood Disorders* (4 Volumes)

2005 *Photographic History of Nineteenth Century Dermatology* (4 Volumes)

2005 *Photographic History of Early Podiatry*

2004 *Oncology: Tumors & Treatment A Photographic History 1845–1945* (4 Volumes)

2003 *Respiratory Disease: A Photographic History, 1845–1945* (4 Volumes)

2002 *Sleeping Beauty II: Grief, Bereavement and The Family in Memorial Photography, American & European Traditions with Elizabeth A. Burns*

1999 *A Morning's Work: Medical Photographs from The Burns Archive & Collection 1843–1939*

1995 *Forgotten Marriage: The Painted Tintype & The Decorative Frame, 1860–1910, A Lost Chapter in American Portraiture*

1994 *Harm's Way: Lust & Madness, Murder & Mayhem* co-author: Joel-Peter Witkin, et al

1993 *Face of Mercy: A Photographic History of Medicine at War* co-authors: M. Naythons, MD & S. Nuland, MD

1991 *Photographie et Médecine: 1840-1880* co-author: Jacques Gasser, MD

1990 *Sleeping Beauty: Memorial Photography in America*

1990 *The American Dentist: A Pictorial History* co-authors: R. Glenner, DDS & A. Davis, PhD

1987 *Masterpieces of Medical Photography: Selections from the Burns Archive* co-author: Joel-Peter Witkin

1983 *Early Medical Photography in America: 1839–1883*

Maiko

By the end of the first decade of the twentieth century, the *maiko* in their flamboyant outfits became the darlings of photographers and tourists. Geisha, to this day, are rarely seen on the streets of Kyoto, but *maiko* are found running between their lessons and other appointments. This photograph, taken around 1912, is typical of the numerous images of groups of *maiko* that became popular and representative of geisha. Kyoto has remained the only city where geisha are trained.

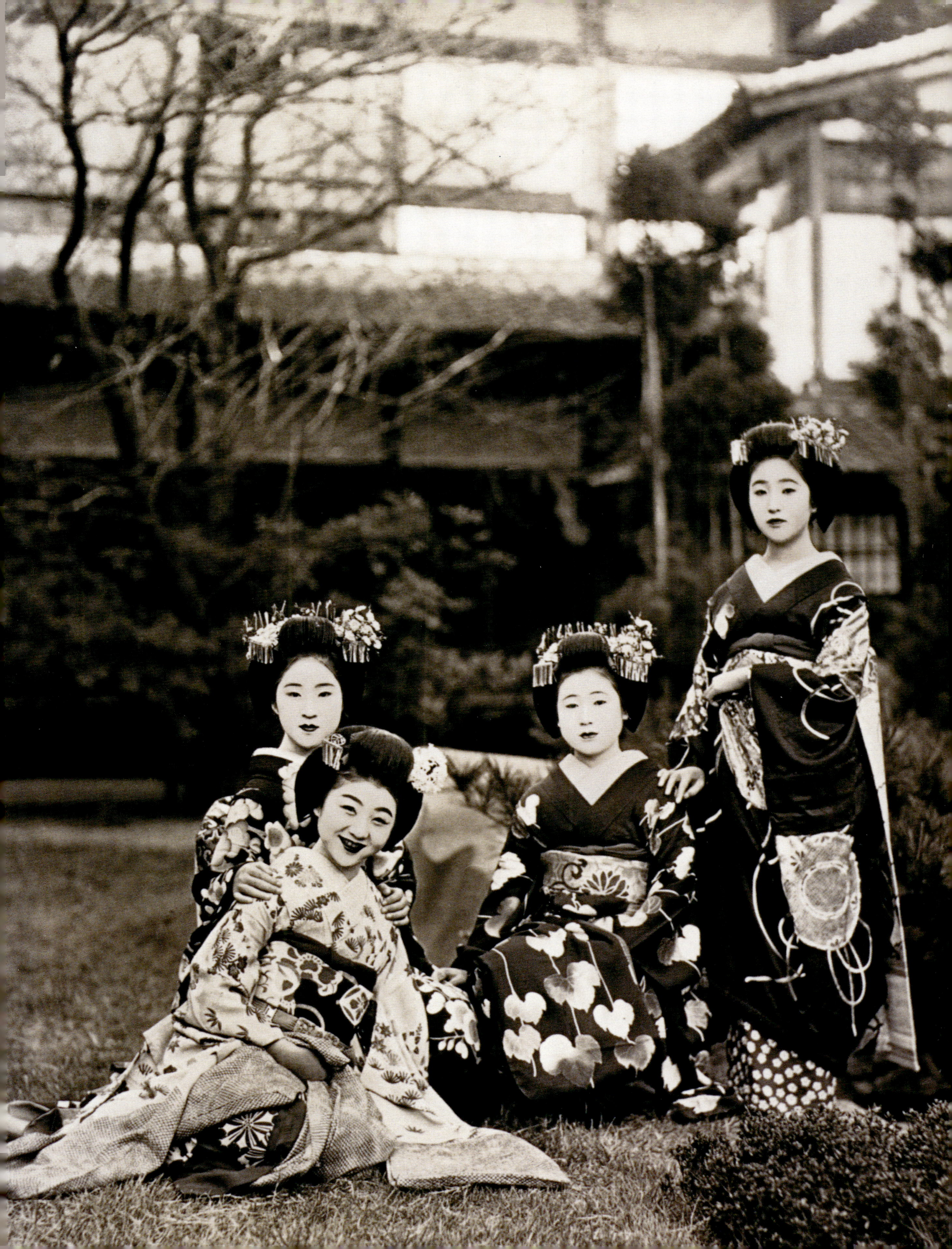

The photographs were edited by Stanley B. Burns, MD and Elizabeth A. Burns.
The book was designed by Mine Suda.

Published in the United States by powerHouse Books,
a division of powerHouse Cultural Entertainment, Inc.
37 Main Street, Brooklyn, NY 11201-1201
telephone 212 604 9074, fax 212 366 5247
e-mail: geisha@powerHouseBooks.com
website: www.powerHouseBooks.com

Library of Congress Cataloging-in-Publication Data:

Burns, Stanley B.
Geisha : a photographic history, 1872-1912 / by Stanley B. Burns and Elizabeth A. Burns.
p. cm.
ISBN 1-57687-336-6
Geishas--History--19th century. 2. Geishas--Pictorial works. 3. Japan--History--19th century. 4. Japan--Pictorial works.
I. Burns, Elizabeth A. II. Title.

GT3412.B87 2006
792.702'8'0952--dc

2006047473

Hardcover ISBN 1-57687-336-6

Printed and bound by Midas Printing, Inc.

A complete catalog of powerHouse Books and Limited Editions is available upon request; please call, write, or *oideyasu* our website.

10 9 8 7 6 5 4 3 2 1

Printed and bound in China